TO THE MOUNTAINS

ABDULLAH ANAS *with* TAM HUSSEIN

To the Mountains

*My Life in Jihad, from Algeria
to Afghanistan*

HURST & COMPANY, LONDON

First published in the United Kingdom in 2019 by
C. Hurst & Co. (Publishers) Ltd.,
41 Great Russell Street, London, WC1B 3PL
© Abdullah Anas and Tam Hussein, 2019
All rights reserved.
Printed in the United Kingdom by Bell & Bain Ltd, Glasgow

Distributed in the United States, Canada and Latin America by
Oxford University Press, 198 Madison Avenue, New York, NY 10016,
United States of America.

The right of Abdullah Anas and Tam Hussein to be identified as the
authors of this publication is asserted by them in accordance with the
Copyright, Designs and Patents Act, 1988.

A Cataloguing-in-Publication data record for this book
is available from the British Library.

ISBN: 9781787380110 *hardback*

This book is printed using paper from registered sustainable
and managed sources.

www.hurstpublishers.com

To God and all His Messengers. To my dear friends Faheem Khan, Ghada, Pana, Registani, Muslim, Aryanpour, Sarmuallim Tariq, Syed Ekramuddin, Bismillah, Abdullah, Amir Mujahid, Syed Najmuddin, Engineer Bashir, Abdel Vader Zabibullah, Abdessabour Farid and Abdullah Azzam and all the martyrs of Afghanistan. Without you the Soviets would never have left. To my wife Summayah and my mother in law, Mrs. Samira. To my parents. Last but not least to my dear friend Jamal Khashoggi who remained true till the very end.

Abdullah Anas

The the special women in my life. You have always been the mountains that I have leaned on drawing strength from your love and prayers.

To Vale, my wife who has the best nose for a story, whose patience with me is unfathomable. To my daughter whose kisses and fearlessness push me on. And to my mother who strove alone on the path urging us always to be human.

And then there is a boy—you have a mighty name may this book be of use.

Tam Hussein

CONTENTS

CONTENTS

PREFACE AND ACKNOWLEDGEMENTS

The idea for this book has been a long time coming and has germinated for six years. But life is such that I have put it off. Initially, I started to develop the project with two journalists, Adam Lively, and then Nick Fielding, then of the *Sunday Times*. Though the project fell through, in Adam I found a teacher who taught me English. I, in turn, hope I taught him Arabic. In Nick I found a dear friend. Both these men are excellent journalists but unfortunately our busy working and private lives prevented completion of this text.

Then I started working with two young men who were inseparable and for whom I have immense love and respect: Alex Strick van Linschoten and Felix Kuehn. I feel a deep connection to them due to our shared passion for Afghanistan. Alex and Felix also knew Arabic and, moreover, they also had that experience of living in Afghanistan and could write about the Taliban with great authority, which was very good for context. But then life in the shape of two women got in the way. They separated! They both became husbands and life's responsibilities overtook them, not to mention the looming deadlines to finish off their respective PhDs.

As for me, my own life took different turns. The responsibility of raising five children, setting up a television channel, al-Magharibiya, and then later the unleashing of the Arab Spring all made me kick this book into the long grass.

Then circumstances were such that I felt obliged to return to complete this book. The post-9/11 world was already highly polarised, yet with the arrival of the Arab Spring, and the Middle East being convulsed by protest, the political climate in the West became increasingly intolerant, with ideas and terms circulating that often meant different things to different people, thereby adding to the overall confusion.

On one side there were men in suits who wished to sully the word 'Jihad', considered sacred to Muslims, and make it synonymous with terrorism. They invalidated not only my labours, rendering me 'a terrorist', but, by implication, also invalidated the Jihad of freedom fighters such as Omar Mukhtar and Emir Abdelkader, figures that we Muslims hold dear. Both these men fought colonialism, showed immense moral courage and were celebrated thus. Yet even these towering figures would be considered 'terrorists' according to some. That was something I could not and will not accept.

On the opposing side were al-Qaeda and her ugly sisters: ISIS, Boko Haram and their ilk. They committed innumerable and horrific crimes including stabbings, truck ramming, burning, raping, looting and God knows what else and called it Jihad. They too have sullied this noble concept by making these criminal acts synonymous with Jihad. Jihad in its essence means 'a morally just war'. I challenge any man to see what good has ever come from al-Qaeda. Absolutely nothing apart from bloodshed and more misunderstanding.

And yet it is this understanding that now colours the minds of the public, whether layman or specialist. For when the non-Muslim hears the word Jihad it conjures up the image of a cruel bearded man, which is far different from what Muslims have in their minds. And so many non-Muslims naturally are gripped by fear, which the media no doubt contributes to, whilst Muslims feel outraged by these masked men who have distorted one of their most sacred concepts. For Muslims, Jihad is a martial tradition with a sublime moral and ethical framework which cannot be transgressed. It upsets them that the wider public are unaware of these ideas and are bombarded with the image of criminals who commit heinous acts in the name of Jihad. These contending ideas surrounding the word Jihad have inevitably led to much misunderstanding and fear, and a return to basic principles is called for.

I therefore felt the need, given my ten years of experience resisting the Soviet Union in Afghanistan during the Cold War, as a *mujahid*—that is someone who fought in a Jihad—to explain the concept of Jihad and its relationship to Afghanistan. Whilst my explanation is by no means comprehensive, I hope that my experiences will go some way towards explaining how the struggle against the Soviet Union contributed to the rise of modern Jihadism. I wish also to draw a distinction between Jihadism, a very modern concept, and the original concept of Jihad. I want to share my experiences of the Afghan Jihad alongside Ahmed Shah Massoud and others in order to shatter some myths, remove some misconceptions and for the reader to have a nuanced and informed understanding of this concept.

It is with this idea in mind that I met Tam Hussein, a Swedish journalist with years of experience studying and covering Jihadism. He also has personal experience of the frontlines, having seen the fruits of this idea first-hand in the ongoing civil war in Syria. He speaks Arabic, and understands Islamic religious discourse and the political currents that I came from. He also knows the West and its culture. I felt Tam would be the ideal interlocutor for this venture and so with his help I returned to it once again. Now, by the Grace of God, the work is complete. We ask that God accepts this from us.

Abdullah Anas
November 2018

PREFACE AND ACKNOWLEDGEMENTS

It will become immediately clear after meeting Abdullah Anas in person that he is not as articulate as the pages within reveal. That is because he is at his best and most persuasive when he speaks Arabic.

I have been extremely privileged to sit and talk with Abdullah Anas over the last two years. In many ways we, the Muslim youths growing up in London, experienced the fruits of his fascinating life story. And in a way I knew of Abdullah Anas long before we met, when one of my friends, a young Algerian, told me that his family was to attend a function in London. He couldn't contain his excitement when he heard that Abdullah Azzam's son-in-law would be there. So, in some respects, Abdullah Anas is responsible for my own fascination with Jihad, war and ideology.

I have also had a behind-the-scenes insight into the stories that some of my friends and acquaintances got caught up in during the 1990s. Pre-9/11, the conflicts in Afghanistan and Bosnia had an immense impact on the streets of London and resonated in the imagination of young Muslim men. One of the first books I was handed at university, as I embarked on a BA in History, was Abdullah Azzam's *Join the Caravan*, one of the key texts in modern Jihadism. It was given to me by that same young Algerian, Mohammed Lameen, who was enthralled by Abdullah Anas' visit to London. He remains to this day on the run somewhere in the North West Frontier Province of Pakistan. His brother, Ibrahim, was killed in a drone strike in Afghanistan and another brother, Anthony Garcia languishes in prison for plotting to blow up a night club, the Ministry of Sound, in south London. Many others that I encountered during the 1990s through my student years went that way too; Zeeshan Siddiqui, for instance, was another. At the turn of the millennium, as a youth worker in Lisson Green, I encountered young men like Bilal Berjawi and his friends who ended up joining al-Shabaab in

Somalia; Berjawi was later killed by a US drone. Many years later, some of his friends became notorious ISIS killers, indelibly associated with the horrendous torture and beheadings of innocent hostages on the plains of Raqqah.

Whilst I cannot speak with absolute certainty, I have a vague recollection of a timid young man, Mohammed Emwazi, trying to get on the pool table as the older guys hogged it during those balmy summers on Lisson Green. Later, after I moved to the Middle East, I encountered other British men, such as Ali Manasfi, who ended up fighting in Syria. All these guys had been captured by this idea; they had a desire to defend Muslims, to fight in the path of God. Many were idealists, many were running from their own demons and most of them attributed their understanding of what it meant to be a *mujahid* to the myths of the Arab Afghans.

Later, as a journalist working in the Middle East and covering many of the major Islamist terror attacks in Europe, again and again I encountered the aftermath of the Afghan Jihad. Not only did I meet Afghans and others fighting in Syria, but I also encountered Westerners smitten by the foundational myth forged in Afghanistan; except now these young men watched YouTube lectures broadcast by demagogues, rabble-rousers and ignoramuses from Walthamstow. Some of these foreign fighters were genuinely sincere and realised that they had come to serve the people of Syria. But there were also many who were hardened ideologues, ignorant and arrogant men who looked down on the Syrian people who are steeped in their culture and history. These men walked around as if they owned the place, schooling the locals on 'real' Islam, as detailed later in this book. I saw gravestones desecrated, heard of convoys being robbed, and sectarian tensions being exacerbated, which fed into Assad's war machine. As usual, there was plenty of infighting over creed. These foreign fighters forgot that they were meant to be guests and servants of the Syrian people and so understandably they became hated even though Assad's forces killed far more people than they ever did. It seemed that many of the events that had occurred in Afghanistan were being replayed in the Syrian arena once again. The fate of these foreign fighters, one suspects, will be more or less the same; just like Ibrahim, Berjawi and Siddiqui, they will probably be targeted in drone attacks, which will no doubt raise ethical questions in the West.

It is a great pity that these young men did not understand that the world is far more complicated than it appears. Many of them believe in foundational myths of al-Qaeda that are historically inaccurate. Some are no doubt intellectually immature, from broken families, and have neither the requisite education nor the critical tools to comprehend the world. Their world is full of uncertainties, conspiracies, cloak-and-dagger machinations and a constant battle between good and evil. Whilst I don't deny that these things do indeed populate human experience, life cannot be boiled down to Freemasons working towards a new world order. There seems to be an urgent need in our times to return to critical thinking, the study of the humanities, literature, culture and religion to avoid the pitfalls of demagogues and the grizzled warrior with his capacity for unfettered violence. The ancients taught their warriors poetry, calligraphy, the art of rhetoric and more, for it humanised the warrior. It taught him empathy and when to sheath his sword and when not to. Empathy is an attribute that is much needed today and I hope that *To the Mountains* will help it to be disseminated further.

I recorded Abdullah Anas' words in interviews that stretched over two years. I have also relied on my notes, recordings, transcripts and his account published in the Lebanese *Hayat* newspaper in 2003. I then translated his text into English and presented him with each chapter to confirm that the content is indeed what he intended and that it is factually correct to the best of his memory. I have checked key dates, added footnotes for further clarification of names for ease of reading. The book presented here then contains, one hopes, his words, his ideas, his spirit and his personality.

Good journalism makes fairness and transparency its cornerstone and I have in that spirit taken the liberty to add copious endnotes. As a journalist working in a world where everyone cries fake news, I felt that I had to highlight controversies, alternative narratives and be as transparent as I possibly could. I wanted to show the reader that we were aware of the other side of the story in order for this account to have integrity, even if one did not agree with it. I appreciate that the notes may be tiresome for the specialist but I hope immensely useful for the non-specialist who might not understand why all fighters seem to be called Abu or why certain rituals and ideas are important in Muslim religious practice and experience. I also sought to contextualise figures that may be viewed in one light but not necessarily in the same light in the Muslim world. Controversial figures too are also explained in order for the reader to understand their significance. So whilst Omar Abdul Rahman might just be that man in Peshawar who Abdullah Azzam tolerates but does not take seriously, my footnotes remind the reader of his involvement in the World Trade Center bombing of 1993. Finally, one of the purposes of this book has been to show that there are similarities with the current conflict in Syria. Afghanistan is the cradle where some of these Jihadis in Syria draw their tradition from, and so I have tried to make these connections clear in the notes.

As a journalist my job is to fact-check, but whilst I have learnt a lot from Abdullah Anas, having been given a master-class in the Afghan Jihad, Jihadism and Algerian politics, this is his account. My job here was to make his story readable and accessible. With regard to facts, I have compared them to other accounts that are available. I have also relied on the specialists on

PREFACE AND ACKNOWLEDGEMENTS

Afghan, Pakistani and Algerian history and politics for accuracy. Ultimately, however, this is Anas' perspective and how he looked at an event in history may differ markedly from another vantage point. I am aware that many of the individuals described within these pages are controversial, and they can be interpreted in many ways according to the evidence, but my views are irrelevant to this book. This is why I have tried my best not to meddle with his account.

However, Abdullah Anas is a modest man and perhaps unaware of George Orwell's famous maxim: 'Autobiography is only to be trusted when it reveals something disgraceful. A man who gives a good account of himself is probably lying, since any life when viewed from the inside is a series of defeats.'

Whilst Abdullah Anas tried his best to keep the focus on the men he met rather than himself I have tried to do the opposite. I wanted to focus on him whilst he urged me to strike out the pronoun 'I' and replace it with 'we' because he did not wish to inflate his contribution to the role that the Afghans played in their nation's recent history. If it turns out that he has given a good account of himself then, I am perhaps guilty of that. To get Anas to talk about himself was truly a jihad.

I trust I have conveyed Abdullah Anas' story for posterity in the hope that future generations will learn from his account.

I would also like to thank the team at Hurst, Michael Dwyer, Daisy and Alison for believing in this project and bringing it to fruition.

Tam Hussein
November 2018

INTRODUCTION

These days if you want to write a book about Islam and you want it to do well, you have at your disposal two strategies: you can be an Islamist who has seen the liberal light or you can be a victim of Islam's oppression. I, Abdullah Anas, however do not belong to either of those categories. I am someone who believes that the problems of our world can be solved by adherence to Islam and yet I do not want to impose it on anyone. My Prophet and the message he brought, Islam, is a compelling faith and whoever approaches it with fairness will see it for what it is. I am also a warrior, privileged to be the son-in-law of Abdullah Azzam, the leading ideologue and organiser of the Afghan Arabs. I am proud not only of him but also my record as a *mujahid*. Not only that, whilst I have with the passing of the years reassessed many of my assumptions, I still believe that Jihad—yes Jihad, that word which has become a swear word in the West and whispered amongst Muslims for fear of being accused of terrorism and having their children taken away—is the very peak of what Islam is. For if one can remain noble when all around you men have lost their heads, when everything is permitted, and you remember why, where, when to raise your arms and, more importantly, when you should not, then you have reached the very peak of humanity. For war consumes the souls of men and leaves an indelible imprint on the soul; it is one of the most powerful experiences that a human being can experience. In such tumult, that being who manages to remember his Lord and not transgress His boundaries is indeed worthy of mention. Unlike peacetime when civility and laws dictate the lives of men, in war you can do absolutely anything providing you have the capacity to carry it out. As such, the person who restrains himself during those times is indeed noble.

Someone once asked me whether I have nightmares, whether I wake up in the middle of the night with cold sweats remembering those people I fought. The answer is no, because my conscience is clean, I kept to the boundaries of God and did not transgress them. If one does that, one can sleep in peace. Since this book is about Jihad, it is appropriate here to explain and clarify what I mean by the word and what the reader might imagine the word to be.

The word Jihad must be understood within the context of Quranic revelation and Prophetic tradition. Linguistically it simply means 'struggle', and as such it has connotations of spiritual practice, of restraining the appetites that afflict all of us; it is about temperance and moderation. But it also has martial connotations. When Muslims refer to Jihad they mean fighting sanctioned by God, and most of the time it is used in a defensive context: when one is fighting to defend one's home and hearth as the Afghans did against the Soviets. But historically it has also been for offensive purposes as was the case in the early centuries of Islam, whereby Islam expanded politically and militarily even though it took centuries for the faith itself to spread within the conquered peoples. The Prophet is often depicted in the West as a fighting Prophet, but we must remember that most of the Prophet's life was not occupied with war; fighting Jihad constituted a very small part of his life, peace then is the norm and should be aspired to. Lest we forget most of the Muslim world was converted through trade and itinerant preachers rather than fighting. But that is not to say that Muslims don't view Jihad as a spiritually rewarding endeavour. The Prophet has told us not to look forward to meeting the enemy but if one does, one should stand firm. Jihad then is sanctioned by God and is as intrinsic to the faith as the Ramadan fast or the Hajj, performing the pilgrimage to Mecca. The reward for pilgrimage to God's house is that you emerge like a new-born babe, sinless. The fast of Ramadan's reward is immeasurable. Similarly, the reward for Jihad is forgiveness for sins, salvation of one's soul and one's family's souls, and being honoured by God. The virtues of Jihad are numerous and undeniable in Islam. It is near impossible to separate it from the religious tradition because Jihad is Islam's martial tradition. Our children are raised on its heroic deeds and named after its early heroes. Those in the West who seek to 'reform' Islam by trying to remove this aspect of the faith will have a thankless task and will no doubt alienate and, I dare say, polarise the Muslim world and set it on a course of conflict with the West.

On the other hand there are of course those 'Jihadists' as they call themselves, namely al-Qaeda and its various factions, who commit unspeakable crimes and then call it Jihad and completely abuse the concept. And frankly speaking for me that is the greater and more important struggle, something that I have believed in since 1989–90 when this nascent group came about and I perceived its dangers. I am quite confident that those Western reformers and analysts who wish to separate Jihad from its religious tradition will fail, but those Jihadists from within the Muslim world who sully that word are the greater danger. And I believe it is incumbent on me and Muslims to defend that word from these violent groups and reclaim it and understand it fully within its context. This can only be achieved through self-knowledge, education and learning about the past. And whilst I must admit that for many years now I have hesitated to write about my experiences in Afghanistan, it now becomes a necessity especially as such ideas are proliferating and becoming increasingly merciless.

Afghanistan is a sensitive subject from so many different angles, especially so after the terrible events of 9/11. The media has made Afghanistan out to be the very crucible from where it all began. And with the proliferation of various al-Qaeda franchises and of course ISIS in our midst currently, I feel that talking about my experiences in the Afghan Jihad is helpful. I feel it is incumbent on me to return to the days of those Arab volunteers who fought against the Russians in Afghanistan and to pass on to the younger generation my experiences. I feel I need to recount the tale of those who, through no choice of their own, became transformed by the media into the 'Afghan Arabs'.

And so I have decided to offer, I hope, the unvarnished truth about these volunteers beyond the myth and beyond the sensationalism. There are many authoritarian regimes in the Middle East and indeed in the West who have scapegoated the Afghan Arabs for their own political and economic ends. The shutting down of the democratic success of the FIS (Front Islamique du Salut, or Islamic Salvation Front) by the Algerian military junta, or the crackdown on his political enemies by the Mubarak regime, or the oppression of the Syrian populace by the callous Assad regime: none of these actions had anything to do with the Afghan Arabs.

Moreover, I write to counter those groups in the West who want to polarise the discourse and want to bring about this 'Clash of Civilisations' between the West and the Muslim world. Their declarations and statements attract various firebrands, demagogues and extremists who do not understand what impact their words have on the reputation of Islam and Muslims. If these demagogues had ever studied the life of the Messenger of God deeply, they would not utter such enormities and lies about him,

INTRODUCTION

nor would groups that emerge out of the Middle East commit such atrocities. And what is sad is that many of our young men, filled with the zeal of youth and wanting to do good, fall for these empty hollow slogans that result in the very mosque of the Prophet being attacked. Sadly many of their ideas are based on the myth of the Afghan Arabs as a model of action.

I feel we are at a critical time. Understanding what happened in Afghanistan is key to understanding what is currently going on in the Muslim world with particular reference to Jihadism. This book is divided into four parts. The first part will describe my introduction to Afghanistan and my fighting with Ahmed Shah Massoud, the second part my time with the Arab Services Bureau or the MAK, and the third part will describe my Algerian experiences during the civil war and the challenges I faced in London during the 90s, the heyday of Islamic activism. The fourth part will cover my return to Afghanistan in the hope of bringing peace to the region. I hope by this account to achieve Divine favour and hope that posterity will benefit from the lessons that I, Abdullah Anas, have learnt in the mountains of Afghanistan.

PART I

THE ROAD TO AFGHANISTAN

1

FROM WHENCE I CAME

When an Algerian says 'I am going to the mountain', it means he's angry. The mountains dominate much of the Northern Algerian landscape and are often the place where men go to either rebel or seek refuge. I too went to the mountains: not the Atlas mountain range of North Africa, but those of the Hindu Kush in Afghanistan. My going however, had nothing to do with expressing my rage or rebellion, rather it was in search of martyrdom and wanting to defend my coreligionists.

I am a son of the Algerian revolution: the fight for Algerian independence in the fifties and sixties touched my family in the way it touched millions of my countrymen who experienced the violence of French imperialism. All of Algeria in some form or other experienced French colonisation. In a way my own father was a product of that system. As far as I know, my father was always apolitical and little inclined towards revolutionary activism. This I suspect was due to the colonial system suppressing one's aspirations, cultivating a certain self-hate that accepts indignity and injustice to one's person. Whilst French settlers had the best land and opportunities, he slogged away as a casual labourer and wished for nothing more than to be able to marry and support his family. He experienced and perhaps didn't even see the discriminatory laws of the French colonial system, which was heavily weighted in favour of the *Pieds Noirs*, the colonial settlers of French, Maltese and Italian origin who emigrated to his country following France's conquest of Algeria in the early nineteenth century. More than 100 years of French colonial rule had given birth to a man whose horizons were so limited that he confined himself to his corner of the world while the settlers creamed off the best farm land and offended Islamic sensibilities by producing some of the best wine savoured in the salons of Paris. Like many millions of my compatriots there was an acceptance to live out one's life in a state of poverty accepting it as God's will and that was the end of it.

And so my father, an orphan from the family of Bounoua, and my mother from the Hamdawi family met when my mother moved to Meshria. This was an unremarkable town about 100 km away from her home town in Western Algeria. No monument stands out there, and Meshria was known because it was connected by rail to the nearest town of Mohammedia. In 1957 at the height of the conflict, during the battle of Algiers, my father of nineteen years married my mother who was a year younger. As the FLN (Front de libération nationale, or National Liberation Front) and French Paratroopers were fighting it out in a dangerous game of cat and mouse, the couple were celebrating their wedding.[1] Whilst both sides used morally questionable tactics, it was the French Paras who used techniques familiar to the prisoners of Abu Ghraib, Guantanamo and Tadmor.[2] That is how distant the war was to us in Western Algeria.

And yet, the fight for independence was also very near, for of course there were Algerian activists where we were. They felt the injustice of being considered an intrinsic part of metropolitan France and yet not tasting the full fruits of French citizenship.

Their sensibilities, their customs and Islamic beliefs were not respected. French laws towards women were at the time less progressive than Algerian Islamic law for instance. Moreover, thousands of French Algerians bled and died for France during the First and Second World Wars, they died in far-flung places like French Indo-China, and yet those promises of equality and emancipation were not forthcoming. The French state only granted 60,000 or so Algerians citizenship and so Algerian nationalists, at first, aimed for political change and reform demanding that they be given equal political treatment. The French state gave them a parliament heavily weighted in favour of French settlers. This was the final straw and the political forces changed for nationalists who increasingly contemplated the use of violence to achieve Algerian aspirations. The war of independence broke out in 1954 led by the FLN, an umbrella organisation of leftists and pan-Arabists. And so throughout the fifties the FLN conducted protracted guerrilla warfare against a more sophisticated military machine. It culminated famously in the Battle of Algiers[3] which although foiled showed French rule in Algeria to be morally bankrupt in the eyes of the international community and spelled the beginning of the end for the French presence in Algeria.

Although I was not even a thought when the Battle of Algiers was going on in 1956–57, it did indirectly have an impact on my life. I was born a year later into the cramped two bedroom house of my aunt in Meshria where my parents were living. Algerian custom dictates that the father of the newborn must serve mutton to guests in order to bring blessings, '*baraka*', in the first week. The child is also named on that day. My father intended to do the same. He wanted to give me a traditional Algerian name, Boujouma, but it did not happen. He had already bought the sheep and tethered it at the back; all that was left was to procure the remainder of the food. Armed with my aunt's shopping list he went off to the market to buy the goods but he never got there. A French army jeep was parked on the street and as he emerged from his house, one of the Paras got out and shouted 'Bashir Bounoua? You are under arrest for conspiring with revolutionaries. You are a traitor.' He was bundled into the jeep and driven off to God knows where. His fate was shared by thousands of innocents who were disappeared by French Paras and militias and never came back. De Gaulle's France could touch even a small town like Meshria.

Everyone was surprised by his arrest, my father was not known for troublemaking or revolutionary activity. Some of the more superstitious villagers eyed me suspiciously and blamed my birth as the cause. I was a bad omen personified even though in Islam drawing such omens was prohibited.

As was the case with many police states whether French, Iraqi or Syrian, no one knew where he was for three months. Eventually my mother who had been wracked with worry, received a curt letter explaining that he was in a prison in Meshria and that he alongside twelve others was to be executed. The whole house welled up in tears. My mother went to visit him. The officer or prison guard encouraged her to divorce him because it was almost certain that he would die. But she refused: 'I will', she said defiantly, 'wait for him forever, and if you execute him, I will memorise his grave.'

In this state of resignation to God's will and acceptance that my father would perish, my mother received another letter a few weeks later. It was from my father who wrote:

> I am still alive being held in Sarno prison, outside the city. It's 80 km away. Eleven of the other prisoners have been executed, but just before my turn came an army car pulled up and told them to stop executing people. If you are able to find some food, please bring it to me as I am starving. With joy and happiness, congratulations.

I don't know what the truth of my father's story is. I do not know whether he was really involved or not. My mother told me my father's name had been given to the interrogator under torture. The courts certainly tried him and the case was proven against him. And yet he was given a reprieve when Charles de Gaulle ordered the French to withdraw from Algeria. And so within three months my father was free and at home trying to adjust to being a father and get to know his first born. Apart from that brief interruption my own childhood was unremarkable.

After independence we moved back to my mother's place of birth, Descartes, now renamed Ibn Badis after Abdel Hamid ben Badis who was an Algerian nationalist and religious reformer celebrated for founding the Association of Algerian Ulama[4] and educating thousands of Algerians. Life though, was not easy because we found ourselves moving from one overcrowded family house to another, and whilst all this tumult was occurring my father went to Algiers and joined the army.

I am not sure why he decided to join the army, perhaps he had been infused with nationalistic fervour post-independence and been taken by the spirit of the times as many young men were. For it wasn't just Algeria that had freed itself from the French yoke but the Middle East too was swimming in a current of pan-Arabism and Nasserism. Algeria in particular was experiencing a love affair with Egypt due to Nasser's support of the National Liberation Front (FLN). Gamal Abdel Nasser, the Egyptian leader, had supported the fight against the French vocally on the international stage, and covertly provided military aid, as well as giving refuge to Algeria's first president, Ahmed Ben Bella. In fact, the Suez crisis in 1956 was seen by Algerians as a means of punishing Nasser for supporting the FLN and it was unsurprising that Ahmed Ben Bella remained a staunch Nasserist for the rest of his life. Post-independence Algeria underwent a policy of Arabisation as a response to shedding its colonial past, which resulted in cooperation with Egypt, Syria and other Arab countries. So the wish for my father to serve his country seemed natural, and we didn't see him as someone who was neglecting his fatherly duties—especially as we received intermittent reports that he was serving Algeria's first President Ahmed Ben Bella. He continued to serve until the ascent of President Houari Boumédiène in a bloodless coup.

I never expected that my father would find religion in the army. In 60s Algeria socialism, nationalism and Pan-Arabism flourished whether on the promenade, in the army, the cafes or on the university campuses. These ideas though attractive didn't touch him as strongly as his Muslim faith. But even still in the context of the nascent Islamic movement spreading all over the Muslim world, he didn't adopt the sort of urbane faith one would expect a born-again Muslim to adopt. The ideas of the Islamic movement were sophisticated and geared to respond to those arguments proffered by modernity and discussed in the coffee shops of Algiers. But my father was a traditional man and took a pass on those ideas too and instead became a *murid*, a disciple of a sufi sheikh who would lead him to God.

Contrary to how it appears in modern times, Sufism still had an immense pull on traditional Algerian society, no less my father. Historically Sufism was widespread all over the Muslim world especially in the countryside. My father, like many men whether in the Indian subcontinent, Afghanistan or Algeria would have a spiritual guide who would help him to remove the impurities of character in the hope that the Divine Light would enter his heart and thereby lead to salvation. As such he was like many North Africans of his day: he prayed five times a day, fasted, read the Quran, venerated the Prophet and paid the alms tax, *zakat*. Like his North African compatriots he followed the Maliki legal school of jurisprudence, in creed he was Ashari and adhered to some sort of sufi order. He viewed the latter as an intrinsic part of Sunni orthodoxy. In my father's case he belonged to the Qadiri order named after the great Iraqi ascetic of the eleventh century, Abdul Qadir al-Gilani. Other Algerians belonged to native mystics such as Abu Madyan, Abdel Qadir al-Jaza'iri, Ahmed al-Alawi and the native sufi orders that had sprung forth like the Alawiyya, the Tijania and Khalwatiya. Salafism or Wahabi thought, at the time, had made little headway in the Algerian heartlands.

But as in many Muslim countries heterodox and superstitious practices had crept into Sufi orders that had sullied Sufism's name. Sufism was akin to a white robe; it got soiled easily. Algerian Sufism was no less susceptible to these curious practices. I still remember my mother bringing a black chicken and offering it up to Abdul Qadir's shrine even though the saint had never visited the place. It was pure superstition. My father too, not knowing any better of course, brought some of these practices with him when he returned in 1970.

When he returned he did not move in with us though, instead he would visit us for a couple of nights every few months. In his absence my mother had enrolled me in a government school that followed the national curriculum, and I excelled there. But now my father looked at my schooling with a sense of dread and worry. Perhaps he was worried about the French teachers that had decided to remain and were now teaching me values and ideas deemed alien by him. In his view this secular government school would 'send our son to the fires of hell.' And on the advice of a sheikh, after primary school I was enrolled into a *madrassa*, a religious seminary and thereby, in his view, on to the path to paradise.

At the age of twelve I began my religious schooling and continued with it for another eight years. My early religious schooling was happy, the *madrassa* was just around the corner from my house. It wasn't as strict as the government school and it brought with it status. In Muslim tradition respect is given those associated with religious learning because they are according to a saying of the Prophet Muhammed 'inheritors of the Prophets'. Rural Algeria was no exception in this regard, and I would be offered the best seats, asked to recite the Quran at funerals and carried the prestigious title of *Talib*, a student of religious knowledge, or *Hafiz*, since I had memorised the entire Quran. Those titles meant little in the city but it went a long way in the village and my ambitions and horizons were confined to that. I didn't worry too much about the way studying in a *madrassa* would limit my career options. I would become a prayer leader, an Imam, and draw my salary from the Ministry of Religious Affairs whilst the other boys would achieve their goals and ambitions by having a secular education.

In truth this vocation I had chosen was not out of sincere religious sentiment. I wasn't particularly devout despite my religious learning. I hadn't really tasted the sweetness of the Quran nor taken on its adornments. My religious education had no impact in my day to day life. I was doing it because this is what young men did in small-town Algeria. I neglected my prayers just like the sheikh who taught me the Quran did. I played football, smoked cigarettes in the public square, went to the cinema and sat in coffee shops watching the football. No one blamed me for it, because their horizons too were confined to the village boundaries.

However things changed as I set foot outside of my hometown. The Islamic religious syllabus in Algeria requires that the student or *Talib* goes to further his understanding of Islam in a bigger religious seminary. Travelling and searching for knowledge, I should add, was also connected to the word Jihad, because searching for knowledge might widen your horizons but it also involved a lot of personal sacrifice. Travelling for knowledge followed in the footsteps of many famous scholars in Islamic history who travelled all the way to Transoxiana or Andalusia in order to acquire learning. Despite Islamic learning having stagnated after about 150 years of French colonisation, the tradition of travelling to learn remained part of the Algerian Islamic syllabus. There in those seminaries the student is required to further his knowledge and understanding. He might stay there perhaps six or seven months studying under a specialist, he may read a text, obtain an *Ijaza*, permission to teach, and then continue on to another seminary. The hope is that one not only sat at the feet of great scholars, expanding one's knowledge, but also grew spiritually as a human being.

My own sojourn began in 1977, my father by then had begun a livestock business and we didn't have any wants or needs after it thrived. My three years 'abroad', if you will, were spent in Tunaan, 90 km away from the Moroccan border, al-Khemis and Ga'foor. It was there in that school of Tunaan that I truly met my first giant of a man Sheikh Ben Rabih. I had never met a man who was so sincere and so intensely devout. The sheikh, a man of seventy years, who spent his nights in prayer and most days fasting, was one of the few men I met who was moved to tears whenever the Quran was recited. It wasn't the numerous texts or prophetic traditions and commentaries that impacted me, but rather his outstanding example.

Time had tested this venerable old man: one of his sons was a Socialist studying in Eastern Germany, another was an Arabic language teacher and the third was studying in Medina. The fate of the oldest son must have worried him but then, God tests those whom He loves. Although this sheikh never claimed to be a Sufi, it was in him that I saw the impact that the Quran could have on a person. And it was that experience sitting at his feet, learning from him, that gave me my first spiritual awakening. And with spiritual awakening also began, as it often does in human nature, political and social awakening. For one can't help but think about one's relationship with God without thinking about one's place in the world, and one's role in it. And so whilst studying there I came across two very important Islamic currents coursing through Algerian society which envisaged a society which had Islam at its heart.

Whilst studying with the sheikh, I had become increasingly devout, but the more I adhered to my faith, the more I wanted to live a faith that was devoid of superstition, one which had a transformative effect on society. Whilst studying in Tunan I came across Tablighi Jamaat, a Muslim missionary movement which had started in the Indian subcontinent to revive the Muslim community, the *Ummah*, as it is known. I was very impressed by how articulate its followers were; they weren't just people who knocked on your door encouraging you to come to the mosque, but some of its adherents articulated their faith beautifully. I still remember how one such man, Abdel Majed, a young lawyer with intense green eyes, had stood up after we had offered the Zuhr prayer in the mosque and gave us a talk as we remained seated mumbling our devotions to ourselves. I was stunned by the eloquence and sincerity of his talk: he was not religiously trained, and yet his faith seemed to permeate through his very being. Here I was exploiting this faith for status and position whilst this layman viewed the faith as a responsibility. How could I go to the cinema watching Egyptian movies or Clint Eastwood in *The Good, the Bad and the Ugly* or listen to hypnotic Rai music puffing away on a cigarette whilst he was struggling to revive the faith? I felt ashamed and so I went on a three day *'Khurooj'* with Tabligh, whereby I went door knocking from area to area encouraging Muslims to come to the mosque. But this awakening within still wanted answers to the bigger questions in Algerian society. What about politics? How does one effect change at a societal level? Whilst Tabligh undoubtedly impacted the Islamic movement and had no doubt pollinated the Muslim Brotherhood, Salafism and other groups, at its heart the organisation is missionary and apolitical in nature. It believed that societal change would occur through regular mosque attendance, worship and the perfection of manners and there was no need for politics. Whilst there has been much good that has come from Tablighi Jamaat, their apolitical stance was profoundly unsatisfying, politically immature and unrealistic to my mind.

By the time I left for my national service I was truly a political animal. I had spent this time with Sheikh Rabih, I had matured spiritually and become more aware of my religious responsibilities due to my interaction with Tablighi Jamaat: all that was lacking were the ideas of Hassan al-Banna, the Egyptian founder of the Muslim Brotherhood. He attracted me because he merged the spirituality of Sufism and its organisational capability with practical steps that transformed society. And I found the Muslim Brotherhood in the army.

It is ironic that although Nasser became a vehement opponent of the Muslim Brotherhood it was indeed his pan-Arabism that brought the Muslim Brotherhood to Algeria. Algeria's attempt at restructuring the education system and moving it away from the French educational curriculum meant that Egypt sent many teachers and advisors over to Algiers, to help with the reorientation. Many of those pedagogues sent over by Egypt were graduates from al-Azhar University, one of the Islamic world's most prestigious and oldest educational institutions. Many of these Azharis, as they were known, belonged to the Muslim Brotherhood and so when they arrived in Algeria they were free to spread the message of the Brotherhood all over the country. Their message was quite simple: the revival of the Muslim *Ummah* lay in unity and a return to the original Islamic tenets. By the time I was doing military service the ideas were already diffused, and I had already been exposed to ideas of Mahfoudh Nahnah, an Arabic teacher and graduate from the University of Algiers,[5] who had joined the Brotherhood. At the time I came across him he was languishing in prison having received a fifteen-year sentence for opposing the National Charter in 1976, he had cut the telephone wires as an act of defiance. It was one of his followers, Zubeir, that brought me one of his lectures on an audio tape. It was an awakening and an answer to many of the questions I had with Tabligh. I started to read more about the Islamic movement. I came across the ideas of Algerians such as Abbas Madani the founder of FIS, Mustafa Siba'i in Syria, Abu'l Hasan Nadwi and Abu 'Ala Mawdudi in the subcontinent and many others including of course Egyptian thinkers such as Muhammed Ghazzali and Syed Qutb.[6] By the time Nahnah was out of prison having received a reduction of his sentence from fifteen years to four, I was a fully fledged member of the Muslim Brotherhood. I was an Islamist. I understand that in Western popular culture an Islamist is seen as an extremist who wants to impose Islam on the rest of society. In fact, Islamism is arguably a broad church with a myriad of political views ranging from extremists such as al-Qaeda who view democracy as tantamount to infidelity to Ennahda who are akin to German Christian democrats and are staunch defenders of democracy. The point is whilst all want an Islamic ethos or framework in their society what and how that is manifested differs vastly. Some could be violent, some could be authoritarian others could be benign. Islamists are part and parcel of the Middle Eastern political landscape and vie with Pan-Arabists, liberals and the left.

As an activist, I met Nahnah once he was out and he allowed me and a group of friends to establish a local branch of the Brotherhood in the west of the country. And so I found myself an activist up until my departure for Afghanistan in 1983. For three years I visited high schools, the university campuses and mosques in our locality trying to get the message of the Brotherhood to young Algerians whether that be through speeches after prayer or little study circles. However, up to that point even though the conflict of Afghanistan had started in 1979, I did not know about Abdullah Azzam nor did I know about his call for Jihad against the Soviets.

Of course, as a Muslim and Algerian I knew about Islam's intellectual and martial tradition both academically and historically. North Africa with its intellectual centres dotted around Tunis, Kairouan, Marrakech, Tlemcan and Fez had produced intellectuals who took their endeavours beyond the region. Ibn Khaldun the great fourteenth-century sociologist and historian who wrote the *Prolegomena* (or *Muqaddimah*) was just one such example. As students of the Maliki school of jurisprudence, we had studied the chapters pertaining to Jihad; most students will cover it as a matter of course. We studied various texts that discussed the topic from a legal standpoint including Imam Malik's *Muwatta*, 'The Trodden Path', the key legal text that the jurisprudential school had been founded on. But we were also aware of Jihad's great virtue: a lot of the early Islamic literature concerns itself with the *Maghazi*, the battles of the Prophet, and we were not shy in studying it. This was just part and parcel of our tradition that encompassed all aspects of life, war and peace being no exception. Jihad was just the martial aspect of the faith which was activated whenever it felt under threat.

I was versed in Islamic history and aware of North Africa's ability to produce outstanding fighting men who had contributed to Islamic history. From a young age we learnt about Tariq bin Ziyad, Musa bin Nusayr, Ibn Tumart—the commanders who conquered the Iberian peninsula; Khayreddine Barbarossa who defended the country from English corsairs; of the legendary exploits of Abdel Qadir al-Jaza'iri[7] who fought the French and the likes of Omar Mokhtar who fought the Italians. These things I was aware of but that I would myself be a fighting man in Afghanistan was not something I had imagined at the time of joining the Brotherhood. In fact, I had never purposely looked for conflict and believed in the tenets of my religion that fighting was only prescribed when absolutely necessary, that one should strive for peace and utilise every means to that end. I always preferred diplomacy over fighting. I had never even heard of Abdullah Azzam until I came across him quite by chance in the year before my departure in Medina when I was working as a guide to pilgrims in Saudi Arabia. I would not have been any wiser to his presence had my friend and activist Nordine not drawn my attention to him. I remember I had done the *Umrah*, the lesser pilgrimage in Mecca and had made my way to Medina during the month of Ramadan in 1981. We had just finished the Tarawih prayers in the Prophet's mosque where we had stood alongside fellow Muslims listening to the Quran, when Nordine pointed him out. It was Nordine who suggested that we greet him; of course, at the time his star was ascendant, and the sheikh had just started to publicise the Afghan-Soviet conflict all over the world and as such, he was swamped by people who wanted to do exactly what we wanted to do. He also had people to see, notaries to meet, lectures and lessons to give. I discovered that Azzam was a man who didn't waste a single idle moment, he gave us a fleeting shake of the hand and left us going about his business. It was only later when I read his article in a magazine on the Afghan Jihad that I realised who he was.

Before the article was published I had absolutely no idea as to who Abdullah Azzam was and did not expect to become his son-in-law one day. Abdullah Azzam was born in the West Bank to a merchant family.[8] He studied at agricultural school, then studied Islamic law at Damascus University part-time whilst working as a teacher. He loved teaching and researching and taught in the universities of Jordan, Saudi Arabia and Pakistan. He completed his post-graduate and doctoral studies extremely quickly at al-Azhar University. At heart Abdullah Azzam was an extremely bookish man, a walking encyclopaedia who was learned in many subjects whether religion, economics, history or geography. This is something that I myself witnessed. I had organised a visit to Ahmed Shah Massoud for him and we were at a height of 5000 to 6000 feet, the cold was cutting and all we wanted to do was to get to the next village for shelter before the sun set. And yet even in such conditions he would still find an opportunity to study and teach from the books. This was not because he was overly tough on the men, it was because he did not waste a minute. It was as if he had realised that true capital is not money but time. He knew that Afghans followed the Hanafi Islamic legal school, and this legal school disliked combining the early noon prayer, Zuhr, with the afternoon prayer, 'Asr, unlike us Malikis.[9] Even if we begged them to combine the two prayers the Afghans would have accused us of being Wahabis, a pejorative term for Salafism and all would be lost because many Afghans had an aversion to that brand of Islam that didn't adhere to a legal school. It meant that every few hours they would stop to offer their prayers but that also meant that the horses had to be unloaded and then reloaded and valuable time would be lost. Abdullah Azzam had accepted those aspects of the Afghan national character and instead of grumbling about the cold and time lost, after the prayer whilst the Afghans were packing up, he would open up a book and explain the legal entitlement for the spoils of war pertaining to what a warrior possessing thoroughbred or a pure Arab stallion was entitled to. It was incredible to see this man's appetite for learning and teaching.

Yet at the same time, Abdullah Azzam was very much a frontline scholar and whilst he didn't always take part in the battles against the Soviets, he had already earned his fighting stripes—he was a Palestinian after all. Defying and fighting the Israeli occupation was something that was ingrained in his character. He was one of the earliest Palestinians Islamists who fought the Israeli occupation when most Palestinians were joining Nationalist and left-wing groups dominating the resistance against the Israelis. He yearned to fight in the path of God and every time he buried his companions in Afghanistan he would say bitterly that 'it was proof that he was not deserving of martyrdom.'

There were also other qualities I saw in him, which other people also noticed. He was an ascetic. This was strange in many ways, because a lot of the leaders of the Islamic movement whilst they fulfilled their basic religious observance, often fell short in aspects of worship because of their activism and work-load. But Sheikh Azzam actually was a man of night prayer, *Qiyam al-Layl*, and he fasted incessantly whilst writing, editing and publishing what were, in my view, insightful articles. He edited half of our publications fot *Jihad* magazine in addition to our other publications.

Other things I noted were his eloquence, generosity towards guests and his commensurate sporting ability. It isn't surprising that so many lines of poetry were written in praise of him by those who met him. For in my mind, and the Algerian tempera-ment is not easily influenced, he was Muslim Arab manhood personified, and would have left a lasting impression on me and anyone who met him.

2

ON THE ROAD TO AFGHANISTAN

The Afghan Jihad has shaped who I am today. There is nothing more intense in life than war, and I have had the fortune to have met two titans of the Muslim world—it is not so much my story that I recount in these pages but rather how their stories intermingled in mine. At the time I never thought that our actions in Takhar, Panshir or in Peshawar would shake the walls of Berlin. The mind boggles that someone as minuscule and unimportant as me had a small part in the downfall of one of the mightiest superpowers in the history of mankind. God's ways are strange; but then again it's one rain drop that becomes a vast ocean.

In 1983, I didn't have a clue about what Afghanistan was or even where it was located geographically. And though my horizons had expanded with my political activities, I was to all intents and purposes a country boy from Algeria. All I knew at the time was that I wanted to help my fellow Muslims in Afghanistan who were fighting against the Soviet Union, a godless superpower. I only learnt later of the rich history of Afghanistan and the political causes that led to the Afghan Jihad. I think it is worth giving a brief overview of it here.

TO THE MOUNTAINS

Afghanistan, or Khorasan as it is known in Islamic history, is an ancient land often referred to as the graveyard of empires. This landlocked country has seen ancient civilisations lay their imprints on the people, and is in fact a collection of ethnicities of Tajikis, Pashtuns, Turkic peoples. From the great Persian emperor Darius the Great to Alexander the Great, both left their mark on the people whether that be the tongue they speak— Farsi or Dari—or the green eyes they possess on account of the Greeks. Before the arrival of Islam the country was a centre of Buddhism, Hinduism and Zoroastrianism and a conduit for the silk route which brought goods from the East. It is also a place where peoples sought refuge from the plains because they could not be conquered once they commanded its heights. Mountains made these people tough and hardy. When the Arabs brought Islam to Afghanistan through its preachers, mystics, traders and conquerors, the country experienced a golden age, especially under the warlike Mahmud al-Ghazna and his dynasty. Following him, the armies of Genghis Khan and their offshoots the Ilkhanate, the Timurid dynasty as well as the Mughals became the main players in Afghanistan. Under the latter the country became intrinsically linked to the destiny of the subcontinent. With the Muslim powers losing ascendancy in the world and the rise of Britain, France and imperial Russia in the nineteenth century, Afghanistan became an important bargaining piece in the imperial ambitions of Britain and Russia. Both saw the country as a vital piece of real estate which had to be secured. The British looked at Afghanistan as an essential buffer against the Russians reaching India. The Afghans however were not servile subject peoples: they guarded their independence jealously, and inflicted severe defeats on the British. The people of Afghanistan were warlike and were often termed by the British as belonging to the 'martial' races. It was a great irony that the last Mughal emperor became a figurehead of the 'Mutiny' by Hindu and Muslim sepoys in India, which was put down by Afghan Muslim war-lords in the pay of the British in 1857. By 1838 however, Afghanistan had become a kingdom and continued thus until the lead up to the Afghan Jihad.

There were two stages of the Afghan Jihad. The first stage began in 1973, when the prime minister, Muhammad Daoud Khan, deposed the Afghan monarch and his first cousin Mohammed Zahir Shah and appointed himself president. The ascent of Khan and the ending of the Afghan monarchy resulted in mass arrests all over the country. Khan ruled Afghanistan with an iron fist.

The main threat to Khan's rule though was the political activi-ties of the Islamic movement[1] at Kabul University in the shape of Muslim Youth Organisation or Sazman-i-jawanan-i Musulman, which was founded by Abdul Rahim Niazi in 1969. The univer-sity in those days was the focal point and battle ground of all the currents and ideas present in the country at the time and Abdul Rahim was a passionate opponent of Communism. In it Islamists and Communists of various shades jousted with each other on the intellectual battle field. In 1970 Abdul Rahim Niazi died and the Islamist mantle was taken over by Professor Ghulam Muhammad Niazi (no relation even though they were from the same tribe), director of the faculty of Islamic jurisprudence at Kabul University. Niazi had studied in Cairo in the 1950s and came into close contact with the Muslim Brotherhood there.[2] It was his activism that introduced the more progressive ideas of Abu 'Ala al-Mawdudi and Hassan al-Banna into the university. But the real engine of the movement was Engineer Habib al-Rahman who recruited students to the cause. It resulted in an inner core of leaders of Gulbuddin Hekmatyar, Burhanuddin Rabbani, Abdur Rasool Sayyaf,[3] Jalaludin Haqqani and others joining him.[4] In 1972 Rabbani emerged as one of the preeminent leaders of this cluster of passionate activists and formed Jamiat-i Islami, the Islamic party which mirrored Mawdudi's party in Pakistan.[5]

However, following the Daoud Khan's coup in 1973 things changed: it was no longer mere intellectual jousting between Communists and Islamic movement students, and events took a more serious turn. Professor Niazi was arrested in 1972 by the Daoud regime and eventually executed on 28 May 1979[6] by the Communist Khalqi government after they had come to power following a coup d'état in April 1978. Engineer Habib al-Rahman was arrested and executed in the years 1973–74.[7] Burhanuddin Rabbani fled first to Saudi Arabia and then to Pakistan whilst Hekmatyar laid low for a while in safehouses in Afghanistan before making his way to Peshawar in the North-West Frontier Province in Pakistan.[8]

Violence of course breeds more violence. Those Islamists who remained outside of prison began contemplating an armed uprising against the Daoud regime. The most prominent of those leaders was Gulbuddin Hekmatyar and the engineer Ahmad Shah Massoud. These men after a period of hiding in Afghanistan went into exile to Peshawar, Pakistan, with the blessing of Pakistan's president Zulfikar Ali Bhutto who hoped to use this uprising as a means to pressurise the Afghan government to resolve the border disputes over Baluchistan and Pashtunistan. Pakistan's destiny and national security interests were tied to Afghanistan. The British Partition of India and the creation of Pakistan meant that there were some in the Pakistani political elite who tended to view India-Pakistan relations in hostile terms. They felt constantly encircled by their larger neighbour and so India dominated their security agenda. Instead of having a Canada-US style relationship they viewed their neighbour at best as competitive and at worst as an open enemy. The two countries had often clashed and the memory of Pakistan's humiliating defeat at the hands of India in 1971, resulting in the loss of East Pakistan (later Bangladesh), had not been forgotten in the political hierarchy in Pakistan. Simply put, Pakistan could not afford to have an Afghanistan which it could not control for fear that it would be encircled by India or fall under the sway of any other power for that matter.

The presence of the USSR in Afghanistan was seen by the Pakistani political and military elites as a threat to its national interests because if Afghanistan fell, then the Red Army could steam-roll its way down to the Indian ocean by way of Karachi. And so this fear whether real or imagined led them to support parties and groups who might have been completely antithetical to their own traditions but would nevertheless be supported based on their own political calculations. Whilst the Pakistani elite arguably might have had more in common with the urbane and Western-educated Daoud Khan, they still decided to support the Islamists who could counter Khan's government. Later on they supported for the same reason the Islamists against the Communists, Hekmatyar against Massoud, the Taliban against the United Islamic Front for the Salvation of Afghanistan or, as it became known in Western media, the Northern Alliance.

At the time though, many of these Islamist exiles were living in total impoverishment and took whatever help they received from the Pakistani government. These men were often living on a few rupees a day in Peshawar and so in spite of the exiles being aware of President Bhutto's policy aims and the motivations behind them, they grabbed the life line his government offered. All the exiles could think about at the time was their personal safety and overthrowing the Khan regime. So this small band of exiles were trained up by the Pakistani intelligence agency, Inter-Services Intelligence (ISI), and tried to launch an attack against the Khan government.

The first military insurrection in 1975 was a fiasco. The operation was led by Hekmatyar who remained in Peshawar awaiting the result of the insurrection and the return of his fighters. The first group attacked government outposts in Surkh Rud,

Nangarhar province. But they retreated on account of the hostile and aggressive military response from the Afghan government. The second group led by Ahmed Shah Massoud made its way to his native Panshir valley and after two days in July 1975 reached Rukha[9] and took control of the government buildings, but could only hold them for a few days before Kabul sent a large force to dislodge them and regain control of the territory with little difficulty. By 28 July they had captured some of Massoud's men whilst Massoud escaped back to Peshawar.[10] It was said that Massoud blamed Hekmatyar for that fiasco and the loss of his men. Perhaps it was naive to expect success after spending only a year preparing for the armed uprising.

This then, in short, was the first declaration of Jihad by the Islamic movement of Afghanistan in 1975. It met with little success because Afghans remained ambivalent to the Daoud regime and the *mujahideen* didn't have any popular support and that was the reason for its failure.[11] I learnt that any political or military movement if it does not have popular support will most certainly flounder. But in hindsight, this lesson in humility and hardship was immensely beneficial for the likes of the Islamist opposition, for pain, suffering and hardship are inevitable in life and build character. For the likes of Ahmed Shah Massoud in particular, the formative experience had a profound impact on him in the upcoming conflict against the Soviets.

Exile must have come as a shock to the system because Massoud was urbane, erudite and cosmopolitan and used to a life of ease on account of his father's military background. Unlike the majority of Afghans he was one of the few people who could spend summer in his native Panshir valley. Massoud like many Afghans had a passion for poetry and even in the darkest hour always carried a book of Hafiz or Saadi in his pocket. He had memorised many verses and sometimes during the early hours he would read from them or sit with friends and discuss them. But just like metals are shaped and formed when they are subjected to stress, so too is the human character. With exile and defeat he was taken away from that life of urbanity and ease. In Peshawar Massoud suffered from hunger, homelessness, poverty and alienation. It was there in the small town in the North-West Frontier Province that he read the canons of guerrilla warfare and strategy, he devoured Ho Chi Minh, Mao Tse Tung, Che Guevara and read about the Napoleonic Wars and of course the battles of the Prophet, the *Maghazi*. It was as if he knew that he had been called to this profession against his will and that now that he was in this situation he was going to master it completely. In fact, I heard much later, that Massoud had a premonition of the arrival of the Russians even in his youth. He had told his father, an army officer, that he wanted to join the army. His mother tried to dissuade him and asked why he wanted to enlist in the officer corps instead of becoming an engineer, and he replied that soon the Russians would invade and he wanted to prepare for it.

Gulbuddin Hekmatyar, the man who would become his rival, was perhaps much better prepared for a life of hardship. Hekmatyar was a fellow student at Kabul University but six years older than Massoud. Unlike Massoud, Hekmatyar was from a family of Pakhtun merchants from the Kharroti tribe who lived in Kabul. He was immensely charismatic, a good organiser, eloquent in his speeches and was a formidable leader. Hekmatyar was not scared about fighting nor did he have any issues leading from the front but he had the political sagacity to realise that the most important person in an army is the general who had to lead from behind, so Hekmatyar did the same. But unlike Massoud his political views and ideas on Islam were far more radical and uncompromising. Perhaps that was just his nature or perhaps unlike the others who had political and religious credentials Hekmatyar was a direct product of the Muslim Youth Organisation, and so stuck closely to those ideas. What was certain was that his activism had already led him to see the insides of a prison cell. He had been arrested in 1972 after a Maoist was killed and the Zahir Shah government arrested the organisers of the ensuing demonstrations. He spent a year in Dehmazang jail in Kabul.[12] After the coup by Daoud Khan in 1973 he fled to Peshawar. Therefore, when Hekmatyar arrived in Peshawar, he was already accustomed to much hardship and difficulty. He formed Hezb-i Islami in 1976 after differences with Burhanuddin Rabbani.

But whilst exile in Peshawar certainly shaped the men that would lead the fight against the Soviets, a friend, whose testimony I don't doubt, told me that the initial defeat and Massoud's vocal criticism sowed the seeds of discord between the two. This combined with their different personalities meant that they were set up for conflict. And sadly, the fact that they could not resolve their differences despite the efforts of Sheikh Abdullah and others, led to much blood letting and the victory against the Soviets being wasted. But the fact that events would go that way could not have been foreseen when the second declaration of Jihad occurred and the Afghans began their fight back against the USSR in earnest.

The second declaration of Jihad was altogether different. Afghanistan was undergoing profound changes during this period. It culminated in the assassination of the Afghan president Mohammed Daoud Khan and his family in April 1978. It was followed by the presidency of Nur Mohammad Taraki, the leader of the Communist Khalq party on 1 May of the same year. His rule lasted for only six months. Taraki initiated a series of radical policies intended to modernise the country. He suppressed the opposition ruthlessly executing, it is said, over 27,000 people. This was followed by Hafizullah Amin on 17 September 1979 who continued the internal political wrangling of the ruling Communist party. The country was volatile, unstable and saw mass demonstrations in Kabul followed by the government firing on the protestors; thousands died.

The furore that erupted with the killings nearly led to the fall of the regime had the Soviet Union not stepped in. On Christmas Eve 1979 the Soviets were in Kabul. They killed the Afghan president Amin who they suspected of being too close to Pakistan and appointed his socialist rival Babrak Karmal to the Afghan presidency in December 1979. It was a puppet regime and in some ways a replay of the Great Game, where Tsarist Russia had vied to control the strategically important country.

The Soviets miscalculated the situation in Afghanistan. The religious scholars of Afghanistan couldn't tolerate this usurpation by an un-godly foreign power, and released a religious legal edict, a fatwa, calling on the Afghan people to revolt and fight Jihad. The people had a duty, they insisted, to free their country from the forces of occupation that not only harboured atheistic, god-less ideas, but also aimed to control the country's economic resources whether that be its waters, minerals or energy resources. This was brazen imperialism. This declaration by the religious Ulama of Afghanistan was spontaneous and the Islamic world did not hesitate to proffer its support. By 1980 thirty-four Muslim countries demanded that Soviet troops withdraw unconditionally from Afghanistan. The UN also passed a resolution protesting Soviet intervention. The Soviet invasion was a god-send to the ragged band of exiles in Peshawar still nursing their wounds from their first attempt to overthrow the Afghan regime, for now their insurrection had popular support.

But unfortunately, there was one thing that the Jihad against the Soviets suffered from its very inception: the Afghan *mujahideen* factions were afflicted by disunity. Despite all the leaders in many ways being linked to Niazi's activism, these seven leaders had different visions of Afghanistan and all claimed pre-eminence in leading the country. Despite efforts by Saudi Arabia and others it was very difficult to get them to unite. To just give you an idea of the various parties that fought the Soviets they were the following: Younes Khalis'[13] Islamic and National Revolution Movement of Afghanistan, Gulbuddin Hekmatyar's Hezb-i Islami, Burhanuddin Rabbani's Jamiat-i Islami and an offshoot of the group Shura-e Nazar led by Ahmed Shah Massoud, Abdul Rasul Sayyaf's Islamic Union for the Liberation of Afghanistan, Sayyid Ahmed Gailani's[14] National Islamic Front for Afghanistan, Sibghatullah Mojadeddi's[15] National Salvation of Afghanistan and finally Mohammed Nabi Mohammedi's[16] Islamic Revolution Movement of Afghanistan. This excludes the Shi'ite groups, known as the Tehran Eight under the wing of Ayatollah Khomeini's Iran. Considering such disunity and rivalry, it was a miracle that these groups achieved victory against the Soviets at all. And whilst Sayyaf had been chosen to be leader of these various factions the rivalries continued. Eventually the split especially between Hekmatyar and Massoud led to the final rupture of the *mujahideen* factions, and it made victory against the Soviets taste bitter as civil war ensued in the newly liberated country.

Meanwhile whilst all this was going on in Central Asia, I, Abdullah Anas from Algeria, did not even know where Afghanistan was located on the map or what its customs were let alone tell the difference between the politics of Massoud and Hekmatyar. All I knew was that I wanted to help my Muslim brothers in Afghanistan.

I never thought then, as I stood in a magazine shop in Bel Abbas, that I would play a role in the Soviet Army's withdrawal. I used to come to the city because a newsagent stocked papers wherein I could glean the latest international news. It was an arduous task, and I had to travel 40 km just to do that. But on that day things were different. I picked up the Arab world's equivalent of the *National Geographic, Majalla al-Mujtama'*, run by the Kuwaiti Muslim Brotherhood. In it was a ruling, a fatwa, by a group of scholars including Abd al-Aziz bin Baaz, Yusuf al-Qardawi and Abdullah Azzam. And I had by now familiarised myself with Sheikh Abdullah after our chance meeting in Mecca. I knew he was linked to the Brotherhood and the Afghan Jihad, I was also aware that he was vehemently opposed to communism having published books like *The Red Cancer*, but my attention was drawn to the ruling because of the fact that Sheikh bin Baaz, a leading Saudi scholar, was a signatory alongside religious scholars from the Gulf and other countries. Sheikh Abdallah Azzam was someone who shared my affiliation to the Islamic movement but that was it.

And so I purchased the magazine, more on account of bin Baaz's endorsement rather than Azzam's. I crossed the street to a coffee shop known to make some of the best espresso in Bel Abbas and sat in the shade to read the article. I drank my macchiato, and considered the legal proposition that the sheikh was making: in essence the ruling argued that it was a religious obligation on all Muslim males to go to fight Jihad in Afghanistan and repel Soviet aggression; avoiding this duty could amount to sin. I looked at the evidence and became convinced that Afghanistan had to be saved from this godless Communist ideology that was being imposed on the people. This I should stress was not because I loved war—far from it, I wasn't affected by this unnatural desire to kill and fight the infidel that many of this new generation seem to revel in. War to me was an unfortunate state of affairs, and I wanted to go to Jihad because I viewed it as one of my duties to protect the weak and oppressed, and if I achieved martyrdom so much the better. I didn't hate Russians in and of themselves and even after my experiences in Afghanistan my view hasn't changed. But here I was sitting in the cafe, on a hot sunny afternoon, convinced by the legal arguments, and I had no means of realising them.

Since I had already intended to go on a pilgrimage that very year I thought Mecca might be the best place to start. The initial plan had been to work as a guide to pilgrims and to further my studies in Mecca and Medina with some of the very best scholars that the Islamic world had produced. But now with this new idea in mind I thought that I might find someone there in Mecca who would be able to assist me in travelling to Afghanistan. If not in Mecca and Medina where else could one receive help from the Divine? The pilgrimage was the largest gathering of humanity in the world. Scholars of Islam used the Hajj to meet, congregate and highlight Muslim issues all over the world. Surely, I could find someone who could help? And so I embarked on fulfilling one of the five pillars of Islam, and at the same time, hoping to meet someone who could help facilitate my journey onwards.

I performed the Hajj joining my fellow pilgrims in my *Ihram*, the two piece cotton cloth that pilgrims wear, I partook in its rituals, my voice joined with my fellow pilgrims saying '*Labaik, labaik ya Allah*'—'At your service, at your service my Lord'. In that throng of humanity I found myself entering the Holy Sanctuary of Mecca, where the black stone was encased, where Abraham prayed, where Adam had established the first house of worship, where the cries of the infant Ismail had rang out and the well of Zamzam sprang forth, and where I saw a man in *Ihram* and a child drinking from the waters of Zamzam. I wasn't sure if the man in front of me was Abdallah Azzam or not. It was night and I had little time to verify his identity before the throng would swallow him up yet again as they circumambulated the Kaaba. So despite my shyness, I approached him and asked him if he was indeed Abdallah Azzam and he confirmed it. I can only attribute this second meeting to Divine providence.

I told him that I had read his legal ruling and was convinced by it, but I did not know how to get to Afghanistan let alone participate. 'Simple,' he said handing me his phone number, 'this is my number in Islamabad, I will return to Pakistan after Hajj, get in touch with me when you get there. I will introduce you to the Afghan leaders in Peshawar.' Then he asked me when I intended to travel and whether I had the resources for travel, as if he could cater for that too in case I was short of funds. I told him that I had the means to travel. 'I'll be ready', I said, 'after fifteen days.'

He left me with those words but also made a lasting impression on me which I will take with me to the grave. God has granted me a long life, and I have had the privilege of sitting with some of the best men and women of the Muslim world and I can tell you that I never met a man like him. Although I suffered initial setbacks in obtaining a visa for entering Pakistan, a chance meeting with a religious student from Lahore with strong connections in the Pakistani embassy ensured that I eventually got my visa. I booked my Kuwait Air flight to Karachi and within fifteen days I was bound for Pakistan.

Karachi was a culture shock. Everything was different. I found myself in a country where I did not know the language or its people, I could not communicate with them in English, French or Arabic. It was a bewildering experience. As I emerged from the airport into dusty bustling streets, I discovered that I shared it with all of God's creatures. The poverty was intense, some slept on the streets with dogs whilst a brand new Mercedes drove past oblivious to the pain and suffering of the downtrodden, and then right next to the Mercedes would be a tired mule taking its master to wherever he wished to go all at once. We didn't have such disparities of wealth in Algeria.

The smells too were different, the street vendors who served milky tea with cinnamon instead of espresso, the smell of fried samosas, the colourful clothes, everything I had known had to be reassessed. Somehow—for Google Translate didn't exist in those days—using gestures, Arabic and snatches of English I managed to purchase a ticket to Islamabad, the capital. I called the sheikh from a public phone as soon as I landed. I was hot, tired, and prayed the sheikh would remember me. I went to a phone booth and dialled the number he had given me. When the voice at the receiving end answered, I told him who I was. The voice remembered me immediately. 'Have you eaten?' was the first thing he asked: his concern for my welfare struck me, as he barely knew me. 'No', I replied. 'Then I'll be expecting you for dinner. Take a taxi and give the driver the address.'

I did as instructed and hailed a taxi. It took me to his house in a well-to-do suburb in Islamabad. I stood in front of his door and rang the bell. The door opened and I was met by a man in his late forties, he looked hardy, he clasped my hand and welcomed me so heartily that I forgot the feeling of loneliness and alienation in this most foreign of countries. He led me to the salon and I entered in on a group of guests already tucking into dinner on the floor. I always remember his house being full of his students from the Islamic university. Many teachers like to keep the line between teacher and student distinct for familiarity breeds contempt, but he blurred the lines between teacher and student without a single thought. He treated them more like his younger brothers. After dinner he asked that I stay with him; there was simply no point in travelling on my own to meet Afghan leaders, I would get nowhere without a personal recommendation and someone vouching for me.[17] Etiquette required an introduction, and it was decided there and then that he would accompany me to Peshawar and introduce me to the people of Jihad so I could fulfil my religious duty.

Following the Prophetic custom of hospitality the sheikh hosted me for three days. He didn't know who I was or what I wanted: I could have been a Mossad agent or part of the Arab intelligence services, I could have been anyone. But he wasn't afraid at all, and he bought me tickets to Peshawar. On the day of our departure, as we all sat down to lunch, the sheikh introduced me to a man whose name would ring out all over the world on 11 September 2001.

'This is Brother Osama bin Laden,' he said introducing us, 'he is from the young Saudis who love the Afghan Jihad.' Osama appeared shy and introverted and spoke very little. I didn't get to work with him much during the Afghan Jihad simply because our activities centred around different places. I was mostly based in north Afghanistan, and he was mostly based in the border areas of Jalalabad, Jaji and Paktia, so we never campaigned together nor did we share any battles together but I will come to our relationship in later chapters.

3

THE ROAD TO SHOLGARA NEAR
MAZAR SHARIF

I travelled on the same day I had my fleeting encounter with Osama bin Laden, with Sheikh Abdullah, his son-in-law, Abu Hassan al-Maqdisi, engineer Abu Mu'ad Saa'di, the late Abu Akram and another friend of his. The flight was no more than twenty minutes and we landed in a small airport on the outskirts of Peshawar. There we were met by the driver of Abdul Rasul Sayyaf, the leader of the *mujahideen* parties. Whilst the Afghan *mujahideen* were united against the common enemy they were also split between seven parties, and at the head of these factions was Sayyaf. He had been chosen to lead them. Sheikh Abdullah Azzam made the formal introductions and I noticed that the leader of the Islamic Union had quick intelligent eyes, a beard that reached down to his chest and a generous demeanour. Sayyaf had studied in al-Azhar around the same time Sheikh Abdullah was researching his PhD but their paths had never crossed till the war broke out in Afghanistan. But it gave them a degree of closeness that men who have studied in the same institutions usually have. He was learned and charismatic with a prodigious memory. Once when the hugely influential Abu'l Hassan al-Nadawi, known as the Syed Qutb of India, was delivering a lecture at Kabul University, Sayyaf translated the whole lecture into Persian word for word without mistakes after the former had finished delivering the entire lecture. It was a testimony to his impressive and photographic memory. His fluency in Arabic, Persian and Pashto and his ability to flit from one language to the other was remarkable and made him well placed to become one of the leading men in Afghanistan. But being one of its leading men meant that he had also suffered for the cause. Whilst teaching at the faculty of Islamic Studies at Kabul University he had joined Jamiat al-Islami—the party of his fellow Azhari Burhanuddin Rabbani—and engaged in political activities against Daoud Khan's government. He was arrested for his activities in 1974 and was only released from prison under a general amnesty in 1980.

Sayyaf and his two companions Sheikh Fayyad, a graduate of Medina University, and Muhammed Yasir received us in his guest-house. Over food and tea he summed up how minuscule the Arab presence was in Afghanistan at the time: 'there are only twelve Arabs', he said, 'with you three that makes fifteen.' Despite what some analysts would like to portray, that was the number of Afghan Arab volunteers that were present when I arrived. Our contribution was tiny. None of the famous figures who became proponents of Global Jihad such as Abu Mus'ab Zarqawi,[1] Abu Hamza al-Masri,[2] Ayman al-Zawahiri[3] and indeed Abu Qatada[4] were in Afghanistan fighting the Soviets. It is important to stress this to dispel some of the myths that have grown around these so-called icons or heroes of global Jihadism.

Sayyaf moved us to the small town of Pabbi about 20 kilometres from Peshawar. It was a refugee camp which Sayaaf ran, and alongside it was a training camp called Mukhayim al-Badr or camp Badr, named in honour of the famous battle of Badr, where the Prophet and a small group of Muslims defeated a larger Qureishi force during the month of Ramadan. This training camp would be my home and I would share it with the twelve Arabs, mostly Syrians and Iraqis, that Sayyaf had mentioned. Amongst them if my memory serves me right was Abu al-Jud al-Iraqi and his brother Abu'l Khayr, Abu Muhammad al-Kurdi and Abu Isam al-Libi. The former two never participated in an armed capacity and were involved only in educational and humanitarian activities whilst supporting the Afghan Jihad.[5]

It was during these introductions that the sheikh gave me the *nom de guerre* Abdallah Anas. This was done for the sake of ease: 'Bou Jouma' was hard to pronounce and was the Algerian contraction for Abu Jouma. I don't know if this was intentional or it was because the sheikh introduced me to my comrades as 'this is Abdallah or this is Anas' but it stuck and I take it as a source of pride to carry the name he gave me.

But whilst I was a guest of the Afghans I learnt very quickly how sensitive my hosts were. We had to be extremely sensitive to the needs of the Afghans, we had come to serve them not to impose our ways on them. I realised this quite early on, on the second day of my stay in Pabbi. Sheikh Azzam was out with Sayyaf and we were in the camp when the night prayer, *Esha*, entered upon us. The *mujahideen* put me forward to lead the prayer. And so I led the men in prayer and everyone in the village could hear my voice. After the prayer Sheikh Abdullah and Sayyaf came in and asked who had led the men in prayer, so one of the fighters responded by saying: 'This Algerian here.' 'Didn't I tell you', said Sheikh Abdullah, tongue in cheek, 'that this recitation isn't the way the Afghans recite the Quran?' 'Do you all think that it's only you who can recite the Quran?' Sayyaf added jokingly, 'do you think the Afghans ignorant and that they don't know how to recite the Quran? And its only you the Arabs?'

Though it was said in jest, the points still stood. I was embarrassed and felt awkward, I hadn't realised that perhaps just reciting in a different style could cause the locals problems. My recitation had been in *Warsh*, the Quranic recitation style popular in North Africa, while in the subcontinent they recited in the *Hafs* style. Many ordinary Afghans could easily misconstrue my recitation style as someone distorting the Quran because they didn't know that there are seven different Quranic *Qiraat* or recitation styles, that expressed the same meaning with subtle nuances. The two men had subtly taught me that the Afghan national character was intensely conservative and traditional. My ability to adapt to their ways was probably why I managed to last so long, for many Arabs didn't last long. And perhaps this is something that a lot of our young men have forgotten as they visit countries with ancient and deep traditions.

Sheikh Abdallah left us for Islamabad, as he had to fulfil his teaching commitments having introduced me to the relevant people, and I continued as Imam to the handful of Arabs there. Of course I knew that I hadn't come here to sit around in Peshawar. I was in my early twenties, full of zeal, and like many of our young Muslim men I wanted to take part in active duty. I, along with my comrades in arms, took part in military training and prepared to take part in military operations inside Afghanistan. Most fighters like today were given Kalashnikovs and shown how to use them. We practised how to use it effectively, learnt military drills, tactics and exercises which they taught at military colleges around the world. I had come across much of it due to my military service in Algeria; nevertheless, it was a good reminder. Yet whilst I was full of enthusiasm for the military life, at the same time, I didn't want to rush headlong into a conflict without knowing what was going on in Afghanistan and what service I could render its people.

I was given that opportunity two months later when Sheikh Abdullah visited us again. Our mission was not frontline fighting but intelligence gathering. Sheikh Abdullah understood that the first thing you have to do in a conflict is to understand the true nature of the conflict. You didn't go in with any pre-conceived notions of how things should be run but rather what the facts on the ground were. For only then could you help the people. 'Men', Sheikh Abdullah told us as we listened attentively, 'I want you to spread out inside Afghanistan. I want you to go in to these provinces and really understand what is going on there. Is the situation really like how Western media has portrayed it?'

He also stressed that this mission was voluntary—whoever wanted to join the caravan could do so. We would go in for a month or six months, it was up to us as to where we could go, whether it was the border lands, north, south, east or west. A convoy was being organised to go to the front. I volunteered to travel to the North. Sheikh Abdullah told me that I would join one of the Afghan religious scholars who was with him, Mawlawi[6] Abd al-Aziz, and that I could accompany him to Mazar Sharif where the latter came from. I was to join one of these caravans bound for Mazar Sharif which would set out in ten days' time.

These caravans of Jihad that Sheikh Abdullah was talking and writing about were not metaphorical—they were real and had a practical purpose. The convoys would come into the North-West Frontier Province full of fighters from inside Afghanistan numbering in tens, hundreds or sometimes thousands of men. These men usually belonged to seven *mujahideen* factions inside Afghanistan. But on the whole they belonged to the two most influential groups: the factions of Hekmatyar and Rabbani. Both were politically sagacious: the former in particular had cultivated a good relationship with the Pakistani state. The latter however was more politically astute and an excellent manager of men inside Afghanistan. These untrained arrivals would then be trained up, drilled and armed. By the time the Pakistanis were finished the men had military discipline and were ready to take the fight to the Communists in a new convoy laden with supplies, arms and men. Each caravan would be known by its respective group; so one might be known as the convoy of Muhammad Nabi or Hekmatyar and so on. The return to Afghanistan, however, was dangerous. The Soviet Union knew very well that Pakistan was arming the insurgency and they tried their utmost to cut off the supply routes of these convoys. And so these disciplined fighters experienced heavy shelling and fire as they returned. I would join one of these returning caravans of Rabbani.

Whilst preparing to make my first trip to the interior, I was told that the various *mujahideen* factions were disunited and that it was crucial that we the Arabs remained neutral. The last thing we wanted to do was to aggravate the situation further. In fact, before setting out Sheikh Abdullah handed me a letter to deliver to the local emir and instructed me to make sure I visited him every three or four days around Mazar Sharif depending on my circumstances. For whilst I may have joined the caravan under the auspices of Burhanuddin Rabbani's Jamiat-i Islami, the province was not subject to his party and it was important that I visited the other local leaders of the other factions too. Courtesies had to be paid to Mullah Abdul Salaam of the Hezb-i Islami lest he think I preferred Rabbani's party over his own.

But I did not realise the true extent and nature of this disunity until I actually got there. And so from then on, my focus was not just on fighting the Soviets but also fostering unity and resolving conflict. Diplomacy was just as important as the Kalashnikov in this fractured political environment. As a guest of the Afghan people I made sure I kept to decorum and protocol. If we stayed in the house of one local emir of Hezb-i Islami for two days, we made sure we stayed in the house of the emir of Jamiaat-i Islami for two days too. This may appear pedantic but it helped us maintain political equilibrium between the various factions. If one didn't take into account the various impulses that motivate human nature from time immemorial, grave miscalculations could occur with disastrous consequences in war. The last thing we wanted was an accusation that the Arabs were siding with one party or the other when we had come to help Afghans rid themselves of the Soviets.

Ten days later my convoy belonging to Rabbani set out for Sholgara near Mazar Sharif. Mazar Sharif itself was occupied by the enemy. There were only three Arabs in the convoy: a Syrian, Abu Usayd;[7] a Kuwaiti, Diya al-Rahman; and me. In Islamic tradition whenever there are three travellers one should appoint an emir, or leader, and Sheikh Abdullah appointed me as their emir.

We left for Afghanistan in the depth of winter in 1984 and I was wholly unprepared for what an Afghan winter meant. Not only did I underestimate the weather but I also underestimated the length of my initial adventure: it would take forty days to reach Mazar Sharif, the capital of Balkh province in northern Afghanistan. As we trudged towards our destination for what seemed like forever, the snow continued to fall and the cold penetrated our very bones. One of the men died due to the bitter cold. But there was no choice but to continue since returning to Pakistan was near enough impossible and would have probably taken an equal amount of time. There were of course other difficulties, namely that of language. I didn't know Persian yet, and sometimes it would cause a lot of confusion especially as many Persian words are derived from Arabic words but mean quite different things. But despite these difficulties our hearts were content and happy. For at least we were close to those brave Afghans that had been doing this for at least four years, fighting the Soviets despite their military might.

On the way to Mazar Sharif we also came across an area known as Hazarajat in central Afghanistan which incorporated the provinces of Bamian, Ghor and Oruzgan. It was at the crossroads of the ancient silk route which connected Asia with Europe, and a place of cultural confluence. It was also a testimony to Islam's tolerance of other faiths, for this lush and verdant place stood out in the starkness of the mountains. Bamian housed the famous Buddhist statues that were remarkable in terms of the human endeavour involved. Even though Buddhism was no longer practiced in the country the Taliban decided to destroy these ancient statues and of course provoked a retaliation by angry Buddhists who desecrated the Quran in anger. These Buddhists had nothing against Islam until the thing that they held sacred was destroyed.

But Hazarajat was different because of its population. The emir of the convoy, Zareef, made us aware of it. The twenty-four-year-old young man, with little or no education had throughout the journey behaved as if he had graduated from a military college. He displayed such maturity, skill and proficiency in handling his three hundred men, munitions and arms that he was respected by all. And he seemed determined to carry out his mission to Mazar Sharif and beyond to the Russian border. His care for us left a lasting impression on me even though I never saw him after that. Although there was a language barrier, he managed to convey the idea that we were entering a Shi'ite area. In fact, later on I discovered that the Hazara population had settled there with the arrival of the Mongols. They were Sunnis who converted to Shi'a Islam under the Safavids in the sixteenth century. Their features and indeed language testified to their Mongol Turkic heritage. As a result of their sectarian affiliation I was made to understand that they may not be so welcoming towards us Arabs and might even use it as an excuse to hamper or even sabotage the progress of the convoy. And so Zareef instructed us to travel in complete silence so we didn't draw attention to ourselves. We didn't exchange a single word those three days. We even changed our head gear to the local ones in order to blend in but I think it was unsuccessful for I sensed that the locals viewed our convoy with suspicion. Suddenly, the price of bread rose up to extortionate prices. If a baker from Hazarajat usually charged three rupees for bread, he would charge us thirty. This was the first time I had experienced sectarianism, for in Algeria, except for a small number of Ibadis, most of us were Sunnis and never experienced brazen forms of sectarianism. It was a complete culture shock.

So we travelled through in silence for three days, not fully understanding what was happening around us because asking an interpreter might give us away. Zareef expended much effort to protect us from prying eyes but in the end we were caught. We just didn't blend in. That night we were eating dinner in a res-taurant—now, when I say restaurant, it wasn't the sort that had tables, chairs, candles and menus. Rather our restaurant was a fluttering spartan tent serving one dish—a hunk of bread and a pot of tea devoid of sugar granules. The lack of sugar in particu-lar, was perhaps the greatest discomfort for us North Africans who love our tea sweet. But by now we had become accustomed to drinking plain tea and bread because we had been eating it every day up to now. But this dinner was like no other, for we had visitors. Local officials entered our tent—they were inspec-tors working for the local authorities in Hazarajat and had prob-ably had a tip off. They walked amongst the men staring into their faces, and soon enough one of these inspectors approached Zareef and asked, 'do you have any foreigners with you?' Zareef replied with a negative. But they persisted in their line of ques-tioning. It was as if they knew. 'You do have foreigners amongst you,' they insisted scouring the tent.

Soon they approached me: 'Speak Persian', they ordered. Of course I couldn't and stayed silent. They realised that I was a foreigner and asked me to accompany them to their office. I did as I was told and followed them. As I entered their office of the local Hazara administrators I saw behind them a large picture of

Ayatollah Khomeini. One of the administrators who I presumed was the boss due to him sitting behind a desk surrounded by subordinates, asked me in a strange Arabic accent where I was from. 'I am Algerian, I replied truthfully. 'How did you enter Afghanistan without a visa?' 'I didn't know you required a visa', I replied, 'in Afghanistan you have a government subject to the Russians and the people are fighting them. I didn't know you needed one, we entered Afghanistan with those who wanted freedom. I did not know I needed to have a visa from you people as well.'

Like all bureaucrats he replied, 'You need to have a visa otherwise you cannot enter our province.' I was in big trouble. 'What has happened', I said, 'has happened, what must I do now?' 'I need to look into your affair' said the official raising the level of complication and difficulty a notch higher. There was no way the men I was with could help me. For we would have to travel five days in Hazarajat territory and we couldn't be travelling and fighting the Hazara until we got to Mazar Sharif. They would cut us off and tear us to pieces: we were only three hundred after all.

'In Algeria', I said appealing to their affection for Ayatollah Khomeini, 'I have read that Imam Khomeini is the imam of the weak and downtrodden. And I am at this moment downtrodden and in need. I thought, as I entered Afghanistan, that I would be the guest of the Afghan people. But this meeting has surprised me. I am shocked by this behaviour, obviously I am wrong.' The words had their effect, the tense atmosphere became calmer. And the little administrator behind the big desk waved his hand, 'Go', he said, 'finished—*khalas*, go complete your journey with your convoy.' Diplomacy took me further than the Kalashnikov in this instance. But what I had said about Khomeini hadn't been mere dissimulation. All of us had been influenced and bolstered by the Iranian revolution in 1979. Khomeini—this austere dignified and devout figure—struck quite a contrast to the Shah who flaunted his corruption on the world stage. The fact that the former deposed the latter was interpreted as providence and showed us that Islamic government was possible. Of course this was before I realised that the Islamic Republic could be just as cynical as any other state, secular or otherwise. Nevertheless in those days me and my companions would go to the Iranian embassy in Algiers to collect the translated audio-tapes of Khomeini and the revolutionary magazine *al-Shahid* to distribute them amongst my friends. We even ran the gauntlet of Algerian checkpoints who viewed us with a degree of curiosity and suspicion for having these propaganda materials on our person.

After over a month of walking we arrived in the province of Balkh where the provincial capital was Mazar Sharif. Since medieval times, Mazar Sharif, which means 'the noble shrine', has been a local trading hub for the silk route and had witnessed the rule of Seljuk sultans as well as the hooves of Genghis Khan's army. Locals believe that the shrine from which the city derives its name houses the body of Imam Ali, the third caliph of Islam, nephew and son-in-law of the Prophet. The shrine was also said to have contained the mantle of the Prophet. Others believe that the shrine actually possesses the body of the Prophet Zoroaster whilst Imam Ali's grave is really in Najaf. By 1979 the city was a peaceful place more in love with the poetry of Rumi's *Masnavi* than Communist ideas but that peace was ruptured with the Soviet invasion of Afghanistan. Mazar Sharif itself was under the control of the Communists whilst the *mujahideen* controlled the surrounding areas.

When we arrived at the first check point which belonged to Rabanni's Jamat-i Islami, the *mujahideen* started to magnify God, shouting 'God is the Greatest', and they fired their weapons joyously. The convoy decided to leave me with them for they had another three days journeying and could not wait for me. The journey had taken its toll on me: my nails had become black and fallen off due to the extreme cold and I was suffering from severe frost bite, and I was hampering their progress. The men manning the checkpoint took me to Qari Ibrahim's house, one of the local judges in the area, so I could recover. I stayed there resting my limbs whilst they searched for a doctor and medicine to cure me. But there was no medicine or doctor to be had and so they put me in bed and put an ointment made of fermented grapes on my blackened nails and feet and prayed that God would heal me and left. I stayed in bed for three days until the pain receded bit by bit. And soon I was able to accompany another caravan going in the direction of Mazar Sharif and Sholgara, our final destination.

When we arrived in Sholgara we had expected to be the first foreigners there. In fact, perhaps there was a touch of self-congratulation as we entered the town, that we were the first Arabs, nay the first Muslims to have come to serve the Afghans. To my surprise however, we had been preceded by a group of French doctors who had come before us and had been living there for the past four years! I could not help but marvel at these non-Muslims who were more concerned about the welfare of Muslims than Muslims themselves. Such humanity left a lasting impression on me.

But moreover what was even more disappointing was that we arrived to the sound of tears and wailing women. I was surprised by such a response as previously we had been given a rapturous welcome accompanied by gunfire. What had happened? Why were we received with tears? What did we do? Could it be a different custom or tradition? Everything here was different. Abu Usayd the Syrian, my comrade in arms, scratched his head and wondered why the situation had changed so suddenly.

When we tried to find out what happened, no information was forthcoming. When we wanted to meet the local emir Abdul Qadir Zabibullah, this was not possible. We were not given a reason as to why he was indisposed. Every time we asked about him, the Afghans seemed to obfuscate and keep the truth from us. When we approached a group of fighters sitting down, visibly sad, as they saw our approach they would wipe their tears, smile and tell us that everything was fine. This subterfuge was part of being a good Afghan host. As their guests it was not befitting on their part to be sad in front of us in case we would be offended and made to feel like a burden on them. At the same time they didn't want to worry us so they used various ruses to keep us distracted and prevent us from asking too many questions about this momentous event which had rocked Sholgara.

But we still had to see Emir Zabibullah and went to see the vice Emir Mawlawi 'Alam, a scholar and graduate of Islamic jurisprudence at Kabul University. Whilst he received us courteously he was unhelpful. He didn't want to reveal the news to us. 'Where is Zabibullah?', we asked politely. 'We want to see him. All the men have been talking about him throughout the forty days, and we finally arrive and we can't see him?' During our journey in every town, village or home we entered, every person we met mentioned him with only praise and recounted his virtues. And though we, the Arabs, had not met him, we too wanted to meet this walking legend who was a master in guerrilla warfare and wise governance. Zabibullah used to be a teacher in Mazar Sharif before the Saur Revolt in April 1978 brought the Communists to power. Being affiliated to the Islamic movement he fled to Pakistan, joined up with the *mujahideen* factions in 1979 and worked closely with Massoud in Panshir and Baghlan gaining much success against the Soviets. 'Where', we demanded, 'is the emir?'

But the vice emir evaded our questions, and kept the news away from us until the leader of Jamaat-i Islami announced his death through the wires in Peshawar. He had been killed when his car struck a landmine. We were all shocked by the news. This explained everything. The women of Sholgara, despite the strictness of their menfolk, couldn't prevent their sorrow at home. And though I didn't know this man, I realised his worth just from the impact his death had on the area. Truth was the area never fully recovered from his passing, and the *mujahideen* could never mount a concerted attack to dislodge the Communists after his passing.

The untimely death of Zabibullah had created a power vacuum. Again instead of fighting the Soviets, I turned my attention to conflict resolution and peace building. I sensed that political rivalry was rearing its ugly head and threatening to destabilise the political equilibrium, and the discipline that Zabibullah had managed to achieve through the force of his personality. The consequences of this rupture would almost certainly be grave, for under the late emir's command were nine thousand fighting men. What was more the administrative and military authority were split between different factions which could cause a potential disaster. Political rivalries and dividing up power could escalate into a local civil war. This problem had to be solved as soon as possible.

This is when I started to tout the idea of Ahmed Shah Massoud, for he was held in even higher regard than Zabibullah. Before my arrival to Mazar Sharif I had no idea who this Massoud was but I realised that alongside the late Zabibullah another name was mentioned: Emir Sahib. I did not realise at the time that this name was used by Afghans as a term of respect. It only dawned on me when I visited Zabibullah's successor, Mawlawi 'Alam, who informed us that it was referring to Ahmed Shah Massoud. 'Our entire front', said Mawlawi Alam, 'is under his command, it is he who taught Zabibullah, he is a great teacher of Jihad.' I soon came to realise that all the local factions—whether military, administrative or local powers—respected Massoud's authority, and if I could get to him perhaps the political rupture could be prevented.

I went to Mawlawi 'Alam and requested a visit to Massoud. Whilst not averse to the visit the emir worried about the harsh winter conditions. 'It will take fifteen days to reach the Panshir valley,' he said genuinely concerned for my welfare, 'the Russians might ambush you.' I didn't blame him for his concern. My previously blackened toenails were only now growing back and I was proposing another dangerous journey. To get to Panshir I had to traverse several provinces—Samangan, Kunduz, Baghlan and Takhar—all of them mountainous and harsh during the winter months. However much I insisted, Mawlawi 'Alam was adamant, 'I cannot let you go', he insisted, and I returned back to my lodgings despondent. But Mawlawi 'Alam was probably right, I was still pretty inexperienced and the truth was the situation in Sholgara was bigger than we three Arabs. How could we make a difference when in reality we were inexperienced, young, lacked training, and had no money to speak of?

That is when I realised that the situation in Afghanistan required the sort of fighter who was cultured, who could provide education, humanitarian aid, and religious instruction as well as military assistance. Diplomacy, statesmanship, was just as important as making the Soviets eat Kalashnikov bullets. We were none of those things. And I wagered that there were very few men like that amongst us. There was simply no way that twenty or twenty-five Arabs could deal with this. I had to convey this idea to Sheikh Abdullah and then see how we could deal with the situation.

After six months, I decided to return to Peshawar and inform Sheikh Abdullah about what I had witnessed and seen on the ground. Whilst Mawlawi 'Alam prepared the return convoy, I utilised my time studying the situation deeply. When I left, Mawlawi 'Alam was gracious and generous and provided me with a guide and a steed so that I could travel through the various areas controlled by the different factions. And as I travelled through these mountainous regions devoid of roads, electricity and basic facilities and sitting with men in caves, homes and hearths it became clear that Sayyaf might be the leader of the *mujahideen* in Peshawar, but the real power-brokers on the ground were the factions of Hekmatyar and Rabbani. They were in control. And this is what I conveyed on my return to Peshawar in a written report to the sheikh.

But I barely had a chance to rest for as soon as I arrived in Peshawar, mid-1985, Azzam expected me in Mecca and I did not return to Afghanistan until after my trip which will be covered later. When I returned I decided again to return to Balkh, Mazar Sharif to try to resolve the issues that I had encountered there. I had hoped that the sheikh would give me Wael Julaidan[8] or as he was known Abu'l Hassan al-Madani to solve those issues. It was clear that Julaidan was an organisational genius with a knack for people and was respected by all factions. But Sheikh Abdullah refused my request because he wanted to use Julaidan's talents for serving the Afghans and manage the relationships between the various Afghan leaders in Peshawar. What became increasingly clear was that the infernal politicking between the groups caused much difficulty for all of us whether in Mazar Sharif or Peshawar.

For instance in Peshawar, when I was preparing my return convoy to Mazar Sharif, I made it very clear to the sheikh that the dominant power in Balkh was not that of Sayyaf. The seven Afghan leaders may have sworn an allegiance to Sayyaf in the Kaaba but real power belonged to Hekmatyar's and Rabbani's parties inside Afghanistan. That wasn't an exaggeration: it was just a fact and it was crucial for delivering aid. So when I took shoes, clothes and medicines from the Saudi Red Crescent with me to the interior, Sayyaf accused the other parties of having deceived me. He wanted his party to have parity in the distribution of aid supplies, whereas I believed it should be proportional to the control each party exercised inside Afghanistan. The simple fact was that Sayyaf's group had less control because of his time in prison which allowed the other groups to gain a greater foothold in the country. And whenever Sayyaf members would try to convince me otherwise I would reiterate this statement of fact: I had visited those areas myself and had no reason to falsify my claims in favour of one party or another.

In the end I got my way and I left that summer of 1985 with a convoy that was adequately supplied. Wael Julaidan wasn't with me, but he had helped me to secure the help of some doctors who would accompany me. It took a lot of work, but Julaidan and I made the rounds of the various guest-houses appealing for doctors. It took a lot of convincing since these men were volunteers and Julaidan had no direct authority over them. But he was eloquent and charming and we convinced them using a combination of God's pleasure for helping the oppressed and downtrodden and highlighting the fact that there were French doctors, yes, French doctors in Mazar Sharif helping our co-religionists when it should be us doing that job. Where were the Muslims in rendering help? Should we not be the first? It was a shameful state of affairs. And so a British trained Libyan medic, Dr Saleh al-Libi responded to our entreaties as did Dr Abdul-Zahir from Egypt. Despite the dangers they faced both did immense good for the people of Afghanistan. The former lost his life serving the people and the latter stayed with us for a year before returning.

We entered Mazar Sharif in summer having trekked for thirty days. When we arrived, we found the political rivalry between the various factions still there. And so this time I went to Mawlawi 'Alam and told him that a visit to Massoud was of utmost importance. The weather was no longer an impediment and the Soviet menace was lessening. Mawlawi 'Alam agreed to my request and I set off in search of Massoud.

What I am offering here of course is a glimpse of what I saw in Mazar Sharif. There were other commanders whose legacy is still felt to this day, for instance Qadi[9] Mawlawi Abdullah Alam

Khan and military commanders such as Muhammed Ata Khan; the latter's contributions for instance, in the war against the Soviets and his rebuilding efforts, have been immense.

PART II

MASSOUD AND ME

4

IN SEARCH OF MASSOUD

Now many of my critics have often depicted me as someone with an undying loyalty to Massoud and therefore my assessment of him is coloured by this friendship. It is true that I was a comrade in arms with him, and of course, when you share life and death experiences and war, a bond is certainly formed. It's human nature. But that does not mean that I cannot view him critically. My regard for Massoud is not out of the ordinary: many others, Muslims and non-Muslims alike, hold similar views to mine.[1] Sheikh Azzam penned an entire book entitled 'A Month amongst the Titans of the North' after he met the commander. The book goes into lucid detail as to why Massoud was known as the Lion of Panshir.

It is important to stress that this polarisation of views about the men who fought in the conflict has come about due to the divisive narrative of the war on terror which has been accepted uncritically both by the West and the Muslim world. Instead of looking at the conflict in Afghanistan as being nuanced and multi-layered, we have been straight-jacketed into looking at the world in black and white. And so many figures are depicted as warlords, terrorists, freedom fighters and many other things without taking into account the many experiences and challenges they faced. They have become caricatures and serve nothing but to reinforce one's prejudices. And any attempt to think outside the box is shouted down as showing disloyalty to whatever team one belongs to. For instance, we overlook the fact that Osama bin Laden's victory against the Soviets at the battle of Jaji in 1987 was nothing compared to Massoud's campaigns against the Russians. He repulsed nine Russian campaigns against him over a period of ten years. This isn't because I fought alongside him, but a fact. Whilst there were certainly contacts between Western intelligence services as with other *mujahideen* leaders, I don't think these contacts were as extensive as many writers have suggested.[2] I was someone who was a boon companion from 1982–92: the first three years I was with him constantly, and in all that time I never saw him meet any Western intelligence agents that I was aware of. The visitors he met were either journalists like the intrepid Sandy Gall, academics like Olivier Roy and humanitarian activists. I never saw the help that the CIA rendered the *mujahideen* through the ISI reach Massoud. And I most certainly never saw those legendary stinger missiles that have been so celebrated in Western media reach Massoud; in fact the only ones he got hold of, that I witnessed personally, were in 1987 when Massoud got word that some local commanders had received a batch from Peshawar, and knowing that these local village commanders would never have need of them nor would they know how to use them, he sent some of his commanders to purchase them. That then was the extent of the military assistance that I witnessed. And it wasn't strange that he would receive so little help: the ISI, the Pakistani intelligence services viewed him as too independent for their liking, and certainly there was some truth to that. I have never known him to act under anyone's orders, ISI or otherwise, for the sake of money or power. He acted in the interests of his countrymen and faith. It may have been different for other *mujahideen* commanders but out there in the Panshir, Massoud seemed to take on the Russians alone.[3] Modern day Salafi-Jihadists who celebrate the martial valour of Osama bin Laden would do well to study the history of Afghanistan. To me it doesn't sound strange that an obituary of Massoud in the *Wall Street Journal* stated that the only victor of the Cold War was he, for I fought alongside him and saw what he could do.[4] In the following chapters I shall recount my experiences of him.

When I finally entered Massoud's territory armed with a letter of introduction amongst other things, he was nowhere to be found. Massoud was the master of hide and seek: sometimes it seemed to me that he was almost like a child, wily and clever. They say that he used to love swimming in the river coursing through the Panshir valley, playing hide and seek with the children, climbing into the branches of trees, hiding in nooks and crannies toying with his opponents. And perhaps it was this natural wiliness, not just his erudition in military strategy, that made him like a ghost to the Russians.

But my guide, Abdul Qader As-Sayyar, was confident that he would find us. 'Don't worry', he said studying the crags in the distance, as if he was searching for a hardy mountain lion in the vastness of the Hindu Kush, 'he's here', he said with total conviction as if he sensed that he was. He was convinced that Massoud had us in his binoculars. The Russians might doubt Abdul Qader's judgement, but I didn't. They were 'looking' for Massoud using conventional military hardware but Abdul Qader knew that you didn't find Massoud that way, you had to sense him: either that or he found you. Abdul Qader, like one of those trackers who sensed water in the Sahara, sensed him in his gut. So I believed him when he said Massoud was here.

And if the truth be told the guide's 'senses' had become honed over time, and Abdul Qader was a combination of intellect and gut instinct. For sometimes you have to go with the feeling of your stomach rather than your intellect. Abdul Qader's job was honed to finding Massoud because his job was to walk between the two lofty mountains of Zabibullah and Massoud delivering messages. Both commanders had abandoned sophisticated communication technology reliant on radio waves and satellites liable to interception, and relied instead on the guide's keen memory, heart and courage to convey secret military messages to each other. For five years, summers and winters, Abdul Qader walked through the crevices of the mountains to convey these messages that were imprinted on his heart the way the Quran had been committed to my heart. Abdul Qader travelled to and fro twice a month on foot, just him, the open skies, the mountains, the stars and his God. I cannot prove this but no matter what technology a man develops, one cannot develop that sense except through such journeys. And so I believed him when he said that Massoud was indeed here.

He was right of course, for after fifteen days I came across Massoud's commander of Sultan Shera. The Soviets had launched a military campaign entitled 'The Ferocious Campaign' to liquidate Massoud and his *mujahideen* in the Sultan Shera valley. So like a lithe pugilist he sidestepped and retreated into the Hindu Kush mountain range where Greeks, Persians and Hindu slaves had passed through to be sold in the medieval slave markets of Central Asia, wherein used to reside ancient centres of Buddhism and Hindu kingdoms. Ibn Battuta, the famous fourteenth-century North African traveller, says that the Hindu Kush was named thus because of its deadliness and bitter cold, but Massoud defied this description and retreated to it regularly finding safety there.

When we arrived at the outpost, Abdul Qader informed the commander that there was an Arab guest for Amir Sahib.[5] Massoud had been a phantom for three months. The KGB, Soviet intelligence services, were searching for him everywhere to kill him. They appeared disorientated and in disarray, their press reported that he had been killed, others said he was in the US with President Ronald Reagan and yet he was right here under their very noses. We waited only three days before we could meet him.

Those three days with these fighters at the outpost were memorable and extraordinary. Their calibre was altogether very different from the other *mujahideen* I had met. Previously the Afghans I had met were simple, dignified, with a jealousy for the faith. Often I met fighters who assumed that Khalq and Parcham, the two Afghan Communist parties, ruled the entire world and that the Afghan Islamic parties could be found in Algeria too! Those people were not aware of their place in the world, and I suspect couldn't tell you where Algeria was located. Here, in Sultan Shera, these people asked me if I could explain how it was that the Algerian people fought in the name of God but after independence from the French, this Jihad had turned into something else. This was an extraordinarily complex question. The one who posed the question needed to have an understanding of French rule and the FLN and much, much more. Here were *mujahideen* who were aware of their place in the world and what went on outside. This was a quality I saw in Massoud as well: he often asked questions wholly unrelated to Afghanistan, from news in Washington, to that in France or Egypt. Sometimes he asked more questions of the journalists who visited him than they did of him. It was this inquisitiveness that had diffused down to his rank and file. His soldiers were also not scruffy or undisciplined or wild looking. They didn't seem to have any sign of bombast: here was a regular army that reflected the mind of a man who looked at war as an unfortunate situation; it was nothing to revel in, nothing to relish. It seemed to me that the mind behind these men had renounced hatred, vindictiveness and the path of revenge. I truly believe that the mind who commanded these men in this lonely outpost was the sort of man who embodied what the Prophet had said: 'Do not look forward to meeting the enemy but if you do meet him hold firm.'

After three days I met him. And the first time I laid my eyes on him, I cannot explain it, perhaps it was his magnetism or charisma, but my heart felt at rest. Some people spend all their lives searching for that perfect man, that archetype warrior, the sort of warrior we see in Saladin, Omar Mokhtar, Abdul Qadir al-Jazairi—the pinnacle of chivalry. I believe my heart had found him.

Massoud wore a Pakhoul, his signature trademark. It was tilted slightly to the left because his head moved from side to side when he talked. It gave him an air of nonchalance as if war was a walk in the park, as if he was a son of destiny and he cared nought for Russian cannons that roared at him. His brow was lined and hid a thousand worries and concerns that stretched across the map of Afghanistan: on one end there lay the political machinations of Peshawar and on the other end were the schools being built on the Oxus river. His eyes, soft and yet piercing, stared into your soul. His hands were not those used to holding weapons, they weren't hard or calloused, but delicate. It was as if they belonged to an architect, calligrapher or someone who was used to reading Saadi's *Gulistan* or Ghazzali's *Alchemy of Happiness*, both of which he carried in his pocket even when the Russians were pounding us.

He smiled at me somewhat playfully. 'Do you understand Farsi?' he asked. 'A little', I replied—I didn't understand Farsi and it was just about at survival level. He turned to his teacher, Mawlawi Ghulam Qari, and asked him to be his translator. Qari taught Massoud Hanafi jurisprudence, doctrine and theology come rain or shine, campaign or no campaign.[6] That consistency allowed Massoud to become pretty adept in Islamic jurisprudence. Through Qari, Massoud asked me about my background and I answered the best as I could.

'Do you recite Quran?' he asked me.

'I can try.'

'Please recite the last verses from al-Imran.'[7]

And so I did. Massoud turned to his teacher and jokingly said that his estimation of him had been reduced. 'They recite', replied the Qari humbly, 'better than us.' He had no issues in learning from the Arab brothers. 'From now on', said Massoud as if the thing had already been decided, 'I will learn *Tajweed* from you after the dawn prayer.'[8]

'But', I protested, 'I am returning to Mazar Sharif in ten days.'

'I am well aware of your purpose', he said assuaging my worries, 'don't worry, I know what the situation is in Mazar Sharif.' And then to soothe me further he said, 'I too was affected by the loss of Zabibullah. You cannot imagine what a loss he was.' He brought out some photographs of the late emir and recounted how the dead man used to visit him often. 'I am surprised', he said as we looked through the photos, 'how an Arab with little experience of Mazar Sharif could spot the fissures amongst the leaders.' I expressed my hope that he would be able to resolve the differences considering the fact that all the leaders held him in high esteem.

Massoud instructed Abdul Qader to return. He ordered his financial director to replenish Abdul Qader's funds and asked that he signed off the papers. After that he turned to me again. 'Stay', he said, 'you belong here.' There seemed to be no room for discussion, it wasn't a command, it was an appeal to my heart. 'Live with us, die with us, your fate is ours.' And yet it wasn't a plea either, somehow I knew that I felt closer to him than any of the other brothers I would fight with in the future. 'It hurts me', Massoud said, 'that the Arabs and Muslims are not taking part in this sacred duty and that they have abandoned their brothers here. There aren't many Arabs amongst us. There is only you. There used to be an Iraqi Kurd, Abu Asim who taught us the

Quran, and Nouredeen a Jordanian brother, but that was just a visit and he returned to Pakistan. I hope you will stay.'[9]

It wasn't just me, but all of us felt irreparably entwined with him. I felt estranged from the other regions, like a Darwish estranged from the world. I saw in Massoud Muslim manhood personified, that of a perfectly balanced sword, elegant, sharp, lithe, and strong with a handle made of ivory and verses of poetry and the Quran engraved in the finest calligraphy. I had no choice but to stay.

5

INTO BATTLE WITH MASSOUD

Many of the Arab *mujahideen* in Afghanistan were, to say the least, not enamoured by Ahmed Shah Massoud. Unfortunately, this was partly due to the politicking in Peshawar. Hekmatyar's tongue, in particular, hit the right notes in the ears of many Arabs. The Arabs were young, zealous and sincere and didn't possess the scepticism that life experience gives you, and so were easily influenced by firebrands and demagogues.

Other Arabs didn't like Massoud because he was meticulous in his organisation. Anyone who joined his army was subject to military discipline and obedience was compulsory, there was no room for freewheeling. No dirty uniforms and no firing in the air, even bullets had to be accounted for. His commanders would take you to task for it. His was a regular army not a rag-tag militia which was subject to the whims of the emir. Here no zealous Arab could come fire his weapons, attack the command post at will, do a tour of duty for a few months and then return home a '*mujahid*'. Far from it. Massoud was a strategic thinker: he demanded your time, he expected you to drill and be ready for war. Massoud lost few battles because he planned them months in advance so that when an operation was launched it worked like clockwork.

In other camps, as I myself discovered, the Arabs were given a degree of independence where they were not subject to the commander. The Arabs who joined Hekmatyar, Sayyaf, Yunus Khalis or Jalaludin Haqqani could participate in guerrilla warfare, hit and run strikes, but they couldn't win because they didn't have the capability of a regular army. This is why many Afghans too found his army strange and called it an army of '*Nazm*', or order, because it had passed the threshold of being a militia. It was no wonder that whilst Massoud may have alienated the Afghan Arabs in Peshawar, Sheikh Azzam to his dying day considered him a titan of the North and tried in vain to publish a book about him in Peshawar which was thwarted due to the strong presence of Hekmatyar supporters there.

From a remote cave network in the Hindu Kush Massoud received reports sometimes weekly, sometimes daily, of each and every area under his control. Sometimes when a commander would report on the situation in Kabul he would reply that he was already cognisant of the situation in the capital due to the network of safe-houses and spies he had in the city. And it was all managed from a cave network in the Hindu Kush which housed about twenty *mujahideen* in each cave. The largest cave was for the emir and it was there that Massoud studied detailed maps spread out on the table discussing with his commanders over one matter or another. It was there that he received radio reports from all the areas under his control, and even from areas not under his control such as Peshawar and Kabul. But he never stayed in his headquarters for too long: sometimes he'd go into hiding for weeks or months, other times he would be escorted by his bodyguard carrying specialist military equipment and ammunition. But in 'normal' quiet times he visited the cave of the emir three times a week, and yet even during times of work, he couldn't resist asking his commander about the meaning of one or two lines of Persian verse, and then for a moment those lines on his forehead would soften and he would get some respite from his worries.

But that lined forehead could comprehend his country in its totality, he could think at both the microlevel and the macro-level, he had a vision for the whole of his country. He had that extraordinary gift of being able to look to the needs of his army, to the education of Afghan girls, and yet at the same time care for the woman who had sacrificed her six sons for him or the woman who had saved his life in the early days of the Jihad. I had the good fortune of watching and learning keenly how to run such a big operation.

I also understood through the constant stream of visitors and commanders from all parts of Afghanistan what the situation was in the country. Not only was I honoured and formed lifelong friendships, but I also had the fortune of being Massoud's favourite Arab, his boon companion he could confide in, and I too could talk with him frankly. So often confidences and ideas were shared with me in the hope that something may be conveyed to Peshawar or to a commander delicately.

When Massoud gave information about his losses he was accurate and didn't exaggerate. When he warned the world about this new force that became known as al-Qaeda this wasn't mere rhetoric, for that was not in his character, rather it was based on carefully considered intelligence. But few people took notice of his prescient assessment at the time. But I knew it to be true, for I had often sat with him on the floor drinking green tea listening to him as he explained the situation in Afghanistan, and some-times the situation around the world. There were three things that Massoud always did before going to bed: listen to the BBC World Service, read his poetry, and recite the Quran.

I will give you an example where I understood this most keenly. As a representative of the Arab Services Bureau, I often visited the different parties and commanders in the area. This was part of my role and responsibilities inside the country. My main objective was to unify the various factions. Whilst I could remain neutral, the truth is that this objective was something beyond my capabilities, but I hope it was not for want of trying. If we could only resolve the differences between Hezb-i Islami and Shura-e Nazar led by Massoud who was under the general command of Rabbani's Jamiat-i Islami, the Jihad against the Soviets would prove easier. So often I would travel like a politician on the campaign trail visiting the various factions. This would also enable me to give a situation report to Sheikh Abdullah in terms of funds and resource allocation. So these visits with the local commanders were absolutely vital. On one such visit to Engineer Bashir in Takhar province, Ishakamish directorate, I saw the difference in mindset between Massoud and Engineer Bashir. Engineer Bashir was a generous host, a vigorous and capable commander much younger than Massoud but he did not have that broad vision that Massoud had. As he hosted me in his salon he joked with me. 'Why', he said with a wink in his eye, 'have you come to Afghanistan to live like a wolf in the Hindu Kush? Come down to us, live with us, walk in the markets and meet the people. Which man comes to Afghanistan to live with the wolves in the snow and the mountain caves of Massoud? Come live with us!'

Of course Engineer Bashir said it in jest, but there was an underlying message that was serious. What he meant was this: if you come and live in areas controlled by Hekmatyar's Hezb-i Islami, you will see areas that are gushing with life. Hezb-i Islami was much more important than those desolate mountains that Massoud controlled. But what Engineer Bashir didn't grasp was that if Massoud wanted he could do that too, but his concern was that his presence would attract Russian bombing on the civilians living there, so he preferred to remain in the Hindu

Kush. He had the strategic foresight to weigh up the consequences of his actions: his prestige may certainly have risen in the eyes of the world but he would have lost the hearts of the people he was defending. When I went back to Massoud, he asked me what I thought of Engineer Bashir, and I replied that he was a man of vigour and energy and encouraged him to reconcile with him. 'I wish', he replied, 'please try to convince him.'

It struck me that Massoud wasn't a partisan, although here perhaps I am the one being biased due to the time I spent with him. But I never felt he was trying to influence me towards siding with one group or another. In fact, he would consult and take every man's opinion including mine in military affairs just to see as many different perspectives as he possibly could before taking his decision. Massoud's vision and approach gave me a political freedom and confidence to allow me to act according to my own judgement. This was something I could not do with other commanders. For instance, I could praise an opposition commander in front of Massoud and he would not mind it—he might even encourage it because it fostered discussion and tolerance—but in front of other commanders the same praise might turn you into his opponent and you had to hold your tongue. That was perhaps one of the greatest aspects of Massoud's personality.

6

MY FIRST BATTLE WITH MASSOUD

I don't like talking about battles and exploits for fear that it will sound like a Hollywood film. And Massoud's battles probably require a separate book or study. But since war is a big part of our story, some account of it is a necessity. I could mention the outright victories that Massoud achieved like those of Farkhar, Khuja Gar, Shahr Buzurg, Taloqan, Kalafgan, Nahrain or Kiranumanjan for instance, but I want to give a glimpse of what it was like. Moreover one never forgets the first battle that one takes part in, so I will recount it. For in many ways, the first .battle is always the one that changes you.

It had been three months now with Massoud. The snow was several meters high when there was a knock on the door. I didn't want to get up and wanted to stay warm under the blankets. It was cold and still very dark. I went to the door and it was Tajuddin or uncle Kaka: though he was 54 years old, he never left Massoud's side. Uncle Kaka soon became Massoud's father-in-law, for when Massoud decided to get married he asked for the hand of his beloved Uncle Kaka's daughter who was his most loyal and trustworthy companion.

'The emir', said Tajuddin, 'is waiting for you.' 'Let us wait a while', I responded. He understood what I meant—it was cold—but he insisted: the emir requested my presence. I got up, got myself ready and trudged through the deep snow, my breath steaming from the cold, and my day began. Massoud was waiting for me, ready and eager with the Quran at the ready. His eyes were alert, *pakhoul* as usual tilted to the left. We sat down and he recited the verses to me and I corrected him trying my best to eliminate that '*zay*' or z-sound which non-Arab speakers tended to pronounce instead of the '*dad*' or d. This was a common problem for non-Arabs, the same way we Arabs often pronounce the 'p' as a 'b'. And so we sat there reciting and me correcting him and explaining the Quranic rules that were appropriate.

Usually Massoud would have enough information about the activities of the Russians but that day we were caught slightly unprepared. Massoud's disappearance with 150 hand-picked elite men into Sultan Sheerah had been discovered by the Russians. For a while now Najibullah, having been a former head of KHAD, the Afghan intelligence service, had planned to shut down the northern front which was most perilous to him. Namely, Kandahar, Panshir and so forth had to be under Afghan government control for it was vital for supplies and reinforcements from the Soviet Union. The northern front was mostly under the control of Massoud. The Russians and the Communists had led several campaigns against Massoud but his forces were intact and illusive. So Najibullah set up a unit in close cooperation with the KGB to take him out.[1] This unit had discovered that Massoud was moving his campaign to the north, and was using Sultan Sheerah and Anjiristan, two remote places in the Hindu Kush, as a resting place, and as a place to plan a campaign which would take the battle to the Russians. However, they were discovered. Najibullah informed the Russians that he had intelligence that Massoud was in Sultan Sheerah with only fifteen men and that they should ambush him and kill the target they had codenamed '*Zhagh*' in Persian. The Communists mustered their forces. Najib was right about Massoud's location but not the number of men he was with. Massoud's network of informers however, gave him an inkling of what Najibullah was planning which bought him enough time to radio for reinforcements. I remember hearing him ordering Hussein and Muslim to meet him within twenty-four hours. The unit made it having marched for twenty hours straight without sleep or rest to rendezvous with Massoud and his men in Sultan Sheera. They arrived the day before the attack. These fifty men were split up into two or three groups. But the intensity of the onslaught took him aback.

And so on the day of the attack we were 150 men whilst thousands of his men remained behind in the Panshir valley. We were startled by the ferocity of Russian air strikes hitting the mountains. Massoud listened, he was calm as if he was catching his breath, and then sprang into action. He made radio contact to find out what the state of play was. He was told that the Russians had launched an operation. The shelling focused on an area more than ten square kilometres.

Ten minutes later the shelling stopped. And then we heard that eerie rumble of the Sukhoi 25 jets strafing the area. Half an hour later another flock of Sukhoi jets came and unloaded their deadly load on us. We were trapped for fourteen days while jets bombarded us. Massoud made us aware that this intense bombardment was merely an aperitif, it was designed to demoralise and weaken us in preparation for an attack.

Through the radio Massoud ordered his fighters to ascend to the Hindu Kush mountain peaks, some of which touched the heavens at 7,000 feet. He wanted to use the element of surprise on the Russians. When the Russians would send their paratroopers and Spetznas fighters in hoping to surprise us, their helicopters would be faced with RPGs and the air drop would be halted at best or at least hampered.

Whilst our fighters scaled those peaks, we were faced with hourly bombardment from the Sukhoi 25s. Their bombardment only gave us thirty minutes respite in between the Sukhois returning to base whilst the other jets came to relieve them. This continued for fourteen days. We found it difficult even to make our ablutions in the river which was about sixty meters away from the cave. Whilst they couldn't get to us in the caves with the bombs equally we couldn't get out either. The walls became white from the shelling. Some of the men posted on the peak outside couldn't be supplied with food and Massoud became immensely concerned for their welfare. Massoud lost communication with the men who had reached the mountain top, whose only job was to wait for these Russian choppers to land and drop their forces. But the resilience of these men was extraordinary, for some of these brigades subsisted on grass for one day.

On the fifteenth day we heard the sound of helicopters: it had begun. We looked out and saw the Russians landing on the mountain face outside. Seyyed Yahya was given permission to engage as and when he saw fit. The paratroopers and the special forces didn't expect our forces to last that long, nor did they expect any resistance. But Commander Seyyed Yahya's unit who had scaled those peaks were waiting for them. Their helicopters were about to land when Seyyed Yahya's brigades opened up on them. They released their RPGs so that the Russians thought that the valley was filled with *mujahideen* waiting for them. This setback forced the enemy to land on another mountain.

Altogether the *mujahideen* downed eight helicopters: the noise was terrifying as they crashed, the sound of whirring rotors, burning and black smoke filled the sky, and felt as if it was something out of Judgement Day. And as God's will would have it, the first helicopter that went down took out the commander of the operation so the enemy was now carrying out the operation blind. The *mujahideen* though, managed to get to the first helicopter and obtain the brief in which were the plans of the operations and those maps were sent to Massoud. Commander Massoud now had in his possession the enemy's map and plan of the operation. It bought us time to prepare for the commandos. But the Russians managed to penetrate Ishkamesh district in order to push towards Sultan Sheera. Artillery positions had been established there in order to target Massoud's cave less than thirty kilometres away. And so we sustained shelling for another one or two days.

Massoud knew that Sultan Sheerah had no strategic value to him. He had entered the area because he wanted to relieve pressure from his Panshir valley. So he made the decision to leave but he didn't want to leave any trace of his retreat. Because he knew where the Russians were situated he could plan his retreat in an orderly fashion. And so he would have to march through the middle of the river that would cover our tracks. We set out towards Farkhar carrying everything with us: luggage, ammunition and more importantly prisoners. Massoud had brought them because he hadn't finished trying them. Everyone—even the Russians—will testify that Massoud always treated his prisoners well. If they were Afghans he'd let them go, if they were senior officers and they had done something wrong they would stand trial. He believed that the Prophet had commanded him not to torture or abuse prisoners whilst they were under his power. It wasn't like now, when they might just be shot and killed because they were a 'liability' and a drain on resources. Massoud assigned twenty guards and instructed them to keep them safe at all times and yet remain vigilant for they might use the confusion to escape. He delegated Commander Mohammed Sayyed Khan and instructed him to escort them to Takhar and secure them. Mohammed Sayyed Khan assured him that he would and that he must make haste to Farkhar before the Russians arrived.

We set out during the middle of the night with icy cold water up to our knees. Sometimes we walked through the freezing cold for several hours. On one such night we had waded through the river and found a spot in which to shelter as the sun rose. We were so exhausted that we just unfolded our tent and slept right there on the spot. I watched Massoud make his tent. We were about a hundred men, some of us were ill and injured, and our feet were blistered and bruised. We were hungry and tired from carrying rockets, RPGs and ammunition and our arms. Some of us just put our heads on a rock and closed our eyes, we were too tired to even unfold our tent.

I barely slept an hour when I woke up to the sound of rockets raining down on us. We thought we were protected—we had burrowed ourselves into a natural hole—but we were wrong. Three men were struck by the rockets and died. Carnage, the acrid smell of explosives, the iodine smell of blood and death was everywhere. It was unimaginable. We lost the wounded within ten minutes and it dawned on us that the commandos and paratroopers had tracked us from above and given the coordinates to the air forces. We had to bury the martyrs under a few rocks because there was no soil to bury them and there was little time. We had to keep going all the way to Namak Ab village, in Takhar province.

We pressed on for one day until we arrived in Farkhar consumed by tiredness. But we had a problem, and here I witnessed how divisions between the *mujahideen* could impact on the Jihad. In Farkhar province we had to cross into Hekmatyar territory, that is territory under the control off Hezb-i Islami. We were not sure whether we would be received well due to Hekmatyar considering Massoud his rival. But fortunately, the local commander had heard of our predicament and was gracious enough to allow us to pass through. We lodged in one of the houses of Rabbani's

Jamaat-i Islami in Farkhar province whilst the Russians took control of Sultan Sheerah in the distance. They seeped in through the gaps, and seized the cave that Massoud had been in to gather intelligence against their enemy. But whilst they could claim victory, Sultan Sheerah was strategically unimportant, and we licked our wounds after the setback having survived to fight another day. Back in Kabul the Soviets and the Communists bickered between themselves over the failure to eliminate Massoud and his men. And what was worse, Massoud returned, within a few weeks, after organising his men, and attacked. With the help of local commanders Abdullah Kazastan and Sayyid Hashimi they seized the Farkhar directorate from the Communists and captured 150 prisoners. And by so doing Ahmed Shah Massoud gained the hearts of the local population who were not Panshiris, and showed them that he was working for everyone, not just his own valley.

7

HEKMATYAR

I realised early on that the key to victory against the Soviets lay in resolving the dispute between Massoud and Hekmatyar. Otherwise the victory would be an empty one. For it would result in intra-factional conflict not dissimilar to the situation that the Syrian rebels found themselves in after their attempt to overthrow Assad's regime. I made my views quite clear to Sheikh Abdullah when I returned to Peshawar in early 1986. The sheikh was convinced by my arguments even though he knew very little about Ahmed Shah Massoud.

At the time I thought that the crux of their dispute was partially due to their shared history, partially their strong personalities and partially their ignorance of each other. Both were incredibly strong personalities whose differences infused their respective parties, and disagreement improperly channelled could be very harmful. I have so far mentioned Massoud in glowing terms, but Hekmatyar too had immense charisma; he was a gripping orator and immensely fearless. But he was also a leader who understood that he had to stay back to administer his party in Peshawar. It is a testimony to his leadership that he could be in

Peshawar and still exercise power over his party inside Afghanistan. Ultimately, it was their irresolvable disagreement that led to the infighting of Kabul.

But I should add that despite their rivalry, I do not believe it was personal. But it has to be said that Massoud talked of Hekmatyar in far more respectful terms than Hekmatyar did of Massoud. Massoud always used the appropriate titles—'Sahib' or 'Engineer'—for him, as Afghan culture dictates. There was also not an issue with regards to any of them questioning each other's beliefs. Neither side declared the other an apostate, unlike nowadays, when this is common. Moreover, I never saw ethnic differences being an issues, since both parties were multi-ethnic. I believe the differences between the two men went back to their shared history. But could the issues in Afghanistan be resolved if they had been reconciled? That is a question I am still trying to answer. Nevertheless resolving their differences would have certainly saved many lives.

When all the Islamic movement leadership were rounded up by the Daoud regime, Massoud was instructed by his mentor Engineer Habibur Rahman to find Hekmatyar. Hekmatyar was older and more established within the Islamic movement and part of the inner circle. Initially, Massoud had no problems in being under Hekmatyar, however according to what Massoud told me, disagreements occurred because he found Hekmatyar's statements were at best exaggerated and at worst untrue. It led Massoud to question Hekmatyar's leadership. But then again, men grow, develop and change over time. Hekmatyar was a different man from the early days in Kabul University and to the days of the Afghan Jihad. Hekmatyar in turn, did not give much time to Massoud—who became known in the Western media as 'the Lion of Panshir'—and viewed him instead like any other *mujahid* commander.

And once distance—seven mountains' distance to be precise—was placed between them, their differences could not be fully resolved. At the time our feeling was that if only the two could sit with each other over a cup of chai then all the disagreements could be resolved. We were convinced that both men were rational actors and could come to an agreement. Sheikh Abdullah became convinced that Massoud would never refuse a request for both of them to meet if it came from him. The sheikh was too highly esteemed by both. If one could break the other's prejudices, and show that Hekmatyar was not the same man Massoud believed him to be, and Hekmatyar viewed Massoud as an exceptional commander who could win campaigns and wars, then perhaps they could start working together.

It was with this objective in mind, that the mission of the Arab Afghans became increasingly well defined. In Peshawar Sheikh Azzam instructed me to gather around me Arabs that were capable enough to deal with this fractious dynamic. We needed Arabs on Hekmatyar's side who would act like a neutral point of contact. Whilst I was certainly respected by Hekmatyar's Hezb-i Islami in Takhar and North Afghanistan and did not discriminate on goods and support, I was still partial since I spent most of my time with Massoud. Whether I liked it or not, I was Massoud's man. It was important then, that they had their own man, and we could come to a meeting point and bring the two parties together. My recommendations would not be accepted unless their man also accepted. What we needed was a group of Arabs dotted around their factions who could work with Engineer Basheer, whose job it was to persuade him to come to the table. I hoped that this would be a great trust-building exercise which would eventually result in peace and the expulsion of the Soviets.

Our choice fell on Qari Abu Ibrahim who would take a convoy to Engineer Basheer in order to be that bridging point—he would be the Arab Services Bureau representative to Hezb-i Islami. My instructions to him were clear: 'Your job,' I said, 'is to serve his needs; from tending to the orphans, widows and the wounded and providing medical assistance and education.'

We had high hopes in Qari Abu Ibrahim, an Iraqi engineer and a memoriser of the Quran: just that very fact imbued him with respect in the eyes of the Afghans. We hoped that a good word from Qari Abu Ibrahim here and there, along with his impeccable manners would thaw relations between the two groups and lead to genuine cooperation. This was of course bolstered by Hekmatyar who sent a message to Engineer Basheer telling him that the Arab Services Bureau had selected a representative and sent him the *crème de la crème* of the Arabs from Peshawar to serve them.

I also picked men who possessed a degree of maturity who could deal with the buffeting and peculiarities of Afghan culture. But it was difficult to find men who could transcend the disputes between the various factions—sometimes they could not even deal with disputes between local leaders in the same party. Instead of trying to build bridges between Hekmatyar and Massoud, what many of the Arabs found themselves doing was getting embroiled in the partisanship or trying to seal breaches in the faction they had been assigned to.

Whilst the first convoy was dispatched to Engineer Basheer with this project in mind, there was a second convoy that I took to Massoud. The men accompanying me, it was hoped, would prove to be morale boosters to Massoud and his men, and help to facilitate reconciliation between the two groups.

In my convoy there were several men who later played a significant role in the future of militancy in the Muslim world. These men were not particularly remarkable. Qari Saeed, unfortunately, went on to have close links with the GIA (Groupe Islamique Armé), the Armed Islamic Group that caused havoc and bloodshed in the Algerian conflict.[1] At the time, I considered him to be a restless young man sitting around in the guest-houses of the Arab Services Bureau wishing to fight Jihad. On one such occasion he gave me an ultimatum: 'If you don't take me,' he said, 'I will abandon Jihad ... and if I leave Jihad, you will be accountable before God.'

I took him in unsure whether he was the man for the job or not. But it would have been unfair of me to pre-judge him so I gave him a chance. It was only later that he turned his back on the MAK and joined al-Qaeda. Other men however remained an enigma to me to this day. For when they approached me they were already deemed to be extremists by the rest of *us*. Abu Ubaida al-Panshiri[2] and Abu Hafs al-Masri[3] both became senior al-Qaeda operatives, and were at the time members of Zawahiri's Egyptian Islamic Jihad, an extreme *takfiri* organisation. So when the two men approached me asking me if they could join the caravan I was hesitant to accept them because of their background.

But I agreed on the condition that they promised to enter Afghanistan as individuals not as part of Egyptian Islamic Jihad and that they obeyed their Afghan commander. They agreed and were true to their word. Neither man followed or pushed their group's agenda under Massoud. And I am unsure whether they even subscribed to Egyptian Jihad's ideology because both men esteemed Massoud. This was in stark contrast to their leader Osama bin Laden who fell under the sway of Hekmatyar's influence. Perhaps if bin Laden had met Massoud he might have shared his views.

Of the thirty Arabs that I took to Massoud, Abu Hafs al-Masri couldn't make the arduous journey through the mountains. We marched through the Chatral mountain range which involved crossing seven or eight majestic mountains at eight thousand metres above sea level. Abu Hafs al-Masri's suffered from a bad knee and couldn't continue and excused himself, finding his way back to Peshawar in the end. As for the rest of us, we were welcomed by Massoud and honoured in true Afghan fashion.

When we arrived he was right in the middle of preparations for conquering Annahrayn. He had been scouting out the place for months in order to minimise his losses. Massoud hated wars of attrition and preferred hit and run attacks or outright conquests as opposed to two forces facing off against each other; that sort of battle would inevitably favour the enemy since they had the advantage of air power and numbers.

It was in such circumstances that Massoud took me to a quiet room, where he had his sleeping bag, his maps and operational secrets. Uncle Kaka was also there beside him as he broke the news. 'We attack Annahrayn in two or three days' time', he said. 'From Takhar we go to Annahrayn, two days' march from here.' He studied my face closely as if to see what sort of reaction I might have. His weather-worn face, the way his head moved from side to side added, 'If the Arab brothers want the honour of battle, they are most welcome.'

Massoud honoured the men by allowing them to participate in that battle. In our tradition, one day in the path of Jihad was better than the world and what is in it. Massoud gave the men an opportunity to get to paradise even though he did not know the men. In fact, it was Massoud who made them. Abu Ubaidullah, Osama bin Laden's most capable commander for instance, became known as al-Banshiri, on account of Massoud allowing him to take part in the battle of Annahrayn.[4]

The next day, I gathered the Arabs and gave the men the option to go to battle with Massoud or remain here.

All the men shouted 'God is most Great!' signalling their pleasure and said, 'How can we stay? This is why we are here.'

I understand that the non-religious mind finds it difficult to grasp this idea; it may even appear somewhat morbid and perverse. Sacrificing one's own being in God's service, to defend one's home, the weak and oppressed, was the ultimate testimony of one's faithfulness to God. One preferred God's pleasure over one's own comfort and love of life and this is why none of the men could refuse such an offer. This is why one of Islam's greatest Generals, Khalid bin al-Walid, relished Jihad. For him the best time was at dawn before the battle when he was dressed in full battle array watching the eastern horizon as the rain smattered his face. He knew that every wound sustained would not enter the hell fire. He knew that except for the martyr, there would be few men who would want to return to earth after they have beheld the bliss of eternity, and so the martyr would be dragged into paradise in golden chains because he wants to return to the battle field to sacrifice himself for God's pleasure. This is why Sheikh Abdullah wrote that 'Men need Jihad more than the Jihad needed men.'

We marched at dawn with the crisp mountain air on our faces. We were unsure as to where this Annahrayn was—Massoud kept the operational details from us—except that it would be linked to two rivers since that is what the name 'Annahrayn' meant. As we reached a mountain pass, Massoud distributed his forces. In addition to approximately fifteen Arabs, mostly medics, Massoud had 200 fighting men. Alongside his local commander Abdel Hayy Haqq Jue, he divided up the arena of battle into various zones. Under Commander Muslim, Abu Ubaidah and Abu Dujanah moved closer to the front line to attack.

First contact with the enemy took most of the day and night. That was unusual, as Massoud relied heavily on lightning strikes which lasted a few hours: this one was tough as the enemy fought well. I saw eighteen Afghan *mujahideen* fall and I lost two men who had become beloved to me, Abdul Jabbar and Abu Dujanah. Abu Dujanah was carried away mortally wounded from the battle field. Dr Abdullah Abdullah did his best to save his life but it was too late. He got what he had prayed for. Abu Ubaidah was also injured. The following day, after Massoud had worn down the teeth of the enemy we moved into the district and took possession of it. He took 200 enemies prisoner and despite losses to his own men, he treated the prisoners like gold. Any mistreatment of the prisoners he would recompense. Many, if he was an ordinary Afghan, he would return to his village in the hope that he could be won over to his side; the only people he kept and interrogated were members of the Afghan Security Services, the notorious KHAD.

We remained in the newly conquered territory for a month or so. The Arabs including Abu Ubaidah returned back to Peshawar to get treatment for their wounds and were duly celebrated by the Arabs in the guest-houses of Peshawar as well as in the Arab media.

I remained for another nine months trying to finish my projects in Afghanistan. Due to the infighting, operations against the Russians was severely hampered as is happening in 2018 in Syria. Sometimes one journey which might take half an hour would take several hours because one could not cross the territory of the other party. The situation had become ridiculous. It expended the effort of the rank and file. Often the Russians and the Afghan government would play one group off each other, sometimes feed the rivalry by way of assassination, by way of rumour mongering and so on. It is the same strategy that has been used by the Assad regime in Syria and the worst thing about it is that with the benefit of age and experience it is glaringly obvious. The same misunderstandings, the same tinderbox between personalities, existed then as it does now. Human nature changes little.

I recall one incident that could have turned into civil war between the various groups. On that day, mid-1986, I was sitting with Massoud in Sultan Sheera when the radio crackled into life. It was one of his commanders Ekramuddin: he was the joint governor of Ishkamesh with Engineer Basheer and was a thoroughly good man. This time though he sounded nervous and agitated. 'There has been', he said, 'a catastrophe between us and Hezb-i Islami.'

Commander Ekramuddin requested my presence. Massoud promptly got up and hugged me, patted me on the back as if to say, 'Go, and may God be with you'. I made my way to Commander Ekramuddin, a typical hardy Afghan with intelligent eyes whom Sheikh Abdullah held in high regard. 'My brother,' said Ekramuddin who grasped immediately what this could mean for the fight against the Soviets, 'that crazy one has just killed Engineer Abdul Wahab!' The latter was the Hezb-i Islami commander for Ishkamesh.

Ekramuddin lamented Abdul Wahab's loss; the latter was a good man and Ekramuddin's brother Abdul Jabbar Jora the brother of one of the local heads, Kadi Islamuddin, had recklessly killed him for no apparent reason. He cursed his brother as the countryside in Ishkamesh was mobilising for war. Engineer Basheer, one of the most powerful leaders of Hezb-i Islami in northern Afghanistan, was preparing his forces to avenge Abdul Wahab. 'He has already declared a state of emergency,' said Ekramuddin worried, 'if this continues I think this fight won't end till two months from now.' You could almost see the 3,000 troops mobilising against him on the commander's face. 'Could you act as a mediator?'

I was not optimistic about the success of this mediation effort. We had tried before and it had failed. So I didn't want to get his hopes up. Nevertheless resolving conflict was a religious duty, even if it fails, so I set out for Engineer Basheer.

I had to walk for six hours to see Engineer Basheer: had I taken a helicopter it would have been shot down without a thought from the men manning the rooftops or hills. The situation bristled with tension between the various lines held by each faction. Each man possessed weapons and anger, not a good combination in any circumstance let alone for initiating dialogue. As I entered the region controlled by Engineer Basheer I began to quietly whisper my prayers to myself, asking God Almighty to sustain me, keep me alive and make me successful with the task at hand. I did not have a sign on my forehead saying: 'It is I, Abdullah Anas, an Arab. Don't shoot!' I worried that I was already in the scope of the sniper. As I drew closer I took off my white turban and started to wave it in the air as a sign of peace. At the first check point I started shouting that I wished them no harm—that I was a foreigner and had no interest in this ghastly business. Some of the men at the check point unlatched the safety of their weapons. One amongst them stepped forward and screamed angrily ordering me to come closer.

So I stepped forward slowly, step by step, no sudden moves, ever conscious that each step may just be my last. Some of them recognised me and I could hear them saying 'He's one of Massoud's Arabs', as if this mediation attempt was some sort of ruse. They thought I was here to kill off the impending battle that they had set their hearts on. They were not about to let Abdul Wahab's blood be spilt in vain. There was anger, loyalty and fear in those voices.

I sensed that these men, indeed the region, was not ready for reconciliation especially as men were pouring in from Kunduz, Khanabad and God knows from where else. In response Massoud's men too were mobilising in fear of the overwhelming force that Hekmatyar could exert. And yet both factions were for the moment, holding their nerve.

When I entered in on Engineer Basheer, sitting on the mattress surrounded by his men, I knew the situation was not looking good. The fire of fury was burning in his eyes. There were rumblings of *'Allahu Akbar,*[5] *La Hawla wa la Quwwata illa billah'.*[6] These phrases were used every day but especially so in moments of conflict when men are trying to draw courage from the words. There were the usual actions of men going into battle: cleaning weapons, counting and recounting bullets, checking their equipment and all such things that men do so that their arms don't fail them at the crucial moment. Sometimes when men are in such a state and their hearts are set on a course of action, dissuading them against such a course will often be countered with suspicion or accusations of cowardice. It is hard to extinguish once the process has begun. These men were determined on revenge and I deemed it inappropriate to broach the subject at that moment. If I mentioned the word 'reconciliation', Engineer Basheer, even if he saw reason, could not accept it on account of his men. And if he didn't accept it on his own account then he may just kick me out and any prospects of peace would flounder.

In spite of his anger, Engineer Basheer received me well and bade me sit, he was a gracious host considering the circumstances. I can only attribute this to firstly, the unseen fraternal bond in Islam which made us brothers in faith—he realised that I had left everything for the sake of God and that had to be respected. Secondly, there was also a worldly reason: I represented the Arab Services Bureau and Abdullah Azzam and it would be unwise to alienate such an important figure that could mobilise the Muslim world with a whirlwind tour, speech or publication. He sat there pensive and brooding, his thoughts would be interrupted by crackles from the radio. His mind was everywhere, one moment jumping from Kunduz, to me, to one commander and Peshawar. Thousands of calculations were going on in his intelligent mind and yet with the calm stillness of a mountain. I offered my condolences to his fallen companion. 'We pray', he replied, 'God accepts his martyrdom, his killing was unjust.' 'Amen', I replied, and there was no doubt about it: Engineer Abdul Wahab had been a devout righteous man and one of the best men in the region. I did not even touch on the issue of reconciliation allowing time to soothe him. I stayed that night as his guest.

The following day, around noon, Engineer Basheer asked me to lead the prayer. I led the men in prayer and after we had offered our prayers to God, and things were still I touched on the subject tentatively. 'Engineer *Sahib*,' I said respectfully, 'Engineer Abdul Wahab was killed is that correct?' 'Indeed', replied Engineer Basheer, eyeing me suspiciously to see where I was going with such a rhetorical question. I knew very well how his man had been killed. The other men twisted their beads, their tongues moist with the remembrance of God, and watched me too.

'And you have mustered your forces, they now stand ready to march at your order to strike Ishkamesh? Correct?'

'Correct', he continued looking at me. Where was I going with this line of questioning? His forces were ready, we could see them from the window.

'Will Engineer Abdul Wahab revive once you have ordered the attack?'

'No', replied Engineer Basheer annoyed at the question.

'Then, we'll lose fighters on both sides?'

'Most certainly.'

'In avenging the death of Abdul Wahab and the losses from the dead and injured, who will it benefit? The Russians or the Jihad?'

'The Russians', he replied gruffly.

'I understand your pain and your anger at this moment in time. But the fact that the Jihad will suffer is undisputable. Even if you don't agree with me and you still want to deal with the wrongdoers the way you want. This is one fact that is undeniable.' He knew what I said was true. I could read it in Engineer Basheer's face. So I pressed him. 'Look, both your forces are mobilising. Why don't you stop this and begin dialogue?'

Perhaps I had said too much.

'How could I sit with Ekramuddeen and Moallem Tarek those backstabbers!' he responded.

'As God is my witness,' I said, 'they were in tears over his death. They studied together. They have already arrested that foolish criminal, Abdul Jabbar, and are ready to do anything you want to solve this.'

The men around Engineer Basheer lost their cool: 'We don't talk with dishonourable people,' they said, 'don't worry the Kalashnikov will do the talking.'

Here I eased off the pedal. There was no point in trying to pry the door open so I didn't pursue it further. So I waited till their guard was down. At dinner time, over the breaking of bread I returned to the subject yet again.

'Engineer *sahib*', I said addressing the commander respectfully, 'we must talk to them.' This time Engineer Basheer agreed his anger had subsided and he had the time to mull things over. I asked for a radio and contacted Ekramuddin and Moallem Tarek. I asked Engineer Basheer to give me two guides to escort me to the other side. It was only on the pretext of breaking the ice between the factions. When Ekramuddin's men saw me being escorted by men from Engineer Basheer they drew good omen from it. I hoped that the guides would return to their camp with a good impression of their treatment, but also that they saw that the leadership of Jamiaa-i Islami were genuinely sad at the loss of Abdul Wahab. In the presence of commander Ekramuddin I contacted Engineer Basheer and told him that they were ready to accept responsibility. It was time to meet.

Engineer Basheer asked that I return and I took with me two guides from the Jamiaa-i Islami alongside the original guides, in order to ease the tension. This to-ing and fro-ing continued for five days culminating in a planned meeting at an agreed neutral place.

I then called Qari Saeed to bring an entire Arab unit with him to Ishkamesh. Qari Saeed and his unit were to be neutral arbiters between the factions as they reconciled and negotiated. But since one bullet could cause a bloodbath no faction was allowed to carry arms in case tempers flared or in case any saboteur from the KHAD or KGB infiltrated the meeting and put a stop to it with bombs or bullets. Qari Saeed's unit would provide the armed protection to the reconciliation.

Qaree Saeed and his men guarded us as the meeting convened. I sat as an interlocutor between the various parties: I was by now a competent Farsi speaker and able to negotiate with the various parties. I had also brought along several religious clerics and Imams who were also determined to resolve the issue. And so in the end the factions were reconciled and for a while at least, the truce held. It was also testimony that Arab Afghans could play a valuable role in resolving the conflict if they stayed neutral.

8

POLITICKING IN PESHAWAR
AND THE ENTRY OF EXTREMISTS

But why did the truce between Massoud and Hekmatyar not last? It was definitely not, as many analysts believe today, due to ethnic differences. I never saw this: Hekmatyar was a Pashtun with many Tajik followers, and the fact that Massoud and Rabbani were Tajiks did not figure in anyone's calculations. However, later, after the war ended and after the arrival of the mainly Pashtun Taliban in the south of Afghanistan, ethnic tensions certainly came to the fore.

When the *mujahideen* government collapsed these men who had initially just carried a white banner with nothing written on it, claiming to fight for peace, started to absorb the disgruntled forces of the old order. The Taliban movement seemed like a protest to end all the infighting.[1] Its leader Mullah Omar appeared to be a pious local commander who had fought commendably against the Soviets. But in the grand scheme of things he was inexperienced, lacked vision and did not know statecraft. This left his movement open to manipulation, infiltration and exploitation by Pakistan who could not tolerate an independent

Massoud. The Pakistanis required a pliant ruler who would do their bidding. Massoud, whilst not averse to Pakistan, wasn't made that way. He had never been anyone's pawn.

The Pakistani military realised this in March 1989. The Pakistani military wanted to deal a knock-out blow on Kabul by taking Jalalabad and expected Massoud to be compliant to their wishes. General Hamid Gul had reassured Benazir Bhutto that the battle would be won swiftly, and that a pro-Pakistani *mujahideen* government would soon be sitting in Jalalabad, their provincial capital. Massoud was expected to hold the Salang pass, a crucial mountain pass that connected Northern Afghanistan to Kabul. But Massoud advised against it, saying the plan was unsound and would risk the lives of his men. Realising that Massoud wasn't making headway he refused to take part. It came to pass exactly as he had predicted: the initial success evaporated; Hekmatyar and Sayyaf's forces met heavy resistance; and it resulted in a severe blow to the *mujahideen*. Osama bin Laden suffered a heavy blow that day, and we lost many good Arabs in that campaign.[2] Hamid Gul was sacked and morale in Peshawar fell to an all-time low. But many in the Pakistani military circles instead of taking responsibility for their miscalculation blamed Massoud for the fiasco. They took it as further proof that Massoud was intransigent and too independent. Whatever admiration they may have had for his fighting skills, Massoud had to go for the sake of the Pakistani national interest. He was too much of an unknown quantity. And so they encouraged dissent amongst the various factions in Peshawar. Unfortunately, there were even jealous members within Massoud's own party in Peshawar who spread calumnies against him. And there was little Massoud could do to counter these rumours as he was busy fighting the Soviets. Protecting the Pakistani national interest meant that the Taliban movement suddenly became very adept in war, and possessed a fleet of new land cruisers, weapons and technical know how very quickly.

POLITICKING IN PESHAWAR AND EXTREMISTS

The political machinations in Peshawar led to the balance of power tipping in favour of Hekmatyar. The latter had no problem in accepting ISI's support since both their interests converged.[3] After all why should Hekmatyar reconcile when he could, with added Pakistani funds, take all? There was simply no interest in reconciling. Meanwhile Sheikh Abdullah insisted that the Arabs remain neutral and stay out of Afghan infighting, but this could not be maintained forever in the volatile political climate where the Afghan Arabs were young and politically immature. The Arabs were gradually swallowed up by the factional vortex, which made them side with Hekmatyar. Osama bin Laden was perhaps the foremost example of this, so close were his ties to Hekmatyar that he was even unwilling to enter Kabul when he fell. He worried that it would alienate Hekmatyar who was at that time ready to take Kabul by force. Instead of enjoying the fruits of victory which he had worked on for so long, he flew back to Sudan in 1992 instead, and only returned to Jalalabad in 1996.

As for us, trying to get the Arabs to stay neutral and being facilitators of peace became near impossible. In the mid 1980s there was a trickle of Egyptian extremists and radicals coming into Peshawar.[4] The political intrigues of Islamic Jihad, who had fled the Egyptian secret police and settled in Peshawar, began to indoctrinate the men against Massoud, Abdullah Azzam and others and further poisoned the atmosphere.

When I returned to Peshawar in late 1988 after nine months with Massoud I sensed that the atmosphere had dramatically changed. I discovered that the Arab Services Bureau was no longer the main organisation in charge of the Arab *mujahideen*. It was naïve perhaps of me to think that only Sheikh Abdullah's organisation should be the sole custodian of the welfare of the Arabs. But in some ways, we were not a state, we were miniscule and other groups could also do what we were doing. Now Arab guest-houses like Bayt al-Ansar had proliferated, *takfiri* ideas had begun to diffuse into the rank and file, and they appeared more ideologically driven. The men I encountered had a more pronounced theo-political outlook, fusing the realms of theology with politics, thus someone voting or not voting—both valid positions—could mean being out of the fold of Islam and such things. Men like Massoud were the bad guys and men like Hekmatyar the good guys.

In mid-1989 I had to interrupt an important officer training course in order to deal with a group of Arabs who accused Massoud of outrageous slanders that had huge repercussions for him in the politically volatile climate of Peshawar. Now, I will deal with this in greater depth later; however, to sum up, this early instance of fake news alienated the Arab foreign fighters and pushed them into the arms of extremists. The accusations ranged from him ill-treating the Arabs to French women frequenting pool parties! As God is my witness, I never saw any of those things they accused him of. Their testimonies were riddled with inconsistencies and falsehoods. How could it be that we who had lived with him never witnessed such things but they who had never lived with him had seen such things? It was a testament to how politically immature these men were. Curiously, the tracts of these accusations were translated into several languages—Pashtu, Urdu and English—within a week and spread all over Peshawar which suggests that there was a serious political campaign afoot against Massoud. I can only conclude that either Afghan factions, *takfiris* or the intelligence services were exploiting the case to serve their own agenda.

This is why I noticed the consternation in Sheikh Abdullah's face as he counselled both leaders towards patience. He wrote to Massoud stressing the importance of remembering God, of trying to reconcile with Hekmatyar and keeping his eyes on fighting the Soviets. When I was there in Peshawar and as I stayed with him over the three months he made his fears explicitly clear and constantly stressed that I should work towards this goal. And whilst the Arabs did not hurt Massoud in the short term, it was indeed from this pool of Arabs that his death eventually came.

9

THE BROKEN TRUCE

By 1988 as things stood all of us knew that the Russians were planning to withdraw. We had known this since 1987, when the Soviet politburo showed signs that they were thinking of withdrawing especially with the arrival of Mikhail Gorbachev, the last leader of the Soviet Union. The question for all of us was what comes next? Fighting the Russians had unified us, since they were a common enemy, but what happens when that common enemy is gone? On 14 February 1989, the Russians began their withdrawal. The war had created 5.5 million refugees, not to mention the amputees, widows and orphans affected by everything from chemical weapons to sexual violence. These were the real heroes of the war. It was they who had precipitated the collapse of the USSR. The mind boggles when I think that I, this insignificant person, had a small part to play in the collapse of the Berlin Wall. I relished the vision of those Soviet troops returning back to their mothers and fathers, some of course would never see their sons returning as they lay buried in Afghanistan where only the mountain goats keep them company. As I watched the Soviet convoys return my joy was limitless.

This Jihad had begun with sticks, daggers, stones and I had been fortunate to participate in defeating the best trained army in the world; an army that had defeated the mighty Germans and controlled eastern Europe creating a spiritual and cultural wasteland for millions of people.

With my binoculars I spied the metal hulks that lay there, abandoned in the Panshir valley, it was as if they had come to die there. I made my way down the valley and walked amongst these fallen machines, I started counting them, but after one thousand I stopped—it took me an entire day. There was no doubt that it had been the Lion of Panshir who had inflicted defeat after defeat on the enemy. And I still remember the vindictiveness of the Soviets as their squadrons strafed and bombarded us as if they were wishing us a final farewell. They were sore losers.

I attribute this victory first and foremost to God. Then to Massoud's leadership and his capable commanders.[1] There were so many other reasons why the Jihad was successful. Pakistan's vital contribution by acting as a conduit for Saudi and US aid, had proved crucial. Pakistan provided the training, the camps, the arms, and they lobbied Muslim countries to get behind the Afghans. It also demonstrated how the West had played a positive role in defeating the Communists by providing the necessary political and military support. They had shown that things could be different between the Muslim world and the West, that we didn't have to be the inveterate enemies of each other. But above all, had it not been for Afghan resilience, sacrifice and courage the battle would have been lost. Had it not been for their sacrifice and their support of the *mujahideen*, victory would have been impossible.

But hubris overtook many of us. We assumed that the Kabul government would fall very quickly after the Russian withdrawal in February. And so a lightning-fast grab against Jalalabad occurred in preparation for an interim government to sit at the provincial capital. The head of the Inter-Services Intelligence (ISI), General Hamid Gul, had promised Islamabad that Jalalabad would fall quickly and that he would be installing the selected candidates there pretty soon.[2] Whoever would be running Afghanistan whether Hekmatyar or Abdul Haq would be dancing to Pakistan's tune, he assured Islamabad: that at least was the plan. But it was a failure. Partly because the Russians had left plenty of hardware behind for the regime to stand on their own feet and the regime was also fighting an existential fight for its survival and so was more determined. Kabul still had loyal military commanders willing to defend the Kabul administration like the formidable General Abdul Rashid Dostum with a capable militia force that ravaged its enemies. Thus taking Jalalabad would not be an easy task. Massoud of course knew it, and Abdul Haq,[3] another able commander knew it, but Hamid Gul didn't. The latter insisted that Massoud do what he was told and hold the Salang pass, but Massoud refused, not because he wanted to be difficult or take a contrary course, but rather because Gul's war-plans were unsound. Massoud was proved right. The Afghans as well as the Arabs were routed and we lost plenty of good men unnecessarily. However, whilst many journalists and analysts have attributed this defeat to sealing Massoud's fate, I saw myself that Gul had immense respect for Massoud's judgement. Gul lost his job as a result of the military fiasco and after the fall of Kabul there were rumours that he had had sought political asylum in Afghanistan. In fact he had gone to meet Massoud several times inside Afghanistan incognito, staying at his safe houses in the heart of Kabul and Panshir. I was there at some of the meetings myself, and saw the mutual respect the two had for each other. I believe Gul's hostility towards Massoud turned to affection by the end of their relationship. Gul always lamented the way things had turned out between the ISI and Massoud and wished to rectify it but sometimes the prerogatives of state are bigger than one man.

Nevertheless the Jalalabad offensive in early 1989 really demoralised us. How could it be that the regime could still fight when the Soviets had withdrawn? But all of us knew that despite the setback eventually Kabul would fall, it was just a matter of time. And so resolving the dispute between Massoud and Hekmatyar was paramount otherwise a full scale civil war would break out once Kabul fell.

It was at this low point that I pressed Sheikh Abdullah to come to Afghanistan to resolve the issue between the two commanders. The tension between the various parties were increasing and the prospect of a civil war was very real despite efforts to build an interim government incorporating all the various factions. Only a man of his stature had the ability to bring them together. And after making his own inquiries he agreed to meet Massoud. He travelled with Burhanuddin Rabbani, Sayyid Saqik Taskhuri, his press officer, Sheikh Abdullah's middle son, Ibrahim, and me. We travelled to the Panshir valley to meet Massoud and spent approximately a month there. He marvelled at the valley littered with the flotsam and jetsam of the Russian attack, the once mighty tanks, personnel carriers and trucks rusting in by the Panshir river. 'I fear', he said, 'that these trucks and tanks, these historic monuments will perish with rain and snow. I wish I could preserve them for future generations to remember.' He had never seen such a thing and he realised, like many others, that Massoud was a general, not a militia commander leading a rag-tag army.

I recall this as if it was only yesterday, sitting down with the sheikh peering down the valley and declaring his love for Massoud. 'I want to tell you' said Sheikh Abdullah turning to Massoud and leaning close as if he was telling him a secret, 'you know my relationship with you has three stages. At first, I was an enemy, I hated you and campaigned against you. I depended on a lot of misinformation from your rivals. They accused you of being a French agent and that you do this and that.' Massoud listened attentively as Azzam continued, 'I even wrote a small pamphlet sending it all the way to Beirut to publish it but God willed that the letter perished. The brother delivering it had a car accident. The second stage was after hearing more about you from Brother Nour Eddine, I neither praised you nor did I blame you. I was neutral. The last stage, where I am now, is when I love and respect you and am working to assist you. This is when Anas came to me after visiting you. As friends I just dismiss all these allegations as lies and rumours.'

The month-long tour with Massoud restored Sheikh Azzam's confidence and he returned rejuvenated. His wife after watching the videos of him smiling asked him why he never smiled like that with them in Peshawar? 'How could one be happy in Peshawar', he replied, 'when there was so much political turmoil?' He was so fulsome in praise of Massoud's virtues that he was accused of exaggerating. In one press conference in Kuwait he even described the man as Napoleon reincarnated. On another occasion the sheikh was sitting with Hekmatyar and praised Massoud so extensively that it appeared like a poetry recital for his beloved. He got up realising that he had nearly forgotten to offer his prayers when Hekmatyar replied wryly, 'Do you still pray?'

Hekmatyar implied jokingly that Sheikh Azzam's praise of Massoud had reached the level of worship and that he was committing a form of idolatry by praying to Massoud instead of God! When we returned home Sheikh Abdullah told me that at least we know that those things they say about Hekmatyar weren't true.

'Since he's allowed me to live,' he said tongue in cheek, 'it means that he doesn't send his assassins after you if he doesn't like you.'

That may be true, for Hekmatyar did have that reputation in Peshawar for killing his opponents and there were regular accusations that Hekmatyar's men were committing incursions and assassinations inside Afghanistan.[4] However, although Sheikh Abdullah was still alive he didn't have any luck in being able to publish a tract he had written about Massoud entitled 'A Month amongst the Titans of the North'. No book shop or printing press in Peshawar would publish his book, and that some said was due to the influence of Hekmatyar's strongmen.

What the sheikh may not have realised is that increasingly his support of Massoud had started to cross political fault lines; it was okay to describe him as a Napoleon but another thing to become critical of the Pakistani intelligence services' attitude towards Massoud. That crossed the red line and must have worried many of the Afghan Jihad's stakeholders. There were members of the Pakistani ruling elite who always felt the impending danger of encirclement and insecurity.

Nevertheless, as we saw it rapprochement between Massoud and Hekmatyar was of paramount importance. Hekmatyar seeing that Sheikh Abdullah had visited Massoud could not but extend his invitation to visit his territory. Sheikh Abdullah accepted his offer. The opportunity came in July 1989 when Hekmatyar wanted to tour the territories under his control. Although Hekmatyar was in constant communication with his leaders he wished to forge a stronger relationship with some of the emirs in the harder-to-reach areas under his control. They entered territories in the north-eastern areas venturing as far as the north of Kabul, Abu Hajar al-Iraqi and I accompanied them.[5]

When Hekmatyar visited central Afghanistan, Parwan and Kapeesa were ruled jointly between Hekmatyar and Massoud and the latter's bases were only two to three days' march on foot. We pounced on Hekmatyar and pressed him to meet Massoud. Hekmatyar had to overcome comments from his entourage that belittled Massoud. Initially, Hekmatyar was reluctant to go against his men but Sheikh Abdullah pressed him using the sheer force of his personality, his religious position and of course the political influence to prevail on Hekmatyar to agree.

'The situation' said Sheikh Abdullah reproachfully, 'is like that of a father and his sons. The father sends them to fetch some gold. But the place is perilous. So the sons instead of being honest with their father lie to him saying that they have been there and nothing came of it. The gold, however, remains where it is.' He turned to Hekmatyar's leaders and added, 'Be honest with Hekmatyar about the good that will come from meeting Massoud.'

Of course the leaders frowned and denied it, but they knew that it was true. And so Hekmatyar agreed to meet Massoud whilst the former was visiting Professor Abdul Sabur Farid in Parwan and Kapeesa, one of the senior leaders of the Islamic Party in Kabul and soon to be the Prime Minister of Afghanistan's coalition government in 1992.[6] Professor Farid's territory was the closest to Massoud and so Sheikh Abdullah instructed me to go and convince Massoud to meet Hekmatyar.

I reassured the sheikh that it could be done. Massoud was not an unreasonable man, he was at the time four days' march away in Farkhar in Takhar province. I prepared my gear and had barely set out towards Farkhar when I got a call from Sheikh Abdullah.

'Come back', he said.

'Why?' I asked.

'I will tell you when you come back.'

I found him sitting with Hekmatyar, both men looking tense and extremely worried, something major had happened which had changed everything. 'The BBC', said the sheikh, 'has reported that thirty-one leaders of Massoud's men have been massacred by Sayyid Jamal.'

I gritted my teeth exasperated, I looked to the heavens for succour. How could it be? I got up and paced up and down asking myself that question. How could it be? I was shocked, I sat down to get my bearings. The same questions coursed through my head. How could this happen? Why? We were so close to peace talks. 'All our preparations', said Sheikh Abdullah, 'have been for naught, the peace that we have been working for has just evaporated.'

This time the massacre in Farkhar, on 9 July lay at the feet of Hekmatyar's man, Sayyid Jamal, a senior commander of Hekmatyar's party, Hezb-i Islami.[7] His rivalry with his collegue Engineer Basheer over control of Takhar had spilt over to violating treaties and truces. As the unarmed leaders, the Shura-i Nazar, of Massoud passed through the territories of Hezb-i Islami, Sayyid Jamal slaughtered them in cold blood. Some of the men were Massoud's close friends.

Sheikh Abdullah looked to Hekmatyar and asked, 'What now?' Hekmatyar looked as lost as all of us. 'I don't know,' he responded, 'this is a disaster.'

I got up to go indicating that I needed to return to Massoud; I could see what the news of the massacre would do to his men. Sheikh Abdullah said he would accompany me, Abu Hajar al-Iraqi and Abu'l Harith, Sheikh Azzam's nephew and personal bodyguard. We got hold of some horses and rode down to Takhar province to meet Massoud. It took us four days and when we found commander Massoud he looked at me concerned. 'Anas I am afraid for you,' he said referring to the truce I had negotiated with Engineer Basheer and Sayyid Jamal a few months ago, 'the region is in tumult, the men are blaming you for negotiating the truce that allowed Sayyid Jamal to kill our leaders.'

Sheikh Abdullah agreed that the situation was a catastrophe but had to be contained at any price. Massoud shuffled awkwardly: he was embarrassed but the outcome of this massacre was beyond his control. 'You know,' he said apologetically to the sheikh, 'if this disaster had happened in Panshir I could act decisively, but we are dealing with commanders here in Takhar province whose loyalty is to the party. I don't have direct command or personal links to the men of Takhar and Badakshan. I don't have the power to pardon them, and if I did, I would be expelled from the party.'

Massoud told us about one of his commanders Seifullah who had been ambushed by a Hezb-i Islami commander. 'Many of the leaders', he explained, 'wanted revenge but I restrained them. I told them that killing a group from Hezb-i Islami, would not return Seifullah to us, may God have mercy on him.'

Sheikh Abdullah remained with us for three days trying his best to diffuse the situation with great difficulty. Massoud felt embarrassed to have to start this military operation against Hezb-i Islami whilst the sheikh was with them. He pulled me aside. 'Brother,' Massoud said, 'it's not befitting that the sheikh is with us when the fighting starts and he is unable to stop it. His stature and credibility might be undermined. This is bigger than me, and I can't stop this. Take him back to Pakistan.'

I agreed: the role that sheikhs play is an important one in Muslim societies, they often act as mediators in disputes, and Sheikh Abdullah being present in such a circumstance would not be good if at a later point he would be required to step in and diffuse the situation. His gravitas would be diminished. I informed Sheikh Abdullah and he agreed to return to Peshawar, and a convoy was prepared for him to return. As we left for Peshawar Sheikh Abdullah asked Massoud to promise that 'the war targets the culprit.' And he continued to write letters till the day of his assassination reminding Massoud of being patient, of not shedding Muslim blood and to remember God and His Messenger's injunctions against shedding blood.

Our convoy set out for the Afghanistan-Pakistan border and as we headed towards the Chatral border crossing we heard the BBC World Service announce that Massoud had captured the culprit of the Farkhar massacre. Their dawn operation had resulted in the arrest of Sayyid Jamal, his brother Sayyid Mirza, and one of his relatives; casualties were kept to a minimum. The repercussions though were far-reaching. Massoud could have retaliated against the men, but instead he put them in prison awaiting trial. I breathed a sigh of relief, he had kept his promise.

And so when I returned back to north Afghanistan, I found Sayyid Jamal chained hand and foot. God had raised him a *mujahid* and he had abased himself by shedding blood unjustly. I was saddened by the dejected state that Sayyid Jamal had been reduced to: that ambush should have been directed against the enemy not his own brothers. There was a long-standing friendship between us. On a personal level I really liked him. Seeing him that way really touched me and I remained with him during the afternoon. I asked one of the interrogating officers if it would be possible to see Sayyid Jamal at his office. After all, this man used to command one thousand *mujahideen* and I didn't like to visit him in a cell unworthy of his status and dignity, he had hosted me many times as his guest.

The Commander agreed and they brought him to me unchained along with his brother, Sayyid Mirza. I asked the interrogating officer if we could have lunch together and he agreed. I would never have done that if I thought that Massoud would oppose it.

'Are they treating you well?' I asked.

'If Massoud', replied Jamal, 'had spent millions of dollars he would not have captured my heart the way he has done so now. I swear it. I am receiving excellent treatment. It is as if they are honouring me.'

I was pleased, Massoud always treated prisoners well.

'So what do you want to eat?' I asked.

'Raisins and almonds.'

I went out and fetched him some. 'What else can I do?' I asked.

He ate the almonds and raisins and replied, 'If Massoud releases me,' he said, 'then I will finish off Engineer Basheer, the road will be clear for him. Just give me a week and I will bring him back dead or alive.'

'I cannot do that', I said. 'I will mediate but to be party for one Muslim to kill another, this I will not do.'

THE BROKEN TRUCE

I left him and he remained in jail for five months before being sentenced to death on Christmas Eve 1989. He was hanged on a cold day alongside his brother and relative in a public square in Taloqan, Takhar. He earned disgrace solely because he had hankered after the world instead of paradise. It was true the crisis had ended. All-out war did not break out but the massacre left an ominous shadow over the *mujahideen*: even though Hekmatyar had condemned Sayyid Jamal's action as betrayal, reconciliation between the Massoud and Hekmatyar was near impossible.

More than that the interim government that had been formed by the fall of Kabul on 23 February just before the launch of the Jalalabad offensive was now in tatters. The formation of the interim government led by Sayyaf as Prime Minister and Mujaddidi as President and the rest of the portfolios distributed amongst the rest of the *mujahideen* factions had been encouraging despite the problems. Whilst there had been infighting between the factions, even assassinations—Commander Hajji Abdul Latif of the National Islamic Front had been poisoned—the interim government could have been salvaged. After the Farkhar massacre the interim government was dead. It had gone so badly that Hekmatyar was even willing to put his Islamic principles to one side to collude with a putschist Communist General Shahnawaz Tanai in order to grab power. General Tanai's failed coup attempt in August 1989 had received support from Hekmatyar whilst the rest of the *mujahideen* forces accused him of brazen treachery.

10

WHEN KABUL FELL, MY WORLD FELL

Although I will discuss the assassination of Abdullah Azzam and the causes below, suffice to say that my world shook when he was killed on 24 November 1989: it was such a low after seeing the back of the Russians. On the eve of his assassination he had knocked on all the leaders' doors asking them to unite. I was in Takhar province when Ahmed Shah Massoud informed me. I cannot tell you how the situation changed after his passing in Peshawar. He was like a great spiritual dam holding things together between the various factions. He tempered the Afghan factions and kept the *takfiris* at bay. With his passing it signalled the beginning of the madness. Now we had Afghans and Arabs who claimed to be caliph and anyone who didn't give them the oath of allegiance was an apostate. Sounds familiar? The Arab Caliph in particular ended up on the Edgware Road in a council house whilst many of his followers conducted banditry and smuggled drugs in and out of Afghanistan. You had foreign fighters being influenced by extremists and these ideas were spreading amongst them. By 1993 these men who really had very little experience against the Soviets, were involved in the civil war that followed between Massoud and Hekmatyar and they took on the title of being *mujahideen*, when in reality they were souls caught up in the net of various agendas.

By January 1990 barring a few glitches I was now running the Arab Services Bureau (MAK) and I split my time between Massoud and the MAK. The atmosphere in Peshawar had become poisonous and oppressive, trust had been eroded and suspicion reigned. It was a time of immense stress and indecision. Sometimes I felt almost besieged from every angle; even a lecturing tour in the US could turn out to be a nightmare. After Sheikh Abdullah's death it fell upon me to take over his lecturing and fund-raising tours in the US. It was in this context that I met Mustafa Shalabi or Abu Du'a in December 1989.[1] Shalabi was an American citizen of Egyptian decent who lived in Brooklyn with his family and was a generous host. Sheikh Abdullah had recruited him to the cause and Shalabi had proved adept at being the MAK's representative in the US and ran it out of Al-Farouq, a *musalla*[2] set up by some Lebanese Americans. We had over fifty-two branches in the US spanning the country: Phoenix, Boston, Chicago, Tucson, Minnesota and in the capital, Washington DC. But the main office was in Brooklyn, New York and Shalabi ran the MAK's operations from there. We didn't call the organisation MAK or associate it with the Afghan Jihad because that would contravene US law and instead called it al-Kifah, which was also a synonym for struggle. After my brief stay with Shalabi I went on the speaking tour in the US and returned back to Peshawar. Shalabi and I stayed in touch and he would occasionally call me requesting more issues of *al-Jihad* magazine and consult me on other administrative matters. When I met him again in 1990 on another speaking tour at JFK airport, Shalabi was a totally different man from what I remembered: he was a nervous wreck. Shalabi was distressed and complaining that he wanted to leave the MAK for good. I was puzzled and pressed him further until I got the truth out of him: the reason was Sheikh Omar Abdel Rahman, the spiritual leader of Gamaa al-Islamiyya of whom I will discuss in greater depth in Part III.

Even though Sheikh Abdullah used to disagree with Sheikh Omar profoundly, the relationship between the two men was amicable. Sheikh Abdullah used to give him a small allowance on account of his blindness and the fact that he was an al-Azhar alumni. When the former passed away I continued this legacy started by Sheikh Abdullah. Sheikh Omar left for Khartoum following the military coup in June 1989 by Omar Hassan al-Bashir. In September 1990 I received a phone call from Abu Talaal, the spokesman for Gamaa al-Islamiya, asking me whether the MAK could contribute couple of hundred dollars for a flight to the US. Sheikh Omar was going on a visit there and if any assistance could be rendered him whilst he was there, it would be greatly appreciated. Seeing that he was blind I agreed to it. Shalabi received him and hosted him in his house for several days expecting that this was enough. But as Shalabi explained, 'You know I gave him my car, everything! But the visit became more than that. He started using the phones to call his family and followers and started to use our money. So I told him he couldn't use Arab Services Bureau's money. He got very upset and now he supplicates against me after every prayer.'

For a devout Muslim that was a very grave situation to be in. So I had to resolve the matter and visited the late Sheikh Omar and found him in a small room above al-Farouq. After our usual pleasantries I told him respectfully that maybe it was time for him to return to Peshawar. 'This place', replied the sheikh, 'is ripe for the Islamic message.'

I continued to press him saying that America wasn't suitable for him. 'You need', I said, 'ten years to learn the language, and ten years to understand the society.' After all in our traditions the prophets were from the people and understood their societies well. The sheikh said he had found a way to stay in the US, that he would marry an American woman. I said it wasn't befitting someone like him to marry an American woman just for a green card. 'Come back to Peshawar,' I urged him.

But the sheikh wouldn't have it any other way and decided to stay. I couldn't just tell him what to do and I left him travelling the length and breadth of this vast country on the usual speaking tours. For two months I encountered people from diverse backgrounds and faiths that really made me admire the genius of these people. Their civilisational achievements were immense and admirable and it taught me that credit must be given where credit is due. Whether that is the greatness of Rome, the US or Islamic caliphate. The two months had been so taxing that when I returned I slept through three days straight, so tired and exhausted was I from crossing different time zones and places.

A month later I received a phone call from Shalabi's wife saying that Shalabi had been killed by an unknown assailant. As he was trying to go to the airport, he was knifed, shot and beaten to death.[3] Shalabi's death coincided with the murder of a far right Jewish Zionist Rabbi Meir Kahane who was also killed by an Egyptian-American El-Seyyid Nosair. There were some reports claiming that Nosair had even been to Afghanistan: I am unsure about this assertion, but if he did, it must have been for a short visit. None of us remembers him ever taking part in any fighting. Whatever the case, Nosair was a *takfiri*. What was worse, Nosair and the sheikh became linked to the World Trade Center bombing in February 1993. Ramzi Youssef and Mohammed Salameh detonated a truck bomb inside the World Trade Center causing immense damage to life and property. The sheikh became linked to these men and was seen as their spiritual guide. I am unconvinced that the sheikh had much to do with it. What happened was that this sheikh being blind and having no context as to who the questioner was, was asked a general question about killing and attacking non-Muslims and so forth, in several circles. And he started rattling off verses from the Quranic chapter of Repentance, *Taubah*, which deals with fighting the Meccans during the Prophet's time.[4] *Taubah* was also the subject of his PhD thesis, and this was recorded by an FBI informant on tape and the prosecution linked this to the World Trade Center bombing. The case of Sheikh Omar was just one of those unfortunate events where extremism led to the death of innocent civilians in the World Trade Center bombing and the imprisonment of an old man who said things out of place, out of context and without wisdom.

To return to the death of Shalabi, it added another extra layer of stress on me, one felt almost beset with one problem after another, trying to run the MAK in Peshawar as well as trying to keep the war effort focused on Kabul. But if the truth be told I was struggling, since the assassination of Sheikh Abdullah Azzam had left a massive vacuum in the *mujahid* body politic. The warmth and unity had disappeared amongst the Arab *mujahideen*. The spiritual influence of the sheikh had disappeared. Now men sat in groups, suspicious of each other and their views.

One guest-house for instance, could be run by Algerians and that very guest-house would be split into various factions. As the great American Abraham Lincoln said, 'A house divided can not stand' and so it was with the Saudi- and the Egyptian-run guest-houses too. Whilst Afghans fought each other inside Afghanistan, the Arab foreign fighters were bickering in Peshawar and sometimes the animosity spilled out onto its streets. This made the Pakistani authorities increasingly impatient with their activities. Everything was topsy-turvy, now if you fought in Afghanistan for ten years it was the same as a fighter who had spent a week inside Afghanistan, and both were considered *mujahideen* even though the former had participated in crucial battles. We were struggling with the calibre of Arabs coming to us. Once we gave forty thousand dollars to a small thin Arab to transport to Logar and he just disappeared for months. We eventually managed to locate him and demanded the money back that belonged to orphans but his heart was made of stone devoid of any chivalry and honour and he would not return it. He had spent it all. This would never have happened in the early days.

Sometimes I wandered the streets of Peshawar dazed, unsure of what I should make of the whole situation. Sheikh Abdullah encouraged his daughters to study, learn and teach. Now you knocked on a brother's door, his wife would throw a stone over with a note saying that he was not in. Or if you called the brother, there would be a tapping on the receiver presumably by his wife, indicating that he was not home. It was absurd as to what lengths many of these people went to. The women were kept in total isolation. Even Osama's wives and daughters would respond over the phone. My mind boggled as I saw men you would stop on the street becoming the self-appointed 'caliph' of monotheism overnight. There was Abu Humam who ran his caliphate from a Lisson Green council flat in London and there was the Afghan Mawlawi Jamil ur-Rahman Hussain.[5] The latter declared himself the Emir of Islamic Monotheism in Kunar province and ran it like his own fiefdom. The Salafi banned tobacco and forced men to grow beards as a sign that he was applying Shariah. His imposition jarred with the Afghans because they were Hanafis in religious rite and Sufi in outlook. But many Saudi clerics from the Gulf issued a fatwa or legal ruling declaring his emirate to be an authentic and legitimate caliphate.[6] And so we had the curious prospect of an underling of Hekmatyar now leading the faithful. Hekmatyar of course wouldn't stand for such insolence and insubordination, and he accused Rahman of being a 'wahabi'[7] and a heretic, while Rahman made counter accusations. Hundreds were killed in the conflict that ensued between Hekmatyar and Rahman. Some Arabs wanted to mediate a solution but most sided with Hekmatyar, and thought that the situation could only be resolved by the gun. They adopted Ottoman or medieval modes of behaviour found in Islamic history: when there were two emirs, kill one of them to stop civil strife. This doctrine, still adhered to in some parts of the Muslim world to this day, has caused much bloodshed. After Rahman's cabinet were killed by a bomb and he was severely weakened the emir fled to Pakistan allowing Hekmatyar's forces to to take over Kunar. Meanwhile Abdullah Rumi, an Egyptian living in Peshawar, got himself invited to Rahman's house for lunch. They broke bread together, they prayed the noon prayer together and then Rumi brought out his revolver and shot him point blank and blew his brains out. And so on 30 August 1991, the reign of the Afghan caliph ended. It shocked everyone, made the Pakistani authorities nervous and set a dangerous precedent for the future. Distrust between Arabs, Afghans and Pakistanis increased. Later when Mullah Omar emerged leading the Taliban fighting the forces of Massoud, Osama bin Laden too got it into his head that killing Massoud would end the conflict, and so he ordered Abdus Sattar Dahmane[8] and Rachid Boraoui el-Ouaer to assassinate him. Massoud's assassination didn't solve anything, for the tribulations continue to this day—blood only engenders blood.

And yet, despite all the madness Najibullah's government was slowly crumbling as Massoud sprang his trap around him. Around March one of Massoud's commanders came into my office—he was aptly named Commander Muslim Hayat, he was a beautiful man in manners and grace just like a Muslim should be. We sat in the office reminiscing, drinking tea and catching up on the war effort when he told me: 'You know, Anas,' he said confidently, 'Najibullah may fall soon.' I sat up from my chair. 'How?' I said. Najibullah Ahmedzai had taken over after the fall of Babrak Karmal in 1987 and seemed to be a far better political operator especially as he had a KHAD background.

'There is a serious scandal afoot between Najibullah and the General Jumu'a Asaq', said Commander Muslim. 'He's been sacked from Kandahar and Dostum too in Mazar Sharif.'

'Really?' I said, surprised: these men were able generals you couldn't just discard them without feeling the consequences.

'Najibullah told General Asaq to be the commander in Mazar Sharif and Dostum didn't accept it. Dostum became angry; he didn't want a southerner ruling over the people of Mazar Sharif.' I was surprised yet again, one of the biggest and perhaps longest battles that I had participated in was against Dostum in 1990. There was no doubt that Dostum was an able commander. Dostum, however was not a Communist, the only ideology he believed in was money. He was a mercenary warlord, ruthless and violent just as the men he lead. His Gailam Jama was synonymous with rapine, brutality and destruction. And Najibullah used this Gailam Jama as a stick to go and fight wherever he wished.

My own encounter with Dostum was in 1991 in Khoja Ghar on the border with Tajikistan. This was a strategically important battle because it was a supply hub where the regime received supplies from the Soviets. This was also the first time I experienced the formidable Scud missile used in the Gulf War with devastating effect. The first time I experienced it, the whole place became day as it lit up the sky. We lost twelve friends that day and one of them, Syed Yahya, died in front of my very eyes, suffering a mortal trauma wound to the head. I could remember all of us crying including Massoud when we buried him. Syed Yahya was an important and capable commander and a great loss to all of us. Dostum had come up from Mazar Sharif and the battle against him was long and hard. Usually Massoud's battle lasted a few hours or maximum a few days; this one lasted twenty days. Villages changed hands regularly, one day we would capture the village, the next day Dostum would attack and we would retreat to reorganise. By the time we finished many tanks and military vehicles had been destroyed. By His Grace we defeated them and we sensed that it was a turning point in the battle against the regime, but it also gave us a good sense of Dostum's fighting ability. Dostum and his men might be mercenary and fickle but they were no cowards.

But now as a result of Kabul's decision to shuffle the military portfolio, Najibullah had become embroiled in the rivalries between his general Dostum and Momin Baba Jan. He could no longer secure the northern supply routes which were more important than the southern supply routes. The northern supply route was key to the Soviet Union; moreover by 1991 the Soviet Union was struggling to supply Kabul because they were at the brink of collapse. This meant that the likes of Benon Sevan, the UN Secretary-General's representative in Afghanistan, was trying hard to bring the various factions together for an interim coalition government. Massoud however, knew that the breakthrough would never come from the south, that is Peshawar. They simply didn't have the political skills nor the experience to come together. So he invested in encouraging the rivalry between Najibullah's generals. He reached out to the generals such as Momin Baba Jan in order to encourage them to abandon the Najibullah government which they did in February 1992. Whilst at the same time Massoud slowly prized apart the Najibullah government, he was also setting up a *Shura-i Nazar*, a ruling counsel inside Afghanistan, where negotiations could be conducted with all the various factions because Massoud did not want to act unilaterally. By defeating Najibullah, Massoud didn't need to rely on negotiations between Kabul and the *mujahideen* as equals but rather the *mujahideen* could dictate terms to Kabul and sort out their differences amongst themselves. And this was the course of action he pursued: he wanted an all-out military victory.

When I told Osama that Massoud was at the gates of Kabul his reply was 'You always exaggerate about the exploits of Massoud', and he dismissed my news. Truth was he was still smarting from the defeat at the hands of the Najibullah government in Jalalabad. The battle had failed disastrously. Many Arabs lost their lives in the battle and bin Laden's morale had been understandably dampened.[9] But fourteen days later Najibullah's government collapsed like dominoes; Mazar Sharif fell, the Salang pass was taken, Bagram captured by Massoud and Dostum retreated after a small skirmish with the *mujahideen*. Massoud and his generals gathered in a location in Charikar, northern Afghanistan, to deal the death blow to Najibullah's government when the dark green helicopter carrying Kabul's foreign minister landed.

The foreign minister Abdul Wakil landed, and made his way to Massoud and his men. Once inside the safe-house, Abdul Wakil congratulated Commander Massoud on his victory. He offered the government's full surrender with only one condition: the new government must give political recognition to all parties including the Communists.

At the time I was immensely pleased with Massoud's response. 'We fought you for fifteen years for an Islamic State.' Massoud said, 'now you want to have a legitimate party after all these years? The only thing I can offer is to pass this on to the leadership. That is the only help I can offer. And even then that is something that I cannot guarantee, this is up to the *mujahideen* leaders.' Now, in hindsight, I believe the *mujahideen* should not have deprived these people of expressing themselves politically, even if they disagreed with their political doctrines. It would have prevented a lot of bloodshed in Afghanistan's political future. Accepting difference amongst each other is a sign of political maturity and the Muslim world lags behind on this issue.

The Najibullah delegation said that they would return to their comrades and discuss these terms, which in reality, weren't really terms but an ultimatum. 'Give us two or three days' said the foreign minister and he flew back to Kabul to pass on the message to Najibullah. The foreign minister's entourage returned a day after with a smile on his face as he descended from the helicopter, he put his hands up in jest in mock surrender and informed Massoud that Najibullah had sought refuge at the United Nations guest-house and the head of Intelligence, General Yaqoubi had fallen on his sword and taken his life. The regime had fallen, the *mujahideen* had won, the road to Kabul was open to Massoud.

Massoud never liked acting unilaterally, and knew that entering Kabul with his army without the Afghan factions would lead to civil war. Already people were saying Hekmatyar's men were ambushing convoys, attacking *mujahideen* factions and so on, and this would stoke the fires of conflict even more. Men would say that Massoud was like the rest of them, a power-hungry warlord looking for glory. He took into account the ethnic and sectarian patchwork that Afghanistan was made out of and called on the Afghan leaders to come together to form a coalition government. He asked them only to halt any international initiatives and form a government that could enter Kabul as if it was the conquest of Mecca. 'Now,' Massoud said, 'you are the leaders, form your government.'

We didn't believe it when we heard the words, especially bin Laden. But once the reality sunk in we went into action. I, Wael Julaidan, Abdel Majid Zindani, bin Laden, Adel Battarji—the founder of the charity Lejnat ul-Birr, the council of piety—and Jamal Khashoggi started to bring the leaders together in various Afghan leaders' houses and pressed them to form a government. In many ways, our links to the Islamic movement meant that our access to the Afghan leaders was more direct than that of many of the UN officials. We sat mostly in Sayyaf's house over tea urging them to resolve their issues. We called in the scholars from all over the Muslim world who could bring hearts together, advise the various factions and smooth out the process of coalition forming. After sixteen days of Massoud waiting in Charikar we were still frantically to-ing and fro-ing between the different groups in

Peshawar, but eventually the Afghans themselves through Sayyaf's efforts came up with a list of nominees that would form a new interim government in an agreement known as the Peshawar accords, signed on 24 April 1992.

Sibghatullah Mojaddedi[10] would be president for two months, and Rabbani would follow him for four months. After these six months elections would take place so that there would be a legitimate government. Gailani would be foreign minister, Sayyaf would be interior minister, Massoud defence minister and Hekmatyar the prime minister. The UN had endorsed the interim government. It seemed all but resolved. There was joy in the air, and people celebrated on the streets of Peshawar, Pakistan and Afghanistan and around the Muslim world. Thousands of Afghan refugees displaced by the conflict hoped to return home.

But the Peshawar accords soon fell apart. Hekmatyar declared that he was not happy with the agreement at all. 'How could this be a victory when Mojadeddi was president?' Hekmatyar quipped. It effectively meant that Mojadeddi was giving his loyalty to George Bush Senior. It was commonly believed that Mojadeddi, was a royalist with links to the last king of Afghanistan, Mohammed Zahir Shah, and was seen as Washington's man. It was widely believed that the Americans hoped for a return of the Afghan king who was living in Rome at the time. But whilst these accusations can be thrown at Mojadeddi, equally Hekmatyar forgot that all the parties received money from the CIA so, whether he liked it or not, he was also George Bush Senior's man because he received the bulk of the CIA funds through the Pakistani ISI.

My take on it was that Mojaddedi was the compromise candidate, as the main powerbrokers such as Hekmatyar's Hezb-i Islami and Rabbani's Jamiat-i Islami were suspicious of each other's intentions. If one of them held the presidency, each party feared that the other might seize power for themselves. At the same time the smaller parties didn't want one of the big parties to control the presidency for fear that one of them would monopolise power; so Mojaddedi became their compromise candidate. In many ways it made political sense in such a fraught political environment. But Hekmatyar ratcheted up the rhetoric: 'How can this be a victory', he said, 'if Dostum and the Communists are still in government and Massoud is working with Shi'ite factions? How can this be a victory?'

Hekmatyar was determined to march on Kabul from where he was in Logar. The initial flush of victory disappeared. Bin Laden, Wael Julaidan, I and others urged them to reconcile. There was more to-ing and fro-ing, flattery, threats, scolding—we tried everything, but Hekmatyar was self-centred, proud and very stubborn and did not think about what the consequences of his actions would be.

During those days, we tried our best to calm the tensions between the various parties. We got Haqqani to meet with Hekmatyar face to face in order to resolve the conflict. But the hardest meeting was for Hekmatyar to meet Massoud. The truth was it wasn't Massoud who was the obstruction as history testifies, but Hekmatyar. We tried our very best to set up conversations between the two on the wireless having it all transcribed and it became very clear that Hekmatyar was behaving in such a bellicose way that he had already determined to march on Kabul and take it by the sword.

Hekmatyar in the end declared that he would march on Kabul on the pretext that there were still Communist insurgents within the city. Massoud respectfully urged him to think again, to come to the table and thrash out their differences within the interim government. When Hekmatyar told him that he had taken his position based on accurate information and the onslaught could not be stopped, Massoud realised that Hekmatyar could not be reasoned with. He simply informed him that as minister of defence he had pledged to protect Kabul and he would do so robustly. Any aggression on Hekmatyar's part would be responded to forcefully. So when Hekmatyar's men began their military movements, Massoud's commanders got ready to defend the capital. Hekmatyar was reaching out to former Communist power-brokers and began to start his military advance but Massoud thwarted it with deadly force. It was only after Hekmatyar saw Massoud's determination to protect Kabul and that he could not beat him without considerable losses, that he informed the interim coalition that he was willing to participate in the political process after the end of Mojadeddi's presidential tenure.

And so finally Kabul fell on the 25 April 1992.[11] Najibullah went into hiding under the auspices of the United Nations having resigned. Sibghatullah Mojaddedi entered the capital on 28 April and declared Afghanistan an Islamic state. At least for me, if felt like the conquest of Mecca. Thousands upon thousands of cars lined the road to Kabul. The Muslim world rejoiced, from Mecca and Medina to Indonesia. But we did not realise that now the real battle had begun; it is easy to destroy and expel an enemy but building your country, creating stability, healing souls—that was the greater challenge, that was the greater Jihad.

11

POWER AND ITS BITTER FRUITS

In the spring of 1992, we entered Kabul as victors. We brandished pure unadulterated power in the warm sun, we were exhilarated. I got a taste, perhaps, of what the Companions must have felt as they entered Mecca when their enemies surrendered in 630 AD. But little did we realise the full extent of what that meant. For the battle may have been won but what one did once it had ended was the greater challenge. And perhaps this is why the Prophet entered Mecca with his head bowed in peace and submission, or Umar the second caliph entered Jerusalem with his servant riding his horse; he refused to pray in churches even though the Patriarch of Jerusalem had invited him to do so. Umar did not want to set a precedent for future generations, he did not want to see them turn the church into a mosque. I suppose it was in recognition that not only did victory come from Him, but also of the great responsibility one had when one wielded such powers. The challenges we faced as we entered were not unique to us: all of human history has wrestled with this question and will continue to do so, some like the Crusaders led by Godfrey of Bouillon failed when they conquered Jerusalem in

1099, others like Salahuddin Ayyoubi succeeded when he took it back in 1187.

In Kabul I took a room at the Intelligence Ministry where Massoud, now defence minister, had decided to establish himself. I worked there or at the presidential palace. I would spend three weeks in Kabul and then make the seven hour journey to Peshawar looking into MAK affairs. My time in Kabul was in many ways a transitional period for me: on one hand, I was an Afghan national, I had been offered an Afghan passport and could settle there without any restrictions. Massoud kindly offered me a home where I could move my young family in if I wanted to. I watched affairs in Afghanistan and could see the clouds of civil war already looming on the horizon. Yet at the same time I watched the success of FIS in my native country eagerly, and so I was torn as to what I should do. So I stayed in Kabul flitting from ministry to palace sitting with various decision makers and going to Peshawar to deal with the affairs of the Arab Services Bureau still trying to figure out what to do next.

Whilst I could enjoy the fruits of power, and the freedom to leave, Massoud could not. Massoud was a man who never wanted power. But being the minister of defence was overwhelming. He was the de facto power in Kabul. I don't think anyone could deal with the immense challenges that faced a post-Soviet Afghanistan. The problems were just too immense, especially as the civil war worsened between Dostum, Hekmatyar and some of the Shi'ite factions of Hezb-i Wahdat who were trying to carve up Kabul and create a situation similar to Beirut.[1] In those days I watched Massoud's hair turn grey and his brow becoming heavy with worry. Everything he did had to be planned, he couldn't just up and leave to some mountain sanctuary with his men in the Panshir valley. Whilst in his office one courier would enter upon Massoud saying that they have lost such and such commander, that they needed reinforcements in such and such area; Massoud would react, then an hour later another courier would rush in demanding help on another issue. It was a constant stream of problems, and Massoud complained loudly about it. The reports of problems and the demand for solutions went on twenty-four hours a day. At the same time, Hekmatyar was gathering his men in Charsyab ready to attack Kabul, and Sayyaf had withdrawn to Paghman not willing to get fully involved or fully supportive of the new state of play in the capital. Within two months the interim government was cracking up. Kabul was mostly under the control of the interim government but the rockets had begun and they were launched by the man who was meant to be the country's interim prime minister, Hekmatyar.

Massoud used to reminisce about returning to his childhood neighbourhood, Shahrinau, where he played football and ate artisan ice cream, but he did not have the time to enjoy those pleasures. I remember in the early days, when Muhammed Gul, Massoud's bodyguard, took me on a tour of Kabul in Najibullah's armoured car, we eventually ended up in the streets where Massoud grew up in a restaurant eating artisan ice cream when we saw Massoud striding across the street on a mission to resolve an issue.

'Come join us', I said, inviting him to sit with us, but Massoud refused. 'See,' I said jokingly, 'this is what power does to you.'

'Do you see?' Massoud replied, 'This is the kind of hell I am living in!'

Sometimes the stress would get to him so much that he would break all security protocol and give his bodyguards a heart attack for he would just slip away and play a game of football or wrestle with us. I think he did it just to feel normal again. And I would often return to Peshawar and report to his father about his son's exploits and defeats and his father would shake his head attributing his son's defeat in wrestling to him not listening to his instructions and not eating his greens. A father will always be a father.

I suppose what we the *mujahideen* didn't realise was that taking power was very different from exercising power—that is much harder. Kabulis looked at us with expectant eyes. Finally they thought, the *mujahideen* would deliver them from this oppressive tyrant, this ex-intelligence chief who terrorised his citizens, this dictator who applied the most gruesome tortures on their bodies just to squeeze out some titbit of information. Kabulis hoped to see their children return from exile and return to their ordinary lives. But though we had entered in peace, we failed them.

I remember driving up to the Intercontinental Hotel overlooking the city in our Toyota pick-up trucks. I entered with my men unhindered by check points or enemy forces. Here we were rough looking, pakhouls, Kalashnikovs, wearing the paraphernalia of war—we were the sort of men who were unfit to grace the likes of such hotels in past times. We stepped in to the lobby, and asked for an espresso and after that we had a chat with the manager who ran the place efficiently and well. I don't know whether he was frightened of us, but pulling up like that, ordering an espresso, and speaking to the manager of the hotel taught me something about war and the exercise of power. It is intoxicating, and it has to be used responsibly. It is in those moments, when one could exercise total power, that one truly sees what one is made of. Najibullah's Kabul was still intact when I had that espresso in the Intercontinental, the boulevards, the streets, the infrastructure more or less worked. Six months later I turned up at the hotel and the situation was very different. The manager could no longer provide us with the award-winning service he wished to deliver. The hotel had numerous *mujahideen* commanders who had arrived at the hotel, and decided to occupy part of it garrisoning their men, and they were a law unto themselves. No commander could tell another commander to control his men. And so you had a situation where everyone did what they wished without the management having any control of the events and so naturally the hotel standards declined.

Looking back now, as a Muslim activist all my life I believed in simple slogans and phrases. I had said them without quite thinking what they meant and what the consequences were. Just like you hear it today from the youth waving a black flag: 'We want Shariah!'

–Yes but *what* Shariah? What does Shariah look like in the modern age?

'We follow the Quran and Sunnah.'

–Yes, but what do you mean? Are you saying that Abu Hanifa or Imam Malik didn't follow the Quran and Sunnah? What does one mean when one shouts out: Islam is the solution? We want the Khilafah. Simple slogans but with massive implications.

I uttered 'Jihad', *'shaheed'* and so on without quite realising the importance of these heavy words. I had worked for ten years for this cause. I saw friends and family who had died for this cause and yet what did it all mean? This wasn't an existential crisis but the realisation that life and reality wasn't just made up of slogans. We had showed the world the power of Jihad and what it could do and now it was all over, a vacuum was here. Now what?

The country had more than a million martyrs, a hundred thousand men and women and children disabled, let alone refugees and internally displaced persons. What shall be the fruits of this great sacrifice? Will we see a repeat of the history of my country in 1962? Or will we see a stable, secure, prosperous and ethical country? What will be the outcome of this Jihad? I had never thought about it until now. We were so busy fighting. What now? I had become Afghanistan and Afghanistan had become me. I loved its people and the country intensely. On my trip to the US I had been offered the chance of getting a green card to stay on in the US, a green card that many Arabs dream of, do unspeakable things to get hold of—it was on offer in

1991, and I could have stayed on in the country but I swear I missed the mountains of Afghanistan. But even as I watched Mojaddedi hold on to the reins of power I could see Afghanistan slip away from his hands.

Mojaddedi was a politician, and no angel, but he was also surrounded by men who wanted to see him fail. He made political alliances, he brought back General Dostum in from the cold and promoted him into a gold star general. Dostum's only concern at the time was praying to stay alive, with Mojaddedi bringing him back, his political fortunes changed overnight. He became a general again in Mazar Sharif. It was a profound shock to the *mujahideen* to see that happen, their foe who had killed their comrades was back to holding the reins of power. It completely undermined Mojaddedi's credibility, especially when he gave him the title '*Mujahed-i kebir*'—Great *Mujahid*, a great wolf perhaps, but he was not worthy of such a title.[2] Only in hindsight, only after 200,000 souls had perished in my own country in 1992 did I realise that Jihad, martyrdom is not enough. It needs political maturity and process. We saw this failure in Afghanistan, in Algeria and now in Syria.

And so only two months into the new government and we were in the same place we were when we had liberated it. Now, I sat in the Afghan presidential palace with Dr Burhanuddin Rabbani going over some paperwork and five to six Hekmatyar rockets landed and would have taken our lives had it not been for the bullet-proof windows in the palace. And all Rabbani could do is just smile stoically and say, 'There is no might or power except God' and, referring to Hekmatyar, 'Look at this hypocrite who rains rockets on civilians, God forgive me,' and he continued about his business. I was amazed at the man's resilience and even more surprised when he accepted Hekmatyar into the interim government as prime minister. The unwillingness of parties to compromise, to work for a common good had resulted in the government whose most powerful leader Massoud came head to head with the likes of Dostum, Hekmatyar and others and the people of Kabul wearily began to seek refugee in Peshawar again as the evening night skies were lit up by the missiles and mortars that saw the entry of the Taliban and the growth of al-Qaeda in Afghanistan.

Hekmatyar fought Massoud because he was allied to Dostum and the Shi'ite Wahdat party who tended to switch sides regularly. Hekmatyar claimed Mojaddedi's government was 'un-Islamic' and so in order to 'rectify' the Jihad, he decided to launch a 'corrective' Jihad. How many times have we seen this in history? It breaks my heart to hear how many good and sincere Arabs died for the sake of this wretched civil war thinking that this was a Jihad. How many of Osama bin Laden's Arabs were fooled into fighting in this 'corrective' Jihad? Where was the foreign occupation? They couldn't see the wood for the trees— this was plainly speaking a civil war. It saddened me immensely. They forgot that article in *al-Jihad* magazine published by Sheikh Abdullah Azzam saying clearly:

> O Arabs, if Allah allows the Afghans to gain victory, and take Kabul, if they succeed in bringing peace and working together, then be part of the continuing Jihad in other ways such as reconstruction for instance, but if they do not unify, if they fight amongst themselves, then don't be part of it. Don't support the disputes over who is right or wrong, arguments between north and south, or one party and another. If they come together then continue supporting them but if they turn on each other then do not be part of any group.[3]

But what about Osama? He was well aware of the situation. He was also aware of Sheikh Abdullah's fatwa—it had been formulated in his house. He knew very well what the conflict had turned into and yet he too had taken sides. I remember the words exactly, when I pressed Osama to join me and Julaidan to go to the newly liberated Kabul: 'What', he said, 'would Hekmatyar say?'

'What do you mean?' I replied.

'How can I enter Kabul and Hekmatyar is not there?' Osama explained. Hekmatyar was on the outskirts of Kabul making ready to take the city by force when he could enter in peace with the rest of the *mujahideen*! But Osama was concerned about Hekmatyar? He had no judgement. Wael and I left him to make our own way to Kabul, but it struck me that Osama was unwilling to alienate Hekmatyar and it was a clear indication that the whispers of the *takfiris*, the partisan politics amongst the Afghan leaders and the death of the sheikh had tipped the balance in Hekmatyar's favour. Osama knew very well that he had no business in it. All I knew was that this pure Islamic state was meant to protect life, honour, wealth and belief and yet they were fighting each other. I saw my friend Massoud forced to make hard choices, he found himself working with groups and men like Dostum because he was serving Mojaddedi's government. I learnt from this civil war that power sharing, dialogue, and cultural understanding takes time—a long time. Lest we forget the West took three hundred years to come to this point in their history; before that there were plenty of civil wars ravaging the continent, and the key to such things is patience. What is left for us to ponder is how to create such an atmosphere, a culture where we can develop a stable body politic that respects life, the soul, wealth, dignity and belief.

For me, I was torn in Kabul, I tried to mediate, I understood what was at stake for the parties involved. I could leave for Algeria, but at the same time these men could not, they had families and men dependent on them. What would happen to each party if they lost? I watched Massoud work from the palace itself whilst I dined with ministers observing almost from a distance—somewhat detached, since running Afghanistan was not my responsibility. I discharged my duties, I liaised with politicians, people and Arabs as part of the Arab Services Bureau, whilst Massoud ran the airports, air forces, security forces, foreign affairs and much, much more, and he looked tired. He controlled the heart of the state, but he was also becoming illegitimate since there was no constitution, elections or parliament.

As the civil war became earnest, it was then that I started to think about returning to Algeria. It was not just me, many of us did. Yemenis started to return in order to fight against the socialists in Aden. Many Gulf Arabs felt that it was time to go home: the Saudis and other Gulf countries had no issues with their citizens returning home. For the likes of me, Egyptians, Tunisians, Libyans and Jordanians, returning home was not an easy prospect. We were seen as a threat to the state and could act as a vanguard for further militancy. But in the end, I decided that it was time for me to part company with the mountains. I told Abu'l Qasim, the new director of the Arab Services Bureau, that I wanted to return home but that I had nowhere to go. I was a stranger and if I returned to Algeria I would be picked up by the Algerian security services. So instead I applied for a French visa and left the country. As I left for Paris, news reached me of an obscure movement called the Taliban led by a local commander called Mullah Omar. I didn't know at the time that this movement would one day take over Afghanistan and that Osama bin Laden would ally with them. I also did not realise that in the bosom of their state Osama bin Laden's men would eventually assassinate my dear friend Ahmed Shah Massoud. Under the auspices of this movement, Osama bin Laden's group, al-Qaeda, eventually infiltrated Massoud's group. Under the pretext of being journalists seeking an interview, two al-Qaeda operatives detonated their explosives hidden in their camera killing Massoud. Osama thought that by taking sides, killing Massoud two days before 9/11, the problem would be solved but Afghanistan has remained unstable to this day. I will now give a detailed account of the birth of the Afghan Arabs and how things fell apart.

PART III

THE ARAB SERVICES BUREAU

12

THE ESTABLISHMENT OF THE
ARAB SERVICES BUREAU

So far I have given an account of my experiences with Massoud inside Afghanistan and the internal rivalries amongst the *muja-hideen* commanders. It should be noted that apart from Abdullah Azzam and few others, the contributions of the Afghan Arabs were minuscule inside the country. However, whilst all these events were going on inside Afghanistan, the evolution of the Afghan Arabs was going on in Peshawar simultaneously. Now even that, in the grand scheme of the Afghan Jihad, was of no consequence, for I reiterate again that their role in the conflict was minor. But because they would play an important role after the Soviets left—not only with the rise of the Taliban but also with the rise of global Jihadism—it is worth recounting the story of the Afghan Arabs in a separate section.

I spent over a decade in Afghanistan and Pakistan. I left Afghanistan at the beginning of 1993 as a political exile for London like many Algerians did when the bloody civil war broke out. Many of these exiles settled in France amongst the French Algerian emigre community, others however didn't find France suitable. French Algerians were ghettoised there and treated like second-class citizens; moreover, France had an unsavoury connection to Algeria. There was a feeling that France colluded with Algeria on security matters, and so as an Algerian political exile, one wasn't safe there. As a consequence many Algerian political exiles went to Naples, Stockholm, Brussels, Bonn and London. Many of us flourished there and went back to our ordinary and quiet lives.

However, our peace was disturbed by the arrival of al-Qaeda and the world-changing events of 9/11. Then a profusion of experts cropped up all over the world claiming that thousands upon thousands of foreign fighters had trained in the camps of Afghanistan. These rough and grizzled returnees were now in their home countries planning to cause terror, mayhem and destruction. This narrative continues to have reverberations even as French men have returned from the battle fields of Syria to cause death and havoc on the streets of Paris.

Admittedly, I am getting old, but if my memory serves me right, I don't remember thousands upon thousands of men passing through our camps. Of course some people with the benefit of hindsight may question me as to how we tolerated these extremists? They will say that either I am an extremist or we subscribed to their ideology. It is true, I did meet men who played important roles in the future but at the time I was busy with the events of the moment, I didn't have the benefit of hindsight to realise what these men might end up doing, I just carried on with what I was doing and paid them little notice. But the likes of Massoud did see these men for who they are and the world paid him little notice, so why couldn't we not fully realise their significance?

Only now do I remember a young Abu Mus'ab al-Zarqawi passing through the Services Bureau offices. He passed through a few times inquiring about this and that; by that time the

Soviets were no more. But the man was so insignificant in the grand scheme of things that I didn't even remember him passing through our offices until my mother-in-law showed me his picture on a video tape of my wedding where I spotted him! I was amazed to find that the young man who had attended my wedding was this man lionised by al-Qaeda as a great *mujahid*. To me he was just one of those *takfiris* radicalised in the prisons of Jordan after he met Abu Muhammad al-Maqdisi. I couldn't believe that this former petty criminal became the leading insurgent in Iraq and lionised by his men.

I also met Khattab in Kabul, a young man who later went on to play a leading role in the fight against the Russians in Chechnya.[1] All I knew at the time was that he was a man who would be something, that he had leadership skills and insights, for he was mentioned whenever an opinion was needed regarding a military matter even before I had met him. I also knew by that time that he was not affiliated to al-Qaeda as is commonly assumed. Khattab had separated himself from the orbit of Osama bin Laden and Ayman al-Zawahiri a long time ago. The latter, whilst we were inside Afghanistan fighting the Russians, was sitting in the guest-houses backbiting and spreading their poison. But that was as far as it went. I couldn't envisage the idea that thousands of Arab fighters had passed through our camps.

Admittedly, some of these experts were so convincing that at some point I started to think that perhaps they were right, and it was I who was wrong. Perhaps the Afghanistan that I had experienced in the north was different from the Afghanistan that others had experienced and observed. Some things were undeniable, and it is true that the small city of Peshawar had mushroomed from being a one-street town, as it had been when I arrived, to one that was bustling with all sorts of trade and business. Its preferred mode of transport had been donkey carts and mostly small Suzukis that zipped through bicycles and pedestrians. By 1993 there were commanders in Toyota Hiluxes, Mitsubishi Pajeros and all types of 4x4s on the streets of Peshawar, intelligence agents, market traders, aid workers, fighters—all of them mixed with each other. Peshawar had grown exponentially, and a new neighbourhood such as Hayatabad that matched the classy suburbs of Islamabad was up and running. So if Peshawar could mushroom so quickly was it not plausible that there were more foreign fighters passing through the city into these numerous training camps? Maybe there had been a proliferation of fighters that had been trained in Afghanistan and these Arab *mujahideen* had turned into these global Jihadists that threatened the very stability of their own countries. So I conceded to the analysts.

But the hypothesis played on my mind: I wouldn't let it lie, I reassessed and fact checked, I asked comrades in arms, and still my conclusions returned to the same thing. These Arab foreign fighter figures were blown out of proportion. In my estimation there must have been about a hundred or so Arab fighters inside Afghanistan at any one time—I mean committed fighters—while the rest based themselves in Peshawar.

Moreover, the media and analysts focused on the role of the Maktabat al-Khadamat (MAK) or the Arab Services Bureau and its crucial role in radicalising and recruiting these fighters. They made it out to be some sort of hub that twisted the minds of these impressionable young Arabs and turned them into battle-hardened fighters bent on the destruction of the West; this is the same formula that is used with many of the foreign fighters in Syria. One of my friends, Wael Julaidan, was turned into an al-Qaeda financier when he had opposed them from the very beginning. If we hated the West why didn't we plan a terror attack from one of our fifty Arab Services Bureaus in the US? We had one branch in the very capital of the United States!

Analysts forget that we could not have operated without the knowledge of the various intelligence agencies like the ISI and the

Saudi intelligence services led by Prince Turki al-Faisal.[2] The other intelligence agencies must have considered us too small to pay us too much attention, but you couldn't operate in the way we did under the rule of General Zia ul-Haqq.[3] The ISI knew full well what we were up to when Sheikh Azzam set up the office.

Nevertheless, since I am one of the founders of the MAK it is only right that I address the issue. For naturally some would argue that I, being one of the MAK's founders, should bear some responsibility for the spawning of this monster that became al-Qaeda. But I am adamant that I am not responsible for it. This is not because I am one of those extremists who renounced their works and seen the error of my ways: far from it, I have not renounced my ideas, I may have developed and grown wiser but I still maintain that the MAK was nothing but an agency to render help to what the Afghan *mujahideen* wanted and that was all. We didn't have global ambitions except to serve Afghanistan. I am not ashamed of the MAK's work; rather, I am proud of it. But I do believe that an explanation is in order because al-Qaeda has been mythologised and the MAK's work has been hijacked to serve al-Qaeda's agendas. It is high time to explain that for the sake of posterity.

Maktabat al-Khadamat was set up due to a logistical necessity. How was one to manage this influx of Arabs who had answered the call of the sheikh? So when I returned to Peshawar from Mazar Sharif to report on my findings I discovered that Sheikh Azzam had already established the MAK. I was one of the people whose names was down as one of its founders. The raison d'être behind the establishment of the office was very simple. Very early on there was a recognition that the Arabs had to be organised in order for them to play a vital role in the Afghan Jihad. Afghans revered us due to the fact that the Prophet Muhammad was one of us (an Arab), the Quran was in Arabic and so on. The average Afghan respected us immensely based simply on that. And this could be used as leverage to negotiate the fractious political environment that existed in Afghanistan. If the Arabs could remain neutral throughout the *mujahideen* infighting and rivalry then perhaps great things could be achieved. That was the idea behind the MAK.

The MAK was there to guide many of these new volunteers through the chaotic political environment of Afghanistan. Otherwise these young volunteers could easily be swallowed up by the infighting. For young insular Arab volunteers to navigate through the fractious politics in the ranks of the Mujahideen alliance of Afghanistan was difficult. This alliance had seven members with different aims and agendas. Afghans are notorious for their infighting as indeed are many parts of the Muslim world.

Just imagine how difficult it would be for a young Arab man in his early twenties with very little experience of politics to understand an Afghan Mujahideen alliance. These men didn't come from the fractious university politics or trade unionism or any sort of political movement; the societies they came from didn't tolerate dissent. How on earth was a young man from the Gulf to make sense of the agendas of the Khalis faction led by Yunes Khalis, Hezb-i Islami led by Hekmatyar, the Islamic Union for the Liberation of Afghanistan led by Sayyaf, the National Islamic Front for Afghanistan led by Gailani, the Afghanistan National Liberation Front led by Mojaddedi, the Islamic and National Revolution Movement of Afghanistan led by Mohammedi and finally Jamiat-i Islami led by Rabbani with an off shoot called Shura-e Nazar led by Ahmed Shah Massoud? It was mind boggling. And this of course excluded the Shi'ite groups, known as the Tehran Eight, under the wing of Ayatollah Khomeini's Iran! You could understand what a minefield it would be for a young Arab fighter coming to Afghanistan wanting to fight the Russians.

The MAK was set up to keep the Arabs independent and neutral so they were not dragged into the often fluctuating politics of the various factions in Afghanistan and indeed Peshawar. For the Arabs to be affiliated to just one of these seven factions could have had a negative impact on relations with another. The MAK's purpose then was to maintain this delicate balance. Instead of each fighter being affiliated to one Afghan faction or another, Afghan parties would be forced to deal with the MAK instead of dealing with the volunteers directly.

There was a wisdom in setting up the MAK: just consider what a negative impact foreign fighters have had in Syria and Iraq. Instead of helping the Syrians to rid themselves of a tyrant they have gotten involved in the bloody politics of the region and have contributed to the problem. As Sheikh Abdullah told me: 'Afghans are divided into factions and groups, if the Arabs participate with any group it wishes to, most certainly the differences of the Afghans will impact them and so the medicine we came to administer will have a negative impact on the Afghans.' It is no exaggeration to say that this was a lesson forgotten by the young Muslims who left their homes, families and everything, no doubt sincere in their wish to help the Syrians, but completely unaware of the lessons that Sheikh Abdullah could teach them. Many have taken his slogans but forgot his message. In Syria some of them have become a poison instead of the medicine that they had intended to be.

The principles of the MAK were also clear and we were loath to depart from them. We realised that a number of the fighters who came were completely new to the faith: most had seen a video, heard a tape or read *The Signs of the Merciful in Afghanistan*. They were new, their minds and hearts were impressionable. We all knew that, especially the sheikh—and he didn't take advantage of that. He could have filled their minds with all sorts of ideas, which groups like Islamic Jihad did when they came to Peshawar in the late 80s and filled their heads with a theology of *takfir* or apostasy, making one fellow Muslim look at the other as an infidel, polytheist and whatever else. The sheikh didn't do that: firstly, because he didn't believe in it; secondly, because he was conscious of what opening that door could lead to.

Of course later, some of the men especially those from the various Islamic movements would urge us to teach them theology. They wanted us to touch on issues which afflict Syria and Iraq today. They asked why we didn't teach them lessons about loyalty and disavowal and the issue of *takfir* and the apostasy of this government and that government? We didn't teach it.[4] It wasn't our business to open up the chests of men and examine their beliefs pertaining to God. For as soon as you do that, what happens? Are Syria and Iraq not testimony to why we didn't teach it? Men are killing each other simply because of the beliefs they hold in their hearts. This is why Sheikh Abdullah would always reply by saying: 'Brothers, God blessed you by bringing you here to strive in His path, and the Afghan people are in need of your help which is of immense value, and their interests are your interests first. Don't over extend the battle. The leaders of the Arab world don't interest me. Our battle is confined to Afghanistan.' We were Muslim, we inclined towards the ideas of Hassan al-Banna, the founder of the Muslim Brotherhood, but we were never under the command of their supreme ruling council in Egypt. We were not Sufis but believed in the science of purification of the heart, and we were not Salafists but we did not oppose their ideas. Our sole interest was in resolving the issue of Afghanistan, not in taking part in some fanciful global Jihadist venture which some analysts have maintained.

These principles were reflected in the functions of the office that may have increased in staff but remained more or less the same size as when it was set up in 1984. We ran the service along several lines. We provided education, training, and translation services, and provided humanitarian support for the people of Afghanistan. We saw ourselves as an organisation which could deliver aid anywhere as opposed to the charities and NGOs in Peshawar. Whilst the latter had the funds, they could not deliver their humanitarian aid inside of Afghanistan whether that be medicine, clothes, food or other forms of aid. They did not have men who were willing to risk their lives for aid delivery. Often journeys inside Afghanistan could result in you losing your convoy or result in your own death: you had to be prepared to die when you led these convoys. The employees of the organisations were representatives of their respective countries in Peshawar and many were dedicated and hardworking, but on the other hand they were not expected nor were they prepared to cross into Afghanistan on foot to Kandahar, or Mazar Sharif on a journey that may just cost them their life. So there was no choice but to have the likes of us who were willing to make such sacrifices because we had come seeking martyrdom. We could transport goods from thousands of shoes to convoys of medicine. We saw ourselves as an organisation that was there to help the Afghans fight whether logistically or physically carrying arms. Therefore we provided volunteers and recruited men to join the Jihad in Afghanistan. These volunteers were looked after by us and acclimatised into this completely alien milieu. We also believed that we had an educational role where we sought to provide educational services and schools to displaced Afghans.

But the MAK was in essence a series of guest-houses similar to the student hostels you have in the UK, they were ordinary Pakistani houses. The first two that we opened were named after the first two Arab martyrs in the Afghan Jihad. The first guest-house was named after a postgraduate student, Abu Hamza, who had deserted his studies in Sofia, Bulgaria, for the mountains of Afghanistan. He fell in an ambush in Logar province in eastern Afghanistan. This house had a walled garden, rose bushes, and two cars parked in the front for picking up volunteers. It had one kitchen, three toilets and several rooms where new arrivals came:

there they slept on the floor, the hallways and whatever space that could be found. If we packed them right the Abu Hamza guest-house could accommodate about forty men. The guest-house also had the office where Sheikh Azzam spent part of his week. In the beginning he was there from Thursday to Sunday and back to Islamabad University by Monday. As the MAK grew its staff also increased and became increasingly sophisticated but the office remained the size of a typical bureau de change in London.

The second guest-house was named after Abu Uthman, a Kuwaiti student who had attended a talk by Sheikh Azzam and had subsequently abandoned his PhD in Islamabad and headed for the Jihad. He fell in Herat in north-western Afganistan. Abu Uthman guest-house was far more exclusive and not open to all volunteers. It was reserved for donors and VIPs, in a similar way many NGOs might have a guest-house when their donors visit to see what the NGO is doing with their donations. This guest-house was set up by Osama bin Laden who would also stay there whenever he visited and would hold his meetings there. Osama donated three thousand dollars a month for the upkeep of our project. He would come once in a while from Jeddah and have meetings with various dignitaries, and whilst he did this Abu Uthman is where he stayed.

The guest-houses we had were so successful that in the MAK's heyday, seven guest-houses were under our control, but after 1987 other guest-houses sprang up with the arrival of the Egyptian extremists namely the arrival of Islamic Jihad, a rival to al-Gamaa al-Islamiya. The group was led by Dr Fadl or Sayyid Imam al-Sharif and Ayman al-Zawahiri. These men were *takfiris*, that is they declared you an apostate if you did not have the same creed as them, or if you failed to declare the Muslim rulers to be infidels or you believed in democracy then you were outside the fold of Islam. Of course, it was they who decided who was an apostate or not. And it was they who started to introduce ideas into the heads of these impressionable recruits which were harmful and antithetical to the Islamic spirit. All the ideas that you see currently from the killing of police officers in Algeria and Afghanistan to the indiscriminate massacre of innocent civilians in Brussels and Baghdad—all have precedence in Islamic Jihad. At the MAK we never advocated such things. In fact, these ideas came to a head eventually in Peshawar, when Osama bin Laden left the MAK and entered the orbit of al-Zawahiri's Islamic Jihad and started listening to Dr. Fadl who wrote the *takfiri* text *al-'Umda fi I'dad al-'Udda*, 'The Essentials of Making Ready [for Jihad]', an important text for *takfiris* of today even though he has renounced it.

There were of course smaller guest-houses like that of Gamaa al-Islamiyya and the followers of Sheikh Omar Abdel Rahman. They too had followed the Egyptian exodus following a crackdown by the Egyptian secret services in 1987. These men were far less radical and shared a toned-down version of Islamic Jihad's ideology. They weren't quick to pronounce *takfir* and I never heard the pronouncements be made by any of the leadership. The spiritual leader was Sheikh Omar Abdel Rahman but the dynamo was found in the late Qassem Abu Talal al-Qasimi or Abu Talal: he was a human engine, brilliant, energetic and an eloquent spokesman.[5] There was also Mohammed Showqi Islambouli, the younger brother of Khalid Islambouli who assassinated the Egyptian president Anwar Sadat.[6] Showqi at the time had celebrity status amongst us because of the assassination of Sadat. Sadat was considered a tyrant in many activists' eyes due to the torture they experienced; his assassination was seen in a positive light by many in the Islamic movement. Then of course there was Rifa'i Ahmed Taha Musa who was also another impressive personality.[7] With all these men, particularly Islambouli and Musa, I built strong friendships. I found them to be calm and intellectuals at heart since their movements had begun in the university campuses of Egypt, and they were willing to cooperate to resolve any problems that arose. What was more they did not pronounce someone a heretic or an apostate at least when I knew them. None of these men took part in combat and focused on the internal affairs of their political group. The way I knew these men—intelligent, open-minded, willing to discuss— was far different from the terrorism that they were associated with especially later with the terrible Luxor massacre in 1997. But extremism is unsustainable for too long. Look at them now—after the Arab Spring they formed a political party and some of them even called Anwar Sadat a martyr![8]

What the political trajectories were of these members afterwards I do not know because I lost contact with them after the war ended. I know that some members such as Mohammed Hasan Khalil al-Hakim and Musa joined al-Qaeda.[9] Musa of course, famously shared a platform with Zawahiri and bin Laden in February 1998 declaring war on Jews and Crusaders, but most of them were antithetical to Islamic Jihad. When we were in Peshawar al-Gamaa al-Islamiyaa were rivals to Islamic Jihad; it was therefore quite natural for them to gravitate towards the MAK. And we in turn provided them initially, with a small stipend to live on. They did not stand against us, they cooperated and praised our work. Of course our connection to al-Gamaa meant that we got a lot of stick from the Muslim Brotherhood for engaging with them. The Brotherhood wanted us to isolate and disassociate ourselves from them. But Sheikh Abdullah refused, because while the MAK might have its compass pointed towards the Muslim Brotherhood, it was an independent organisation, and we made it very clear that it should remain so. In any case, we left al-Gamaa to their own devices and we rarely clashed: apart from a few moments of awkwardness in Peshawar and the Shalabi incident, we didn't have any issues with them.

Another aspect of the MAK was giving the Afghan Jihad a voice to the outside world. To that effect MAK opened up offices all over the world and helped to organise visits by donors and journalists so they could see for themselves the plight of the Afghans. All of this would help us with fundraising and raise awareness for our cause. *Al-Jihad* magazine served that purpose: it was a weekly before becoming a monthly publication reaching at its peak around 70,000 issues. In fact, the MAK representative in the US, Mustafa Shalabi, asked me to send over more copies because the offices in the Gulf had run out due to demand and they were now contacting the New York office for more copies. By 1987 our publication services had grown so effective that we were also issuing daily briefings to the press via fax through our publication *Lahib al-Ma'raka*, 'Flames of the Battle' magazine, run by Abdullah Azzam's nephew Abu Adel. I should add that in this respect *al-Jihad* was not a magazine that was out of the ordinary: Sayyaf's group had *Bunyan al-Marsus*,[10] 'the Solid Wall', and Hekmatyar had an Arabic-language magazine, *al-Murabitoon*,[11] 'the Garrison', and did the same thing. What *al-Jihad* was not however, was some sort of precursor to ISIS' publications like *Dabiq* and *Naba*, for these latter magazines in content drew heavily from Abu Qatada's *al-Ansar* magazine which was replete with *takfiri* ideas, denunciations, lies and of course communiqués. In content we were different from ISIS magazines. We were more like a specialist trade paper, we didn't call for an oath of allegiance to an emir, nor did we call for terrorist attacks on the West and our sole concern was for the fight in Afghanistan.[12]

Whilst I was not directly involved with *al-Jihad* magazine I was certainly there when it was founded. Abdullah Azzam had the idea in the first year of my arrival in Peshawar, three or four months in. Sheikh Abdullah came and announced that he had an idea: 'The Afghan Jihad', he said, 'needs a voice outside of Peshawar.' Having written articles and books previously, he understood well the power of mass media and the Afghan Jihad. He was always someone who had his nose in some book, always armed with a red, green and blue ball-point pen, constantly taking notes, studying or writing. Even Massoud used to be astounded by the fact that the man didn't waste a moment of his time. It was with this experience that he took over a room in Abu Hamza guest-house, with two chairs and two tables. Initially he brought in two people to write for the magazine: Imad Abid, or Abu Anas, a Palestinian graduate of Medina University and an extremely humble and peaceful man with impeccable manners; and Muwaffaq Zaydan, a young Syrian undergraduate at the University of Islamabad, who later became station chief for the Islamabad bureau of Al-Jazeera. Zaydan would travel up to Peshawar a few times a month and write up the stories for the magazine. Later on Abdullah Azzam brought in an engineer, Jamal Ismail who later became station chief of the bureau in Islamabad of Abu Dhabi TV channel. I did not stay around to see what became of this fledgling project because I departed for the north of Afghanistan, but after a year the magazine had grown exponentially. It now had full-time salaried correspondents, it had moved offices and now comprised of a hefty edition which included news from inside Afghanistan covering battles, social work, humanitarian efforts, pictures, interviews and of course rousing poems and stories. It was an incredible feat and it went a long way to publicise the plight of the Afghans against the Communist menace.

13

THE EARLY ARABS

Most of the Arab brothers who came to Maktbat al-Khadamat (MAK) or the Arab Services Bureau were blank sheets of paper. Their hearts were filled with zeal, their minds were full of Sylvester Stallone and visions of paradise. Like many young men they sought adventure, glory and a guaranteed ticket to paradise through martyrdom. You see, a martyr doesn't get held to account for sins, he doesn't stand in front of God naked and ashamed ready to face Him. Even the pain of death feels like a pin prick, and suddenly he is in a state of bliss. Some narrations talk of the martyr residing in the hearts of green birds until the Day of Judgement and on that day he is brought forth to the throne of God and shaded under it, he is not held to account but is displayed as an example to the rest of mankind who will be yearning for that shade as hell and paradise are brought close. The martyr's wounds smell of musk and he is allowed to take his family members to paradise. Other narrations speak of the martyr being married to the beautiful maidens of paradise as an aperitif to meeting the supreme felicity which is God.[1] For He is the source of all bliss. The only martyr who will be accounted is the one who decided to be a *mujahid* so men will say he is a hero for he did not do the act for the sake of God.

Idealism and visions of grandeur is something you find in all societies, even in modern times. Look at the motivations of many young white Englishmen going to fight for the YPG (Yekîneyên Parastina Gel, or People's Protection Units) in Syria. Don't they have an idea of utopia? Is it so different? Most of the Afghan Arabs that came were like Abu Hamza and Abu Uthman. They didn't have an Islamic movement background and they weren't ideological. They could easily be manipulated or shaped if one wanted, for like many young men they were impressionable, they had only recently begun to practise their faith and were galvanised by the events in Afghanistan in the same way many young men were galvanised by the Arab Spring. The majority of those who came had read Sheikh Abdullah Azzam's book, *The Signs of the Merciful in the Jihad of Afghanistan*.

The sheikh had collected anecdotes of all the miracles that the Afghan fighters had witnessed. Now, miracles do play an important part in the Muslim imagination for two reasons, for Muslims and indeed Jews and Christians believe that God can intervene and give succour to the believers. The parting of the sea for instance, is one clear example in the Christian and Quranic texts. In Muslim religious tradition God helped the Muslims in many of the battles of the Prophet; Hunayn being an important example. Hunayn saw the Prophet fighting the Hawazin tribe which nearly turned into a rout, until God aided the Muslims with angels reinforcing their ranks and turning it into a victory. This miraculous help in battle is referred to in the Quran. In the context of the miraculous, Sheikh Abdullah's book was immensely important especially in the early years. And there is no doubt that many Arab foreign fighters came because of having read it. For the inner circle who ran the Arab Services Bureau, the book had a lesser impact. Miracle or no miracle, we were ideological, we had a vision and in a way, we didn't need miracles to understand why we were needed there.

But I didn't object to the book: I believe in miracles like all believers do. But I do not base my faith on miracles. The Companions of the Prophet saw few miracles in the battles against their enemies, the reason they didn't see it was because miracles were for those that had some sort of defect in faith. And this is why God sent down angels in the battle of Hunayn because the Companions were bolstered by newly converted Muslims who had joined the faith for more worldly reasons. The Companions believed in God and the Messenger in the same way we know the sun and moon to be true. And so what use were miracles to men of such conviction? Miracles did not increase nor decrease their faith. Miracles were for those who needed assurances and proofs just like Moses did to the disbelieving pharaoh.

But, I did convey the criticism that the book received, for many believed that Sheikh Abdullah exaggerated those anecdotes. 'People', I would say, 'are saying you are paying for these miracles.' And the sheikh would reply that these miracles that he recorded came about as he sat with the men of Jalal ul-Din al-Haqqani in Paktia at the latter's al-Zhawara base.[2] He would ask these men if they had witnessed any miracles. They would reply positively and recount it. The sheikh would then get them to swear an oath to God that what they had witnessed was true. He would then accept the narration and give them a bit of money which is known as an *ikramiya*, an amount given out of respect for what they had seen. The sheikh didn't pay men to forge accounts, in fact that is considered a sin, but it is possible that men forged miracles because they would receive this *ikramiya*; such things are found in human nature.

In any case, as the Afghan Jihad continued, the book took on a less important role. Sheikh Abdullah would always say that the greatest miracle is the fact that a barefooted, hungry and relatively pre-modern people if you will, were fighting and defeating one of the most advanced countries in the world. That to me and many other believers remains a miracle.

To return, it was these men who called on us in Peshawar during the initial stages of the Afghan Jihad. Sometimes we'd get a phone call at the office, a voice shouting down a crackly line saying that they would be in Peshawar on such and such date and that we were to pick them up. On the day of their arrival we would pick them up in our Suzuki, throw their luggage in the back and drive them down to Abu Hamza guest-house. There Abdul Quddus would receive them. Abdul Quddus was an American Palestinian and an organisational genius who yearned to fight Jihad. He used to beg the sheikh to go and fight in Afghanistan but the sheikh needed him there in that office, where he was most useful. He had the skill and the language to sort out the visas so it only made sense that he stayed there. In the end he resigned himself to his fate and realised that he was best utilised in the guest-houses. Here then was a man who put his needs last and did what the cause required of him and so Abdul Quddus and the rest of the brothers at the office would ensure that the young man's luggage was stored away safely and that his needs were met after his long journey to Peshawar. And whilst the young men spent several days acclimatising themselves to this strange and alien country and the routines of the guest-house, Abdul Quddus ensured that they were legal and had the right to stay in the country. There was nothing clandestine about our activities.

Contrary to what the Western imagination might think happened in these guest-houses, the routine was quite straightforward. After Fajr, the dawn prayer, the new recruits would sit and study the Quran with one of us. Sometimes I would lead prayer; other times some of the other men, like Abu Hajer al-Iraqi from the inner circle of the sheikh. Then there would be some sort of religious circle, *halaqa*, consisting of a religious lessons or text or a religious reminder. Then the recruits would line up in rows and we would pray Ishraq, a non-obligatory prayer which one performs after the sun has risen, then breakfast would be served by one of us. After that the new arrival would be free to do what he pleased: he might help out in cleaning the guest-house, preparing the food or perhaps just lie down and have a snooze in the Peshawari sun. We would then pray Zuhr, the afternoon prayer, which would be followed by a small reminder on the virtues or sayings of the Prophet. Lunch would follow usually consisting of some rice or bread and stew with minuscule bits of meat. It was incredible to think that most Afghans subsisted on less than what we lived on. After that the new arrival's time was his own until 'Asr prayer which again was accompanied by a small talk. And so it would continue till the Maghreb prayer, dinner and then the night prayers, after which everyone would sleep on the floor back to back. The guest-house, when full, housed thirty to forty people. After a few days, after one of us had schooled these young recruits we would send them off to one of the training camps where they would go through their basic military training.

Usually we would send the new arrivals off to one of the camps of Sayyaf, the designated leader of the Afghan *mujahideen*. His camps were in Khald and Sada and had a capacity for holding 250 or so Afghan *mujahideen*. ISI officers, the Pakistani intelligence service, were also training Afghan commanders in becoming effective officers: that training took more than six months. As I said earlier in the beginning we, the Arabs, were at most fifteen men but by 1986 we had about a hundred Arabs at the camp. Our impact on the conflict was similar to the meat you found in the guest-house stew. Miniscule.

There were of course other camps such as that of Rabbani's Khalid bin al-Walid camp, named after one of the greatest generals in Islamic and indeed world history. Hekmatyar also had

'Azam Warsak camp and later on as the Arabs began to take sides, they trained there too. As the conflict continued we would also send men off to Paktiya and Patika, to the camp of Yunus Khalis of Hezb-i Islami in Banu Meran Shah that was led by Haqqani, a very able commander. Haqqani was an impressive man, one of the first Afghans to declare Jihad against the Soviets in 1979.[3] He was a trained religious scholar of the Deobandi-Hanafi school who ran a religious seminary next to the camp as well.[4] Haqqani was highly intelligent, spoke fluent Arabic and was an impressive military commander who was often seen amongst his men at the front line. He was one of the earliest men who emigrated to Peshawar to rally the people to fight against the Communists. Whenever I used to return from northern Afghanistan I would pass through his camp. I would be amazed at this *mawlawi* who would have the responsibility of a general, teach his lessons in the afternoon, discussing difficult questions of jurisprudence, and then I would find him at the front lines being hit by mortars and shells. It was no wonder Sheikh Abdullah called him one of the symbols of Jihad in Afghanistan and was one of his greatest admirers. He wouldn't let anyone speak bad of him despite there being some genuine criticisms of the commander, especially later on with the rise of the Taliban. He, as is well known, sided with them.

For the early Arab recruits, basic training lasted ten to fifteen days. One of the most brilliant and one of the worst things about the Kalashnikov is its simplicity and resilience as a weapon. A recruit could learn how to take it apart in less than a minute blindfolded if he applied himself. He also learnt how to use grenades, offensive and defensive manoeuvres and so on. By the fifteenth day some of these young Arabs were itching for a fight with the Russians, thinking that war was a movie.

But there were other things in basic training too. Sheikh Abdullah realised that these men were naive as all young men are before the fight. So he set up religious instruction based on the methodology of Tablighi Jamaat and concentrated on the basics of worship and the perfection of character. Intelligence is the application of what one has learnt and Sheikh Abdullah took those ideas from the Tablighis and applied them to the camp. He gave the recruits religious instruction from the very basics; from how to make ablution to performing the night prayers, Qiyam al-Layl, and moreover how combat allows one certain dispensation and flexibility when it comes to obligatory religious observance. The battle does not necessarily stop when the time for noon prayer comes after all. Thus the recruit did not only learn how to fight but also developed himself spiritually. It was paramount that the men who entered the battle were ready spiritually for the hardships of war. For it is my conviction that this is precisely why war crimes are committed by Muslims and non-Muslims. For once one has lost the connection with the spirit then one has lost the moral compass that prevents one from committing war crimes. So religious instruction was accompanied by drills, running, drills and more running.

And then they went off to join the caravan to fight in Afghanistan. And how disappointed they were! For their mind's eye had envisaged a dynamic war full of heroics but in actual fact most of war is waiting and doing everyday things with intermittent action that didn't last too long. These men filled with Hollywood and Bollywood movies found themselves garrisoned in a village that saw little or no action at all. Apart from an odd air strike very little happened. These men had come to fight and get martyred, and instead found boredom, basic food, bitter cold and a relatively primitive people. Many got homesick, they missed ice cream, they missed Arab customs and friends and so after a few months they would return back to Peshawar, book their flights and return to their normal lives. Most fighters were like this. Many were received as veterans of the Afghan war and viewed as heroes in those days, but are nowadays viewed with suspicion.

Even then, we used to ask ourselves the question whether these Arab fighters really had an impact or was this some sort of war tourism? These men returned and were no threat to anyone, because we didn't fill their heads with anything. We understood that these men were volunteers and had no oath of allegiance to us. Now, had they opened their eyes, had these volunteers understood what our role was, and indeed what this war required of them, they would have realised that for us, this war was about being everything: a diplomat, a journalist of sorts, a fighter, a humanitarian worker, an aid worker, teacher and so much more. Work never ended. Those of us who came from an Islamic movement background understood this immediately. For us there were not enough hours in the day. We had lessons to teach when we were free, we had caravans to take full of aid, we had reports to write. For us this wasn't war tourism—this was more than just an adventure to tell our friends about.

14

THE INNER CIRCLE

There were the Afghan Arabs in general, the *'Amma*: they came, fought and then they left or were martyred. Then there were those who formed the close circle, the *Khassa*. In hindsight, there was no doubt that all of us, whether *'Amma* or *Khassa*, lived in a bubble. Whilst all around us the complex business of the Cold War was conducted between the super-powers—the international community working against the Soviets and supporting their faction amongst the Afghan rebels—we lived in our own world. We were akin to naive children. Whilst the KHAD and Soviets where thinking about how to destroy Hekmatyar or Sayyaf, we were in our guest-houses excited about a dream one of our brothers had had about Abu Hamza.

One brother would walk in and announce that he had seen Abu Hamza in a luscious garden in a dream during the night. And we would all huddle around him to find out more. It would infuse us with zeal, we would sit in that guest-house praying that God gave us the same fate. We would console each other that next time it would be us who God would take to Himself and place us in the hearts of green birds. We sincerely wished for it, and though we are older now and perhaps don't put as much emphasis on dreams, we wish that God takes us as a martyr still when we meet Him.[1] I believe this would be the wish of any Muslim. This is how we lived, there was nothing cynical about it, it was idealistic and almost dream-like.

And yet the Afghan leaders did not treat us as naive children. They viewed us as blessed men, men that would bring God's blessing, 'baraka', to their cause. After all, we didn't want power or control, all we wanted was to fight and die in the Path of God and help our co-religionists. Ours was a blessed project. In fact Sayyaf recognised our value even from a political perspective. He told us that the value of one Arab to an Afghan was a thousand: not because of our fighting ability or character, but rather because the Afghan villager who might contemplate fleeing might, on account of us being connected to the Messenger of God as Arabs and the fact that we had left our homes to fight for them, feel ashamed to flee the battle against the Soviets. What was more we were neutral, we didn't have any political agendas in the early days and Sheikh Abdullah's primary aim was to maintain this balance.

There came a point when Sheikh Abdullah could no longer divide his time between Peshawar and teaching during the week at Islamabad University. The Afghan Jihad became an all-consuming preoccupation. So much so that at times I wondered whether the Afghan Jihad needed him or perhaps he needed the Afghan Jihad. And in my mind, there was no doubt that he was at the heart of the Arab Services Bureau.

Once he had made the decision Sheikh Abdullah spent his days in Peshawar on administrative, educational and humanitarian activities full time. But these activities would not have been achieved if he didn't have a dedicated group of people who worked closely with him such as his two nephews Abu'l Harith and Abu 'Adil, Abu Abdallah and Abu 'Ubada. To us he was the sun and around him revolved the planets. Amongst these planets were some who were closer to the sun's orbit and some who were far more distant.

That is not to say that there weren't men of his calibre at the Bureau—consider, for instance, the famous Yemeni scholar Sheikh Abdul Majid Zindani, currently embroiled in the conflict in Yemen—but in those days the polymath was an important figure in Peshawar.[2] He frequently flew to Pakistan and spent about half a year teaching the Arab fighters and working on administrative issues that needed resolving. Both Sheikh Abdullah and Zindani worked well together and regarded each other with deep affection and profound respect.

The Bureau was also in contact with a coterie of scholars from all over the Arab world because the Afghan Jihad was a concern for all of the Muslim world. And so we were in contact with the likes of Muhammed Qutb,[3] the brother of Syed Qutb, Sheikh Abdallah Zayed,[4] Sheikh Muhammad al-Sawwaf,[5] Yusuf al-Qardawi,[6] and others. All of these men could be called on to give advice and raise awareness amongst their flock. Many of these scholars were also involved in the often heated and difficult negotiations between the *mujahideen* factions, especially when it came to forming an interim government when Kabul fell in 1992. There were others who were oddities and were there for other reasons, for instance the late Sheikh Omar Abd el-Rahman, who became known as the 'Blind Sheikh' in the West. He used to be one of the leaders of Gamaa Islamiyya in Egypt, a group that was known for its extremism and dislike of the Muslim Brotherhood, and yet they were not out-and-out *takfiri*s such as the likes of Dr Fadl and Ayman al-Zawahiri's Egyptian Jihad who came in the mid 80s.

On an ideological level Sheikh Abd el-Rahman was an opponent of the ideas of the Muslim Brotherhood. And sometimes he would openly oppose Sheikh Abdullah. Once when the sheikh praised Zia ul-Haqq, the general who ruled Pakistan at the time in a talk, Sheikh Omar Abdel Rahman stood up and opposed him. He got the crowd to side with his viewpoint that supporting any ruler who didn't rule according to his understanding of Shariah was a sin. Sheikh Abdullah laughed it off, and didn't pay it too much attention. And despite the fact that Sheikh Abdullah viewed him as an extremist, he gave him a pension on account of him being disabled, in need, and an al-Azhar alumnus who had gained a PhD. In the Islamic tradition scholars are honoured and respected, and it would not be appropriate for an al-Azhar scholar to be living in penury on the streets of Peshawar.

If the heart and brains of the Arab Services Bureau was Sheikh Azzam, then the engine that kept it running with funds was no doubt Wael Julaidan or Abu'l Hassan al-Madani. Julaidan had met the sheikh whilst the latter was on a speaking tour in the US. The sheikh would often stay in the US for a few weeks after attending the two main Islamic conferences, namely the Islamic Society of North America (ISNA) and the Muslim Students Association (MSA). He would then go on a tour of university campuses where he delivered talks to the Muslim students of the universities. This would not have been possible in the more recent climate but in those days the US didn't have such a poisonous relationship with the Muslim world. It was on one of those campuses that he met Julaidan. Julaidan was preparing his postgraduate thesis and was already a pillar of the Muslim community centre in Tucson, Arizona. Later he became linked to the World Muslim League in Saudi Arabia. The sheikh encouraged him to go to Afghanistan instead of studying in America and he responded to the call. Sheikh Abdullah did the same thing with another pillar of the MAK administration Sheikh Adnan Tameem, and Tameem too responded.

Julaidan was a force of nature in Peshawar. It was incredible what he could do, he travelled to Saudi Arabia and spoke to worshippers in the mosques and collected donations in their millions. Every day we received cheques worth ten or twenty thousand dollars coming from Saudi Arabia and the rest of the Muslim world. Consequently, we were able to subsidise 50–70 per cent of the price of the air fare for any Arab Afghan who wanted to participate in the Jihad. Julaidan brought all his organisational expertise to not only the MAK but also the whole struggle. As president of the World Muslim League he mobilised immense wealth and influence to the struggle. He lead the Saudi Red Crescent, he devised a system to transport weapons without the weapons finding their way back into the gun markets of Peshawar. He negotiated, mediated and organised. His relationship with the seven *mujahideen* leaders was impeccable. You could find his trace everywhere you looked. Whilst this was excellent for us fighting the Soviets, later on this proved to be detrimental for him. His omnipresence in a way made it very easy to link him to al-Qaeda and Osama bin Laden's organisation and he was easily associated with the group and labelled one of its financiers even though he opposed the group from its very inception.

It was for this reason that I requested that Sheikh Abdullah give me Julaidan as I returned from Mazar Sharif on my first trip inside Afghanistan and he of course refused. I remember sitting down with the sheikh just before leaving for Balkh province again, asking him if he could spare me some men. 'By God,' I said, 'if only we had a hundred men who could be journalists, diplomats, humanitarian workers and fighters dotted all over the provinces, you'd see an end to all of these problems within a few years.' The sheikh sat down and looked at me sadly and lamented: 'And where', he said, 'will I find these sorts of men?'

It was frustrating: can you imagine, only a few weeks before, we had both attended the world conference of the Muslim World League, where all the leading lights of the Muslim world gathered, and in that gathering, we could not find a hundred men such as that? If I felt frustrated I couldn't imagine how the sheikh felt.

'Give me a few men', I pleaded, 'to take with me inside.'

'Who?' he asked.

'Wael', I said. 'Give me Wael Julaidan.'

'Wael?' he said shaking his head. 'He is more useful here than inside.'

He was right of course but if you don't ask you don't get.

Then there was Sheikh Tameem, this man was a complete rock to the sheikh. He was a Jerusalemite from an important family of poets and governors. The sheikh loved him so much that he wrote a book entitled *The Lofty Mountain* as a eulogy to him following his death in October 1989.[7] Tameem was devoted to him, sometimes the devotion verged on that of a capricious child in its innocence. Tameem was a qualified English lecturer who had met the sheikh in Riyadh in Saudi Arabia. The sheikh told Tameem that he belonged in Peshawar, little expecting that the large man would make the journey. But Tameem yearned to fight Jihad and made his way to Peshawar, he was devoted to the Afghan Jihad and was an excellent fundraiser.

Tameem dedicated his whole being to the cause, and were it not for the fact that he had inherited a condition that made him obese I believe he would have fought in the trenches as courageously as many Afghans. And despite his girth, Tameem fought in Jaji for a whole month in 1987 when the Russian special forces attacked a small band of Arab fighters led by Osama bin Laden. But his weight also brought him problems whether that be the fact that sometimes horses refused to carry him or having to use a winch to pull him up the mountain. In fact, he was so determined to fight Jihad, that he booked himself a flight to the US where he fundraised and trained intensely in order to make himself fighting fit. However, it was during this time in the US that he met his end on a hospital bed. His energy was sorely missed at the MAK and many of us were distraught. That's when Sheikh Abdullah wrote *The Lofty Mountain* a eulogy to his dear friend.

But there were others too who supported the Bureau with their hard work and dedication. Abu Hajar al-Iraqi and Abu Ibrahim were two Iraqis who escaped the clutches of Saddam Hussein and travelled across Iran to enter Pakistan where they joined the MAK. They belonged to the Muslim Brotherhood and were engineers by training and had studied Islam. Another man was Jamal Khalifa, a friend of Osama bin Laden who was also his former flat-mate in Medina. Jamal Khalifa, in my view, had the judgement that Osama lacked. And finally, there was Osama bin Laden himself, an energetic, dynamic man with exquisite manners and refinement. He worked tirelessly to keep the MAK afloat and raising awareness for the Afghan Jihad in Saudi Arabia. But perhaps he had too much ambition which led him to separate from the MAK and tear the Bureau apart.

Had we stuck together, rendered help to these poor people, we would have kept that brotherhood and the Arab Services Bureau would have continued to be an organisation that helped the oppressed. But the world is treacherous and our brotherhood was torn apart by political intrigue, ambition and extremism. And because of that this simple organisation became perceived as the forerunner of what became known as al-Qaeda.

There were other names that were added to the Arab Services Bureau in due course as we expanded and grew. For instance, Abu Hafs al-Masri, an Egyptian police officer and Abu Ubaidah al-Banshiri: these members of the Egyptian Islamic Jihad, I met much later. They became very close to Osama bin Laden. But what was curious about the two men was this: whilst they were affiliated to al-Zawahiri's *takfiri* group, Islamic Jihad, for the life of me, I never saw those *takfiri* qualities manifest in their behaviour. And it still surprises me, as to how these men could be linked to such rabid extremists. I knew for a fact that Abu

Ubaidah was an open admirer of Ahmed Shah Massoud and often spoke highly of him. After all Ahmed Shah Massoud made him, if you will.

Post 9/11 these men that I describe herein have been depicted as beastly blood-thirsty terrorists but this was not the experience that I had with them. And I will now try to give an account of these men and show how the MAK was transformed into something that its founders had never intended.

Up to that time the Arab Services Bureau was not that dangerous organisation that became known as al-Qaeda that plotted against world governments. If this was the case Sheikh Abdullah would not have enjoyed the freedom to travel regularly to these countries. Every year he visited the US and the UK to attend conferences, to speak to Western Muslims about the Jihad in Afghanistan. All the *mujahideen* factions had offices all over the West and no one thought them a threat, because the simple fact was, they weren't.

15

INNER OF THE INNER CIRCLE

A combination of ambition, extremist ideas and backbiting led
to the break-up of the Arab Services Bureau (MAK). This epi-
sode is very painful to me because it involved people that I loved.
Nevertheless, I feel that as a witness I have to describe what I
have seen and heard. Giving testimony is a weighty thing in
Islam and giving false testimony is a grave sin. Yet I feel I must
recount it, warts and all.

What passed between me and the men I hold dear is hard to
bear. I have affection for all my comrades with whom I shared
my best years. Some are tied to the very fabric of my life now.
The man who advised me to marry the woman I hold dear,
esteem and respect, this daughter of Sheikh Abdullah who bore
me five children, was Osama bin Laden. This man took the lives
of thousands of innocent people from Mombasa to New York
and killed the man who remains beloved to me, Ahmed Shah
Massoud. Indeed the organisation he led sullied the noble concept of Jihad and sullied the name of my father-in-law. This is
why I am so conflicted and pained by this period.

As I said before, I first met Osama in Sheikh Abdullah's house
in Islamabad in 1983. There in the tidy modest-sized salon sat a

dignified Saudi man in a white *thobe* and red *keffiyeh* with impeccable manners. He quietly ate the delicious *maqloubeh*, a traditional Palestinian dish of rice and meat, cabbages and aubergines. Osama was a man of few words, not because he was unsure of himself, rather because he had gravitas. It was clear that he was someone who did not want to talk unnecessarily and was used to being in control. He was a boss to the employees of the construction company that his father had bequeathed him and his brothers. As we sat on the floor eating I noticed what a contrast he was to Abu Akram and Abu Hassan, two Palestinians who were joking with each other and making wisecracks.

But even though the Saudi spoke very little, I liked him immediately because here was an extremely rich man, who like many of his class, could be gallivanting in the capitals of Beirut, Paris and London committing all sorts of debauchery, but he refrained from that. Instead here he was in this sparse living room visiting the star of his age, Sheikh Abdullah. That was rare amongst the Saudi elite. I found out later that Osama would travel to Islamabad often to drop off donations and return that same day to Jeddah. After that dinner, I did not see him again until I returned from Mazar Sharif eight months later.

I had returned from Mazar Sharif and had given the sheikh an eye witness account of what I had seen. I then went off to organise a caravan for transporting medical aid in Miranshah, Waziristan, on the Afghan-Pakistani border. By now I had *taz-kiya*,[1] a recommendation from the sheikh to all the aid agencies such as the Saudi Red Crescent and others who relied on us to get aid into Afghanistan. After a week when I returned from Waziristan, Abu Akram, one of sheikh's aides and bodyguard told me that the sheikh had been looking for me; I had to go to the Hajj immediately. Abu Mazen or Colonel Salim Lahmoud, the Saudi military attaché to the Afghan brief, fast-tracked my visa, and Abu Akram got me a return economy ticket to Saudi Arabia and so I was on the last flight to Jeddah flustered and stressed not knowing how on earth I was going to locate the sheikh in the throng of the pilgrims all wishing to perform their duty to God. But fate is such that on the ninth day of Hajj when I was performing the stoning ritual at Mina, I found him standing right in front of me. Both of us were exultant with joy at having found each other.

I met Osama again at Mina for it turned out that the sheikh was being hosted by him. Instead of staying with the rest of the pilgrims in large tents, I was in a sparsely furnished house with Sheikh Abdullah's entourage which included the leaders of the *mujahideen*. The house I discovered belonged to Osama bin Laden's family. Whilst pilgrims sweltered in the heat we were inside this air-conditioned house receiving notaries such as Recep Tayyip Erdogan's mentor Necmettin Erbakan, who was a lifelong friend of the sheikh.[2] Osama also introduced us to Saudi notables who asked the sheikh about his book on the miracles of the Jihad in Afghanistan, *Signs of the Merciful in the Jihad of Afghanistan.*

Only later did I discover that only distinguished families close to the Saudi royal family were given houses in Mina to be used during the Hajj period. Bin Laden belonged to such a family: they had helped the royal family when they were in dire financial straits. Bin Laden's father, a self-made man and construction magnate, had built his company up from scratch and had been involved in constructing the Saudi road network as well as having the honour of expanding the holy places in the Kingdom. They had also been crucial when Juyahman al-Otaybi and his followers took over the Holy Sanctuary in Mecca. Otaybi had taken over the Holy Sanctuary and declared that the Mahdi, this Saviour who was expected at the end of time before Jesus' descent, had arrived.[3] The bin Laden family was crucial in putting down the siege, and were rewarded with special privileges and dispensations. So the house was a token of the royal family's respect for the bin Laden clan despite their family hailing from Yemeni stock.

It was in this house in Mina that I saw him serving us food and tea and being true to the traditions of Arab hospitality. He was committed to serving us personally. He didn't rely on his servants, he was like a sufi *murid* devoted to his spiritual master. If the sheikh stood up, he stood up, and if the sheikh asked for something he would run to get it. It was quite an incredible thing.

We spent several days in Mina where we attended a conference organised by the World Muslim League who also had a building there. Hajj season was an opportunity for all the world's scholars and notables to gather there and exchange ideas. The sheikh had intended that I speak at this conference to convey what I had seen and what the Afghan Jihad needed. But I couldn't do it when the sheikh called me to the lectern. I did not rise: it must have been an embarrassing moment for him, but I was only twenty-four and very shy, I couldn't stand in front of the *crème de la crème* of the Muslim world, titans and great scholars and describe the situation in Afghanistan was just overwhelming. But the sheikh saved me from embarrassment and described the situation himself. After this debacle we moved to Jeddah where again Osama housed us in his home and put at our disposal all the drivers and services that we needed.

It was in Jeddah that I learnt how Sheikh Abdullah and Osama had got to know each other. When the Jordanian government prevented the sheikh from teaching at the University of Jordan, he received a contract to teach in Jeddah. It turned out that they had got to know each other then. Osama would attend his talks in the mosques and they lived close to each other, and often their families visited each other. Throughout the Hajj period Sheikh Abdullah had a relentless work schedule. It was only after he left for Peshawar with the leaders of the Afghan *mujahideen*, including Sayyaf and Khalis, that Osama relaxed somewhat. After they left he suggested that we take a short break in his farm outside of Jeddah where he kept his prized Arab horses. There we could train and live simply to reinvigorate ourselves spiritually and physically so that we could return to Afghanistan with fervour. Luxury and soft living often erodes the character of men and removes their martial vigour and can even lead to the downfall of nations as the great North African scholar Ibn Khaldun had written in the fourteenth century in his *Muqaddimah* or *Prolegomena* as it became known in the West.

The truth was I wasn't that enthusiastic about this excursion—I had experienced the toughness of war inside Afghanistan where we dreamed of bread let alone stew—but I was with my friends and I didn't want to be a spoil-sport. Osama's enthusiasm was insatiable and infectious. Most of his friends who accompanied us were like-minded but Jamal Khalifa or Abu'l Baraa, who became his brother-in-law in 1986, struck me as an exceptional figure. He had been Osama's senior in school and had an air of natural authority about him. Sadly following 9/11 Jamal Khalifa was killed by unknown assailants in Madagascar in 2007. There was also Shafiq al-Madani—who died in Afghanistan in Jalalabad in July 1989, sacrificing himself so that Osama and his men could retreat—Ali al-Madani and Mohammed Amin: all of them made history in Afghanistan.

On the first day we exercised, wrestled, jogged and rode our horses in the desert hoping to condition our bodies. I remember there was a particular mare, Anoud, who was very difficult to control and all of us tried to tame her. We all vied with each other in trying to control her but it was Osama who mastered her. He was a good horseman. He loved the *Aseel*, pure Arab horses, and preferred them over the much larger thoroughbreds. Arab horses have always been beloved in our tradition. In times past, Arab warriors and tribes would raise the horses in their own tents and treat them like their own children. So their horses were often soft and gentle. Even when the warriors went to battle, they would not ride them until they had reached the battle field, and only then would they unleash the swiftness of their Arab steeds on the enemy.

The second day, like mad men, we jumped into our jeep and drove into the desert without a map. It was only when our car ended up in the sand dunes without petrol that we regretted not having a map for we got terribly lost. It was funny because some of the men thirsted for water in the scorching sun and Osama harangued them to man up. 'You have only been out for two hours,' he shouted, 'and the *mujahideen* in Afghanistan don't have any water!' Osama always lived an austere lifestyle and did not allow himself to get comfortable despite his immense wealth. We only returned to the farm after six hours of wandering around the desert having abandoned the car in the sand. We decided, rather wisely, to call it a day after that.

We returned to Jeddah and it came time for me to fly back to Afghanistan. Osama decided that he would accompany me to Peshawar. We went to a shopping centre where he bought goods that would benefit the fighters such as binoculars and such things. Then we boarded a Saudi Airlines flight where I sat in economy and he in first class. As we neared Islamabad, Osama realised that my visa had expired so he came to economy and took me into first class. Because the Saudis were VIPs my visa was fast-tracked by the Pakistani authorities whilst waiting in the VIP area in Islamabad and then we travelled back to Peshawar and ended up in Abu Uthman guest-house where he was staying.

Osama spent the three weeks in Peshawar meeting the leaders of the *mujahideen*, networking and building close ties with them. He tried his best to understand what the situation in Afghanistan was like. As for me, I left Osama for Mazar Sharif and the mountains of Afghanistan and did not hear much from him until I

1. Anas (centre) with mujahideen commanders in Panshir by Tam Hussein

2. Anas in Panshir valley with destroyed Soviet tanks by Tam Hussein

3. Rabbani (left) and Azzam (right) Hindukush

4. Massoud (left) with Syed Ekramuddin mujahideen commander

5. Anas (kneeling) and Adnan Tameem (left)

6. Cover title of 'A Month Amongst the Titans' by Abdullah Azzam

7. Anas burying Qari Muhammed Kurdi in 1985

8. Anas with Ahmed Zia Massoud the former vice-president of the Karzai administration by Tam Hussein

9. Anas beside Massoud's grave in Panshir by Tam Hussein

10. Anas beside a tank in Panshir valley by Tam Hussein, 2018

11. Anas riding (left) and Massoud (centre) on horse

12. Azzam (centre) with Adnan Tameem (right, with glasses)

13. Massoud (left) next to Rabbani, Azzam next to Anas by MAK

14. Commander Ikramuddin and Anas by Tam Hussein, 2018

15. Afdal Hayat (left) Dr Abdullah Abdullah (centre) Anas (right)

returned one year later. When I returned in late 1986 I passed by Abu Uthman guest-house, and I met Abu Ubaydah al-Banshiri and Abu Hafs al-Masri who were staying there. These two would become the most able deputies of Osama bin Laden. I didn't how they had met, but this was the first time Osama became linked to Islamic Jihad.

When I met them I was suspicious of them: they belonged to an extremist group responsible for numerous acts of terror in Egypt and declaring those who didn't agree with them as apostates. But they surprised me, for they didn't fit the Islamic Jihad mould at all. They were not *takfiris* at all; of course they were vehement opponents to the Egyptian state but they were not rough or aggressive, nor did they look upon their way as the only way to salvation. Far from it, their manners were impeccable, they were humble and honest. In fact, Abu Ubaydah and Abu Hafs remained good friends of mine and Sheikh Abdullah until their demise as a result of their unfortunate membership of al-Qaeda. The two even attended my wedding and did not take part in the slanders that Dr Fadl, Ayman Zawahiri and the likes of Abu Firas al-Suri[4] were throwing against Sheikh Abdullah when the leaders of Egyptian Jihad arrived in Peshawar in the mid 80s.

When I met them at the guest-house, they asked if they could travel with me to Afghanistan to fight. Although I was suspicious of them I laid my conditions down clearly: if you want to join my caravan you need to leave your group's ideology behind here in Peshawar and do what the Afghan emirs command you to do. It was that simple. Surprisingly, they agreed. I emphasised this a few days later when I gathered the Arabs, around forty of them, in Abu Hamza's guest-house, and reiterated the same message. They all agreed to my conditions.

When we set out the men including Abu Hafs and Abu Ubaydah were instructed not to say a word of Arabic whilst travelling. All of them obeyed and I managed to take them through the mountains to the north, able to buy off corrupt guards at check points hungry for bribes or the goods that we carried.

I did not hear much of the activities of Osama whilst inside with Ahmed Shah Massoud, but Osama was busy for sure and once he had decided to stay he entered into the work with total commitment. I remember sitting in on a discussion he had with Sheikh Abdullah who chided him for coming to the region periodically, saying that he should just stay permanently to help the war effort. At the time, Osama had said that this would disturb the equilibrium between the bin Laden family and the House of Saud and so was hoping that a fatwa from Sheikh bin Baaz, one of Saudi Arabia's leading scholars, would release him from his obligations. But the fatwa never came and in the end Osama's zeal just took over and he just stayed and threw himself into work. Five months later in 1987, news came back from one of the commanders about the battle of Jaji.

Jaji was a district controlled by Sayyaf who had set aside a small corner for the Arabs. There Osama constructed a hospital and storage facilities knows as Ma'sada al-Ansar, the lion's den of the helpers.[5] Whether Osama's project was constructive and the best way to spend his resources was another matter. I certainly expressed my views on that. Jaji was not a defensible position militarily. But he was the boss of his company so it was difficult to persuade him otherwise. Once Osama got something into his head it was hard to dissuade him. Nevertheless, whenever I passed by Jaji I would see his company bulldozer constructing roads and him walking around speaking to workers, driving his digger and looking at maps. It was refreshing to see this tall wealthy Saudi working with such energy and zeal for the sake of the Afghan Jihad. At the same time, I don't think Osama was thinking about establishing his own organisation just yet—the work he was doing was in support of Sayyaf.

To return to the battle of Jaji in 1987, when we received the news of the battle I was with Massoud. We were all overjoyed.

This was the first time that the Arabs had fought by themselves, repelled 200 or so Spetsnaz special forces supported by air. There were many men participating in that battle from amongst us: Abu Ubaydah, Abu Hafs, Sheikh Abdullah, Adnan Tameem and Osama fighting alongside Sayyaf's commanders and others. Abu Ubaydah and Osama led several raids against the Soviets who sustained heavy losses. Sheikh Abdullah too manned the guns. In the grand scheme of things, it was a small battle that didn't add much to the conflict from where I was sitting but for the Arabs and the Gulf countries it was a morale booster and a huge propaganda victory. The news was broadcasted on the air waves and in the papers giving all of us confidence. It raised our esteem amongst the Afghans and showed them that we could fight by ourselves. We were no longer children: finally we had matured, or at least that was the sense. It also helped to create one of the foundational myths about the fighting prowess of the Afghan Arabs and made us overlook many things. It created heroes for a region that needed heroes. Remember the Arab world was still smarting from defeat and humiliation. These Afghan Arabs were seen as invincible who could take on the Soviets singlehandedly, forgetting that the battle of Jaji would never have been won without the help of their Afghan brothers.

But things between us Afghan Arabs were changing. By the middle of 1987 having returned to Peshawar, I noticed that the atmosphere had changed considerably. Osama had more or less separated himself from the MAK and ran his own operation.

At the time I didn't fully realise the importance of this split. My heart was caught up with affairs inside Afghanistan to pay it much attention, but in hindsight I realise that Osama was becoming his own man and had got caught up in the various political currents in Peshawar. That wasn't difficult, you had to be politically resilient and discerning. The subtle changes in his personality were not easy to spot initially. I only realise now that bin Laden in particular was sought after because of the resources he wielded and the influence he could project, and so he was courted by all and sundry: men with integrity as well as unscrupulous charlatans. As such it was easy to have an inflated impression of one's own importance.

So you had Hekmatyar courting Osama and making a big impression on him. He presented himself as the strong man of the seven *mujahideen* leaders. And so Osama, like many of us, was drawn to his charisma as the years progressed. He also began to have a closer connection with the founders of Islamic Jihad, including Dr Ayman al-Zawahiri. How and when that connection was made I could not figure out until much later. It turned out that they had met whilst al-Zawahiri had been living and practising medicine in Jeddah. The Mubarak crack-downs in Egypt meant that their followers trickled into Peshawar and brought their radical ideas with them, and so naturally they began to influence the environment around them.

Many of these men didn't fight the Russians or the Communists, they just sat in Peshawar agitating against Sheikh Abdullah's work. Both of us would complain as to what exactly their role was in this Jihad against the Communists. Instead they were poisoning the hearts and minds of these simple young men with their insane ideas. These men might claim to be *mujahids* now but they are not.

The difference between Sheikh Abdullah's ideas and theirs was vast. The sheikh never introduced political ideas on the fresh-faced young men who came to fight in Afghanistan. He stayed away from *takfir* and issues of theology because he had to maintain a careful equilibrium between all the various stakeholders. These politicians, security attachés and others already viewed him with suspicion; he had the potential for being a trouble maker. Remember he was a Palestinian, he belonged to the Muslim Brotherhood, he was an influential religious scholar and a commander of men. That is a powerful combination. Sheikh Abdullah knew that he had to maintain the status quo in order for the Afghan Jihad to continue smoothly. He knew very well that in order for the Afghan Jihad to continue these stakeholders had to be reassured, and that their contribution both in men and materiel would not end up harming them. He could not give these extremist groups any excuse to hamper his project.

The Saudi authorities for instance, whilst they viewed the Afghan Jihad as a worthwhile and just war, were of course concerned that their sons might fall under the sway of this charismatic Palestinian. There were always reports and counter reports going to Riyadh from Pakistan where one wing of the Saudis feared his influence whilst another wing argued that the sheikh was a positive calming force on its citizens and there was no harm to the security of the Kingdom.

Sheikh Abdullah knew that it didn't make any sense to harm the interests of the Saudis when they were contributing so much to the war effort. He respected the naivety, if you like, of these fighters, without introducing those political ideas that could result in the creation of a vanguard which could start an insurgency inside the Kingdom itself. As a result many of these young fighters could return to their home countries without posing a threat, and many of them did.

Sheikh Abdallah knew that it was essential to have a good relationship with the likes of Abu Mazen, a devout colonel and military attaché to the Saudi embassy who whole-heartedly believed in the Afghan Jihad. It was this man who had the power to reassure the jittery nerves of the Saudi intelligence officers and argue that the sheikh's ambitions were confined to Afghanistan. But these political manoeuvrings and diplomacy alienated Egyptian Jihad and their followers. They believed that the sheikh was selling out to illegitimate regimes and what was more giving their names to the Saudi security services. This was patently false but once such rumours began in Peshawar they never went away.

In fact, the best example was Osama himself, he had immense respect and love for his home country. Sometimes when discussions would turn in a political direction amongst the close circle regarding his country Osama would politely get up and leave, not wishing to entertain such discussions. Bin Laden was not born out of social intellectual struggle; that is he, unlike the Egyptians or the Algerians, Tunisians, Sudanese and others, was not forged from the intellectual jousting of the left versus the Islamists on university campuses. Nor was he involved in the picketing and demonstrations of the trade union or student movements. These movements added to the political maturity and development of many Arabs and gave them the ability to understand nuance and forced them into uncomfortable partnerships, which meant that sometimes principles had to be compromised for the greater good and so on. Bin Laden was not from that sort of social milieu; Saudi society didn't have what would be described as civil society. It made him politically immature and ripe for being pulled in different directions whilst he was trying to find his feet. This combined with his wealth meant that if Osama made a mistake it was like business, he lost financially but he could move on and no one could hold him to account because it was his money. This was not the case with student politics or the trade union movements. Someone—your friend, your rival, your enemy—would hold you to account. There in the rough and tumble of politics political decisions had consequences, and though you suffered political losses you gained political maturity.

Osama's political naivety made him susceptible to the ideas of Islamic Jihad whose simplistic ideas might have appeared very attractive. When he came in contact with Ayman al-Zawahiri who introduced him to the ideas of Islamic Jihad it may have shaped his understanding of how the world worked. But that, of course, did not mean that Osama didn't have agency, for he knew how to be a boss and how to manage employees. He could have stopped those ideas from infecting his men by turning the Egyptian *takfiris* out of his guest-houses but he did not. He allowed the recruiters to keep on coming to his guest-houses and talking to the foreign fighters. I myself came across them as they spoke to these impressionable men. When you saw them you could only assume that this was due to al-Zawahiri having sent them there, or Osama had allowed them to remain.

Slowly but surely the presence of Egyptian Jihad in Peshawar started to have an effect on the morale of the fighters. From the guest-house of Bayt al-Ansar, which had been opened by Osama, their whispering campaign against the Muslim Brotherhood vis-a-vis the Arab Services Bureau began. They accused us of being too soft and compromising, saying that Sheikh Abdullah was a Saudi agent and I was his mouthpiece. The main culprits of this campaign at the time were led by Dr Fadl[6]—the author of *al-'Umda fi I'dad al-'Udda* ('The Essentials of Making Ready [for Jihad]'), a classic Takfiri text espousing Jihad against those who did not rule by the laws of God—al-Zawahiri his friend and fellow medic, and the late Abu Firas al-Suri, a bookseller in Peshawar, who was killed in an American air strike in Syria in 2016.

By 1987 when I turned up in Bayt al-Ansar returning from northern Afghanistan I discovered that Osama had left the Arab Services Bureau. He now ran his own guest-houses. However, that is not to say that cooperation did not occur: Bayt al-Ansar guest-house was run jointly by us and Osama. It was a complete shock. The house was tense and the atmosphere was foul. Moreover, the guest-house was divided between those who sided with the sheikh and those who sided with Osama. I even heard that some of sheikh's closest aides such as the likes of Abu Hajer had said that his star was on the wane. That sort of talk upset me. I was pulled aside by some of the men and told that Osama was allowing the Jazrawis, that is the Saudis and those from the

Arabian peninsula, to slander and bad-mouth the sheikh in his presence. 'He doesn't condemn them,' they said upset 'and he allows them to talk that way.'

Things came to a head when Sheikh Azzam and I were in Osama's car. There was a *nasheed* playing in the car and as the call to prayer, *adhan*, came in, Sheikh Abdullah asked the driver, Abu Qutayba to turn down the sound out of respect for the *adhan*, since it is Muslim etiquette to listen to the call to prayer and repeat the words. As such if anyone travels to the Muslim world, often music and the TV will be turned off when the *adhan* is heard. Sheikh Abdullah's request was an innocent gesture, however, Osama didn't like the instructions that the sheikh had given Abu Qutayba and ordered him to leave the tape playing thereby implying that he was the emir. It was awkward for all of us: I could see the driver torn by his love for the sheikh whom he didn't want to disrespect and Osama from whom he received a salary. And so the driver left the tape recorder on. Sheikh Abdullah didn't say a word and just kept on smiling but it was a smile of forbearance.

But Osama's actions were unbearable to me. Abu Qutayba later returned to the sheikh and got to his knees and begged him for forgiveness. The sheikh would not hear of it and told Abu Qutayba to get up and forget about such things. It was a small issue. The sheikh didn't begrudge Osama becoming a leader, he was unique in that way, I have never met a man who would want you to be the very best that you could be. And despite the awkwardness, the sheikh continued to boast that if there was a saint in this world, it would have been Osama bin Laden. I don't know if it was just to boost Osama in front of the Saudis for political expediency or whether he really believed it. I'd like to think it was the latter because it fitted with his personality. I, however, couldn't accept such things from Osama, he was my equal and moreover I wasn't on his payroll, nor was I intimidated by his wealth. I could tell him what I wanted without any repercussions because as friends we could tell each other the unvarnished truth. And so I went to his house, knocked on the door and told him that this sort of behaviour was completely unacceptable and dishonourable.

'What on earth is going on?' I said. 'You cannot behave that way.' By allowing people to talk badly of the sheikh he was effectively condoning it. Osama was polite and silent. At one point he said that he didn't like it but it was better that the circumstances were controlled rather than allowing it to flood on to the streets. To me that was a poor excuse; such slanders had to stop and if he allowed it he was irresponsible, not to mention sinful. He also had to stop the little slights that maybe Sheikh Abdullah didn't see, but I did. A few months back we were visiting Jalaludin Haqqani in Khost district in Paktia, when Sheikh Azzam and Osama decided to pass by Jihad Well, Osama's training camp that housed about forty Arabs, the vast majority being Saudis. Once there the sheikh delivered a *khutba*, a sermon, and afterwards we sat and talked. When it was time for prayer Osama went to make ablution and he was accompanied by someone who would pour water for him from the water carrier. When it was the sheikh's turn to make ablution no one from Osama's men had showed him the same courtesy, even though his status as a scholar warranted such behaviour according to Muslim etiquette.

Now in Western culture of course it is nothing, can't a man go and do ablution by himself? But amongst Afghans and indeed Arabs, that was saying something and I don't think Osama was naive when he did that. Osama knew etiquette and manners very well. He was from a family that prided itself on those things. Here was a clear signal to the rest of the men that the student believed that he had superseded his master. And so Osama didn't argue with me over that point because he knew it was true. I knew how to treat scholars because part of the Islamic curriculum is to acquire the manners and etiquette of a student; part of learning was to know how to treat one's teachers. In fact, one could fail one's studies based on that alone. I could only attribute such behaviour to people who were working on him. And there were clues to my suspicions. One of our mutual friends was in Osama's house when Osama announced after Maghreb that he was going to Dr Fadl's house for a lesson. My friend looked at him strangely and asked, 'Are you going to take lessons from that mad man?' Osama shrugged his shoulders and still attended his classes. If Osama had just asked the sheikh he would have given him one-to-one lessons. The actions that Osama did later seem to be in line with the sort of behaviour that Egyptian Jihad espoused. Osama had become the adopted son of the *takfiris*.

And yet, I wrestle with the question as to who captured whom? Who influenced whom? It is difficult to judge whether Osama gained their loyalty through his quiet charisma or if Zawahiri and Dr Fadl's arguments influenced him. This relationship must have been one of cross-fertilisation, for Osama had enough religious learning to not just accept Zawahiri's and Dr Fadl's arguments wholesale. Perhaps it was a case of Osama wanting to be that knight in shining armour, and seeing it as an opportunity to gain followers. I remain sceptical and mystified by Osama's trajectory to extremism.

16

ASSASSINATION

It was around 1988 that the first signs appeared that the sheikh's life would end violently. Already the pressure on him on the political front was immense. The Pakistani authorities despite being run by what we believed was a benevolent and devout dictator, General Muhammad Zia ul-Haqq, made it clear that the sheikh was becoming unwelcome.

This was not because the Arabs were causing problems in Pakistan but a lot to do with the internal reports that sheikh's opponents were filing. They were writing critical reports to the Saudi interior ministry claiming that he was a political threat. We have analysts like this even now, they see threats in every nook and cranny even when there is none. These reports were having an impact on Saudi policy. Consequently, the Pakistani security services who were close to the Saudis definitely kept an eye on the MAK's activities after that time.

In fact, a close friend of the sheikh, Dr Abdallah Omar Nassif, visited him that year and advised him that there were rumours that he would come to a bad end.[1] Dr Nassif had procured him a job at a university in Nigeria and advised that it would be in the sheikh's best interest to take up the job offer. But Sheikh Azzam replied that he would not leave the Jihad in Afghanistan unless an enemy of the faith, a hypocrite, or an envier had killed him and so Dr Nassif didn't persist in his proposal.

It was only after Zainab al-Ghazali's visit to Pakistan that the harassment of the sheikh ended. Zainab al-Ghazali, was a courageous Muslim Brotherhood activist who founded the Muslim Women's Association. She was a brilliant intellect and often chartered her own course. When the Brotherhood fell into crisis following the founder Hassan al-Banna's assassination she held the Brotherhood together. Her activities also earned her the wrath of President Nasser. She was sentenced to over twenty years or so of hard labour in the prisons of Egypt. It was during those dark times that miracles were attributed to her. In her book *Return of the Pharaoh*, she recounted her harrowing experiences in Nasser's prisons where she was spiritually fortified with visions of the Prophet whilst unspeakable things happened to her as she recalled in an extract worth quoting in full:

> At sunset, the butchers of the Military prison became active. Their wheels of torture began to roll. During the night they took me back to the cell of water. My intestines screamed with hunger, my throat was cracked from thirst, my bodily wounds scorched my soul. Miraculously, I fell asleep and enjoyed the most beautiful of dreams. Beautiful people wore beautiful clothes made from black silk, adorned with pearls sewn together in gold-embroidered velvet. They carried plates of gold and silver full to the brim with meats and fruits that I had never seen the like of before. I began eating, first from this plate, then another and another. As I awoke I realized I was no longer hungry, or thirsty. Rather, the taste of the food I had eaten in my dream remained in my mouth. I thanked Allah and praised Him for His bounty.[2]

It was her courage, patience and fortitude that made her revered as a walking saint by many Muslims including the

Pakistani General Zia ul-Haqq. She was his distinguished guest when she visited the country in 1987. During that period Sheikh Abdullah came under increasing scrutiny from the ISI to such an extent that life in Peshawar became unbearable. So he left for Sada camp where he could escape their prying eyes, and continued to teach, train fighters and generally feel at ease there. Whilst he was at Sada, Zainab mentioned the harassment of the ISI to the general. Her 'son', for that is how she referred to the sheikh, could not live a normal life in Peshawar she pleaded. When Zia ul-Haqq heard about it, he put an end to the harassment immediately.

But whilst the harassment from the Pakistani intelligence services stopped, the rumour-mill didn't. The epicentre for these rumours was Osama bin Laden's Bayt al-Ansar, which is where they congregated and delivered their study circles. Al-Zawahiri, Dr Fadl, Abu Firas al-Suri, Dr Ahmed al-Jaza'iri and others continued to spread rumours that the sheikh was a Saudi agent.[3] Sometimes there would be a talk by one of the fighters where a jibe would be thrown in and Osama would say nothing as if he was condoning it.

Whilst al-Zawahiri and Dr Fadl's extremism was known, Dr Ahmed al-Jaza'iri's vehement opposition to Abdullah Azzam was a mystery. His story is revelatory as to what was going through the minds of these *takfiris*. Dr Ahmed or Abu 'Amra was one of the earliest *takfiris* in Peshawar and though he wasn't a member of Islamic Jihad or al-Qaeda he was one of their closest allies. Dr Ahmed used to attend the mosque of a friend of mine, Abdur Rahim 'Abbo, who had spent time with him in prison after the military coup in Algeria in the 90s. 'Abbo and his group were followers of the Salafi Albanian scholar Sheikh Muhammed Nasir ul-Din Albani in Algiers.[4] They met Dr Ahmed in 1981 and were impressed by him because despite him being a two-star officer in the army he offered his dawn prayers at the mosque before going to work at a hospital nearby. That was a rare thing as the officer class in Algeria were often secular Francophiles. Over the following year Dr Ahmed started to attend their circles at the mosque and they built up quite a rapport until one day he just disappeared. He must have gone to Afghanistan from 1982 or 1983 onwards when I heard of him in Sayyaf's camp in Pabbi.[5] I was informed that apart from us, there were two other Arabs in Peshawar. I met the thirty year old surgeon in his flat in Peshawar three to four days before leaving for Mazar Sharif in 1984. Sheikh Abdullah, as was his habit, was trying to recruit him to join his efforts. He was gently rebuking him for his actions in Wardak that had resulted in Dr Ahmed barely escaping with his life. The doctor who had sworn to save lives had been working in a hospital in Wardak when some Afghan *mujahideen* brought in one of their wounded at death's door seeking emergency treatment. The man wore a *ta'wiz*—an amulet with Quranic verses—around his neck. With regards to *ta'wiz* there are differences of opinion in Islamic jurisprudence as to its permissibility: some allow it, others do not. Dr Ahmed, who was not a jurisprudent in any shape or form, stated categorically that he would not treat the patient unless the amulet came off. The Afghans were incensed at the request whilst one of their companions was at death's door and here was this Wahabi, as they saw him, concerned about amulets and talismans. I don't know exactly what followed after, but Dr Ahmed had to flee the hospital. After that incident Dr Ahmed developed a deep hatred for Afghans and their Jihad. It was in that context that he sat with the Sheikh Abdullah, the latter remonstrating him for his behaviour in Wardak and the former telling the sheikh that he was betraying the Jihad. 'What should one do?' asked the sheikh. 'You must first start with monotheism and correct their creed', replied Dr Ahmed. It was the standard call that you hear from most Salafists to this day. As for me, I just didn't like the way he was speaking to a learned scholar. Islamic etiquette honours scholars, women and the elderly. 'Have some manners', I said.

He got angry and left us in his flat slamming the door behind him. I didn't see him till about a year later. He had travelled to Kuwait and met with Abu Muhammed al-Maqdisi, a man *takfiris* consider a scholar and was distributing his book *Millat Ibrahim*, 'The Denomination and Creed of Abraham', in the various guest-houses. He was clearly trying to do what he had advised Sheikh Abdullah of doing, unite the fighters on the Wahabi creed. When the Egyptians came he allied himself with them and worked strenuously against the sheikh. After the war Dr Ahmed returned to Algeria and spoke against the FIS victories in Algeria in 1991 and denounced them as heretics for participating in elections. His rabble-rousing in Algeria got him stabbed and later after the military coup he found himself in a dungeon with my colleague 'Abbo who pieced together what happened to him. Of course, there were also rumours that Dr Ahmed was part of the Algerian security apparatus, however that seems to be just that, rumours. He was killed in 1995 or 1996 and even though Dr Ahmed was not linked with the GIA, his ideas and those of Zawahiri were the seed that led to the GIA.

There were also others from the Afghan side who contributed inadvertently to the sheikh's demise. One of Sayyaf's men Mohammed Yasser of Ittehad al-Islami or Islamic Union was upset following my report that recommended that the MAK should support groups that actually exercised power in Afghanistan, namely Burhanuddin Rabbani, Yunus Khalis and Hekmatyar's factions. This report was based on hard realities. The war effort would have been more effective that way, Sayyaf's group didn't have much of a presence in Afghanistan. This wasn't a reflection of his leadership skills but rather because Sayyaf had spent much of his time in jail and could not mobilise support for his party. He had come to the scene late. Sayyaf's role both during the Afghan Jihad and indeed now as an elder statesman seemed to me invaluable, but facts were facts.

My report was not well received by some members of Sayyaf's party. Mohammed Yasser, a senior member, took it especially badly. And so he started a whispering campaign against the sheikh which inevitably contributed to the rumour mill. In fairness, Yasser, a devout man, did apologise for his behaviour after he saw a dream. Dreams in Muslim tradition are seen as a minuscule part of prophecy. Seeing the Prophet for instance, in your dream is taken as a good omen for Satan cannot take his shape. Yasser was part of the delegation led by Burhanuddin Rabbani to meet US President Ronald Reagan and saw a dream whilst in Washington. In the dream he was in a mosque where he had finished the congregational prayer and after the prayer, as was Afghan custom, he gathered around the imam to give his greetings. A crowd gathered around the imam as it became known that the imam was one of the Prophet Muhammad's companions, the famous Abdullah ibn Masood.[6] So Yasser rushed to shake his hands because any Muslim would want to shake hands with such a blessed and holy man. Eventually after much elbowing people out of the way Yasser finally reached the imam and beheld Abdullah ibn Masood who it turned out had the face of Sheikh Abdullah. When Yasser greeted the Imam the latter snubbed him and turned away from him saying that Yasser's breath was terrible. Yasser woke up and immediately understood that he had wronged the sheikh. On his return to Pakistan he made his way straight to Sheikh Abdullah's house and apologised to him recounting his dream about the bad breath. 'It's a true dream', said the sheikh half in jest and half serious. He accepted Yasser's apology but unfortunately once the words are out, they remain out there. This is why the Quran and the Prophet warned against back-biting and slander.

Whilst there had been some cooperation between Osama's group and the MAK, at one point in 1988 Osama completely separated himself from the MAK on the pretext that the men around the sheikh were always denigrating his contribution to the Jihad. He claimed that the Palestinians around the sheikh were always back-biting him and that the sheikh never stopped them. But from what I saw and heard, the sheikh would always praise Osama and even went as far as describing him as a *Wali Allah*, a friend of God. He praised him even when the back-biting against the sheikh from Osama's followers was at its height. He had a genuine affection for Osama. The biggest proof of that was when I got engaged to the sheikh's daughter. When the subject of my marriage came to the fore, Sheikh Abdullah went to Osama for advice. He would never go to someone for advice if he loathed him and considered him his rival, especially not when it came to his daughter's hand.

It was Julaidan who had suggested that I marry Sheikh Abdullah's daughter, Summayah. He had asked me indirectly in the car driving to some destination or another. My mind at first wasn't really focused on marriage: there was work to be done, and I didn't have the means to marry. They were all the excuses that young men use to put off marriage. But when Julaidan suggested Summayah I jumped at the idea. Still, as we drove Julaidan didn't want to get my hopes up and said that he would speak to the sheikh first.

When Julaidan went to his house next he broached the topic. 'Abdallah Anas', said the sheikh, 'as my son in law? That would be a dream.' He had not considered it up to that point. He sought the advice from his wife and she replied, 'Abdallah Anas and Summayah, what can I say?'

The sheikh was surprised by her response. Usually his wife would kick up a fuss whenever a rich Saudi or some other person would ask for her daughter's hand. 'Never in a million years', she would say. But in my case she didn't object at all and was surprisingly subdued. So it made Sheikh Abdullah even happier. So the next time I was around Sheikh Abdullah suggested that I go to Osama for some advice on the matter. 'Summayah', he said 'is young, go and ask Osama what he thinks.'

Osama's opinion was important, especially as he had more experience in such affairs. He had married several times and was a better judge of women in comparison to those of us who had none. Moreover the two families had lived in the same block of flats at one point and Osama had a chance to observe the family closely. Osama's advice was spot on. On my visit to his house, he told me that his experience of the Azzam family had shown him that the girls there mature quickly and that turned out to be true. My wife has been a rock ever since and borne our tribulations with fortitude and patience. Even though the Prophet was forthright in showing his deep regard and love for his wives, I come from a culture that doesn't easily express its deep love for its womenfolk. Suffice it to say my love for her runs deep.

Irrespective of the personal relationship and regard they had for each other on a personal level, when it came to the Afghan Jihad they differed. Osama felt that he was throwing his money towards an organisation that didn't value his contribution. Especially now that there were families and specialists coming to Peshawar that needed more money for their upkeep. And so in the end Osama left the MAK to set up his own guest-houses and camps. Unfortunately, it didn't matter how much the inner circle tried to stop it, the back-biting and the agitation continued within Osama's organisation. Sometimes the sheikh would get upset and frustrated referring to al-Zawahiri and Dr Fadl. 'What', he would say exasperated, 'are they doing here just sitting around in Peshawar talking?' None of them fought inside Afghanistan and were agitating against him in Osama's house right under his very nose. It used to make me upset and I used to blame the sheikh for not stopping it, but he never did.

Eventually the sheikh came to the conclusion that something had to be done for the sake of unity amongst the Arabs. He gathered the closest amongst the original founders of the MAK and instructed them to go to Osama's house and organise an election of sorts where Osama becomes the emir. And so the 'election' was organised in late 1988. Most of us though knew that this was just a way to placate the Arab fighters rather than actually giving the leadership to Osama. Osama, though very capable in many ways, didn't have the respect and, frankly speaking, the stature that Sheikh Abdullah had in terms of knowledge and spiritual presence. He was one of our equals—a comrade—but no way could he command the authority that Sheikh Abdullah could amongst the Arabs and the Afghan factions. But this election was also a very subtle message to policy-makers within the Saudi state who viewed Abdullah Azzam with deep suspicion and the likes of Prince Turki al-Faisal, the head of Saudi intelligence, that they had nothing to fear from him. In other words the MAK was not aiming to tear down the Saudi state. In fact to placate these fears, the MAK had even given authority to one of their own sons, Osama bin Laden who was already on good terms with the establishment. That then, was the take-home message to the Saudis with this 'election'.

But somewhere along the line Osama started believing that perhaps he actually was the solution not only to the Afghan Jihad but indeed to the *Ummah*. He had fallen victim to that age-old spiritual disease: hubris. Hubris lead him to miscalculate the American resolve after 9/11. He had expected the Americans to bomb the country for a few months after 9/11, enough time for him to declare a new Jihad against the West and rejuvenate the *Ummah*. But how wrong he was! The US spent billions, not to speak of blood, to defeat al-Qaeda and the Taliban and thereby changing the very face of the Muslim world and the political discourse that we are still experiencing in our day-to-day lives because of that fatal flaw: hubris. Osama subverted prophetic injunctions which said that one should not wish to meet the enemy, but when one does, one should stand firm. He forgot the injunctions which said leave the Romans when they leave you, and sought instead to draw the enemy into Muslim lands causing much harm.

So Sheikh Tameem went in to Osama's sitting room where the men sat themselves down on the floor. Sheikh Abdullah was not in attendance, he was at the Sada training camp at the time. Julaidan too didn't attend, despite the sheikh explaining why he had to attend. Julaidan had no problem attending the meeting but he categorically could not vote for anyone but the sheikh, and so respectfully declined.

Osama had all his followers there at the gathering and after the usual formalities and pronouncements before starting an important meeting the men began to talk. These were men, some of whom we had never seen before, they had never met the sheikh and I doubted had even fought on the front lines. Some of them began to slander our emir. Tameem, an immensely emotional man and deeply attached to the sheikh, couldn't contain himself. He couldn't stand these Egyptians who he had never seen before slandering his beloved emir. It was as if these devils were insulting his father. 'What is this?' Tameem said bristling with anger, 'I thought this was an election?' This didn't feel like an 'election' but rather court proceedings designed to assassinate the sheikh's character. Osama raised his hands and stopped him, 'Wait, don't speak: I am your emir.'

'Emir?' Tameem said exasperated, 'Who are you? I am not going to sit here and listen to these devils!' He got up, spat on the gathering in contempt and left the room. It prompted others to follow his example and it was left to Osama's followers to elect Osama as emir. So in truth the MAK didn't give authority to Osama but his rabble-rousers who already followed him did. Amongst us veterans there could never be any emir except for the sheikh.

Posterity recorded that day as the day that al-Qaeda was born but the truth was there was no such thing as al-Qaeda. It only became a name when Western analysts began calling it thus and al-Qaeda appropriated and used it much, much later. No one ever used the term al-Qaeda in the way it is used now, it was merely short for Osama's organisation. It did not evoke fear in any of us nor was it taken that seriously. Contrary to modern myth Sheikh Abdullah had nothing to do with its birth even though the people who slandered him appropriated his image to bolster the credibility of the organisation. Al-Zawahiri wouldn't even pray behind him when he was alive and only started to praise him after 9/11. This was just an act of cynical opportunism. Just like nation states need symbols and some sort of national story, al-Qaeda did the same; it is an utter and shameful lie that God will hold them to account for.

And the proof of it was that things carried on as before, except now of course the Arab foreign fighters were even more divided. The closest friends who had come to fight the Communists now passed each other without looking each other in the eye. They didn't stop to talk, hug and inquire into each other's affairs. If they did stop and talk it was for a brief moment consisting of generic chit chat with little meaning. The tension between the Arabs would manifest itself sometimes in childish events and other times in serious incidents that had serious consequences for the parties involved. Two of these incidents that epitomised the tension was the 'Case of Ahmed Shah Masoud' which I mentioned briefly earlier and the 'Judgement of the Tahaddi' project.

In 1989 in April or May, I was inside Afghanistan, in Panshir, Takhar to be precise. Ahmed Shah Massoud used to have a ten-day training camp for his senior commanders and officers. Those ten days taught the commanders spirituality, military tactics and provided an opportunity for Ahmed Shah Massoud to unify his ranks. My responsibility was to instruct the officers in Quran and

Sira, the biography of the Prophet. I was warming to my teaching role, and looked forward to meeting some of the bravest men that fought against the Russians: they were tough like mountains but their hearts thawed like snow at the mention of the Prophet.

On the third day of the programme I received a letter from Peshawar: it was from Sheikh Abdullah requesting that I leave immediately for Peshawar. I was puzzled by the immediacy of the request but I thought, let me finish the ten-day course and then I will set out. A few days later we received a second telegram from the sheikh asking whether I had left. If not, I should leave immediately. It was not often that the sheikh insisted on such a thing. 'It must be serious', said Massoud. He insisted that I return and I prepared for the arduous journey back to Peshawar. I trekked through the mountains for several days before I arrived in Peshawar only to find that my men were getting up to childishness. In some ways I couldn't believe that I had to deal with such matters, and yet, I understood immediately why the matter was grave. It needed to stop and I as emir of the Arab fighters on the ground was the only person who could stop it before it infected the rest of the Arab foreign fighters in Peshawar.

Sheikh Abdullah explained that some of the young Arab foreign fighters, some of whom had fought alongside me and Massoud, were going around the guest-houses denouncing Massoud as being a lustful Iranian spy or something of that sort! These leaflets were not only being distributed in Arabic but had come out in various other languages as well. I couldn't help thinking that some sort of foreign hand or intelligence services were involved in this. Such rumours would have a terrible impact on morale in Peshawar, this hub of activity and entrepôt for the Jihad in Afghanistan.

At the same time Sheikh Abdullah couldn't deal with it directly and stop these rumours because the men looked up to him, and demanded that some sort of 'judgement' was required from his part on Ahmed Shah Massoud. He knew very well that it was childish nonsense but he needed someone like me who had spent several years in the company of Massoud to dispel these rumours. Moreover, my standing amongst the men was high, I was their military emir and the most experienced amongst them, I had taken them across Afghanistan, I had given them their first taste of the Jihad, and they respected me.[7] So it was only fitting that it came from me.

And so as soon as I arrived we set up this 'muhakama', judgement room, in one of the salons of the guest-houses.[8] These judgements were similar to an Afghan Jirga if you will, a gathering of elders to resolve a dispute or a matter. You had Sheikh Abdullah who was the arbiter of the dispute, and several observers who would ensure that the judgment was carried out fairly and independently. Those people were Sheikh Abdul Majeed Zindani, Sheikh Tameem, Osama bin Laden and Julaidan. Then there were the accusers of Massoud around ten of them who had signed the leaflet of calumnies and slanders. And then there were those who had fought with Massoud, three Algerians namely Abd el-Rahim,[9] Abd el-Wahid,[10] and me, Massoud's advocate and defender.

We sat there on the floor, tea cups at the ready for two days and we began. Sheikh Abdullah made the introduction to the sitting with all the religious and Islamic supplication that started all important gatherings to remind us all of our responsibilities. Pretty soon Sheikh Tameem again started to get uncomfortable. He started to make a fuss, and got up to leave. 'Who am I', he said excusing himself, 'to pass judgement on Ahmed Shah Massoud?'

He got up and left. Sheikh Abdullah didn't mind, he always used to say that he had the emotions of a child. He called a spade a spade. And on this occasion he was right. Sheikh Abdullah had seen with his own eyes the damage that Massoud had done to the tanks of the Soviets, hundreds of them lay there strewn and scattered along the valleys of Panshir and here we were discussing absurdities that had been conjured up in the over-fertile imaginations of some Arabs! In any case, did the opinions of a handful of Arabs really matter, what was our contribution alongside those brave Afghans who were daily fighting the Russians? Even the money that the MAK gave them was a mere drop in the ocean, why should they be indebted to us? Rather it should be us who should be indebted to them for allowing us to take part in this blessed path. I made my views very clear and argued that Massoud was doing us, the Arabs, a favour by allowing us to fight in his ranks. After all our contribution to the Jihad had not been anything out of the ordinary. Massoud had hundreds of battles under his belt before we came and would have more after us and did not need a single one of us. As a frame of comparison Jaji had been a success for the Arabs but it had relied on Sayyaf's men. The Arab offensives in Jalalabad had been disastrous because the Afghans had not been there. We needed to have some sort of perspective. Who needed whom? Massoud was doing us a favour.

I had to answer accusations and they were seventy in all, from the fact that Ahmed Shah Massoud's commanders were Shi'ite spies of Iran to the fact that Massoud had a swimming pool where French women in bikinis bathed! The latter was so absurd because it was apparently an eye-witness report by someone who had seen it himself. But when I pinned the witness down nothing stuck, this eyewitness couldn't 'remember' where this place was. It must have been made up in the lurid mind of the accuser. In this ultra conservative society, if Ahmed Shah Massoud walked around without a *pakhool* on his head *Mawlawi*s would question the very integrity of him as a man and Muslim—could you imagine him in a pristine swimming pool frolicking with French ladies in bikinis in Afghanistan?!

The other accusation was that Massoud's men were Shi'ites and Iranian spies. There were no Iranians in the ranks of

Massoud. A simple case of geography had become conspiracy theory. Afghanistan had Iran as its neighbour, and many Afghans were refugees there because that was the closest country where their families could flee to if they lived in the West of the country. Moreover there were advantages too; Afghans were Persian speakers and might feel closer culturally to Iran than Urdu- or Pashtu-speaking Peshawar. Even so there were also many Tajikis in Peshawar. Many of Massoud's men's families had fled there and so they occasionally visited the country to see them; wasn't that a perfectly plausible reason to go to Iran? I even pointed out that Hekmatyar's men did the same. What exactly was the issue?

I couldn't believe I had to answer these question due to their ridiculous nature but it had to be done. I believe that some of the Arab animosity towards Massoud stemmed from the latter not allowing the Arab *mujahideen* free rein like the other Afghan leaders did. You had to fall in line. Point by point I destroyed and rebutted the charges. I didn't expect any of the observers to object to my advocacy. But I noticed that whilst Julaidan was rooting for me, Osama wanted some of those charges to stick against Massoud and I wasn't quite sure as to the reasons. I tried my best and often encouraged him to meet Massoud and he had been receptive to the idea but something always got in the way. Massoud certainly had nothing against Osama and had they met history might have been very different. But I suspect it was a combination of things. Osama had suggested that such meetings might jeopardise his relations with Hekmatyar.[11] Others suggested that Osama fell under the sway of the Egyptians and may have harboured certain prejudice towards Massoud; whatever the case, I noticed that there was something Osama had against the Afghan commander. He began to interfere in the proceedings. Sometimes he would interrupt—'You', he would say, 'did not consider this or that'—and it was likewise countered by Julaidan. At one point I just turned around and told him point blank: 'For two days now you have been interfering between me and my men, now if you won't allow me to carry on this business then you can leave.'

Osama of course didn't like it but he was always a man of impeccable manners and so he got up and left saying not a word. Sheikh Abdullah went after him and conciliated him and brought him back to the gathering. In the end the decision of this 'judgement' was that those charges was unproven but Sheikh Abdullah was not allowed to praise Massoud or fund him through me, and in return they wouldn't spread those things about Massoud in Peshawar. Even though Sheikh Abdullah thought it was absurd and foolish, he stuck to his side of the bargain for the sake of peace, at least in public, just to keep the young men on side. He even told me that no youth would keep him away from funding the Jihad in Afghanistan and even gave me money to deliver to Massoud when I made preparations to return. The agreement however was non-binding: after all the sheikh only exerted spiritual authority. And the agreement of course was not binding on me. So I gave an interview to *al-Sharq al-Awsat*'s Jamal Khashoggi about the incident, and this according to these young men invalidated the agreement and so the young men continued spreading these foolish rumours which harmed no one and nothing but their own afterlife.

I returned to Afghanistan and told Ahmed Shah Massoud how frustrated I was at these young men, and he chuckled and shrugged his shoulders. Even when he discovered that some of the Arabs like Abu Rawdah al-Suri who had served under him had spread calumnies against him attacking the very probity of his honour as a man—that he frolicked with women in a swimming pool—he laughed it off.[12] Later Abu Rawdah saw a dream wherein he gave Massoud a jacket and realised that he had wronged him. So he bought a jacket and asked me if I could deliver it as a gift as a token of his sincere apologies. And I did what he requested and Massoud accepted his gift and forgave him. The sheer greatness of the commander came through when he allowed Abu Saeed back to his ranks without a single word of blame against him.[13]

The second incident occurred a little later after the '*muhakama*' of Massoud. There used to be an Egyptian-Canadian called Ahmed Said Khadr also known as Abu Abdur Rahman al-Kanadi.[14] The sheikh used to call him 'effendi' on account of him wearing Western clothes when the rest of us wore Afghan or Pakistani clothing. Khadr was involved in fundraising and the sheikh had urged him to move his family to Peshawar to set up the Tahaddi or the Challenge project.

The Premise of the Tahaddi project was simply this: that they would try to match the efforts of the Western NGOs. Sheikh Abdullah and Julaidan got Khadr involved in the project. They said that he would run the project whilst they would provide the office space, telephone lines and cover its expenses. Khadr asked for a letter of endorsement for his fundraising and the sheikh gave it. And so it was all agreed, Khadr received the letter of commendation and travelled the world fundraising for this project.

But Khadr increasingly fell under the sway of al-Zawahiri and Dr Fadl. And at some point a disagreement occurred between him, Sheikh Abdullah and Julaidan. Khadr claimed that Tahaddi was his organisation and he could do whatever he wanted with it. This according to the sheikh was contrary to their agreement, for Khadr would not have been able to raise that amount of money without his endorsement.

This dispute poisoned their relationship, and with the poisonous words of the *takfiri*s in the house of Osama the atmosphere became unbearable and tense. Khadr went as far as accusing Sheikh Abdullah of being a Saudi spy and a thief and repeating the accusation of the *takfiri*s. These were dangerous assertions for they put the sheikh's life in danger since the *takfiri*s had no issue in killing a traitor with or without legal process. In fact, the issue came to a head one night when there was a knock on Julaidan's door. It was Osama: he looked flustered and nervous and told Julaidan that he needed to set up another '*muhakama*' to resolve the issue between Khadr and the sheikh for otherwise those 'devils would kill him'. Osama also advised the sheikh to stay away.

This is where I couldn't understand the man: Osama was fearful for the sheikh's life and yet at the same time he allowed these same devils to back bite and slander him? Sometimes I just wanted to shake him up and tell the sheikh to abandon this lost man. In fact, many years later, during the Arab Spring I heard one of these Salafists from the Nour party defending Sisi and saying that they had planned to kill Sheikh Abdullah at the time because he was an agent of the Saudis and had stuffed an ambulance with a cache of weapons, and I realised that Osama had been right—they really were trying to kill him. It was lucky that he didn't attend. Only Julaidan went and sat at the judgement presided over by Osama and Dr Fadl. Julaidan and Sheikh Abdullah renounced any stake in the project and walked away leaving Khadr to do what he wished with it. It was the wisest thing to do. Yet now the threat that people were ready to kill the spiritual master of the Afghan Jihad was real. And then in November 1989, Sheikh Abdullah Azzam was killed.

I remember the fateful day as if it was yesterday. I was in Taliqan, Takhar province in north-east Afghanistan. I was there because the Arab Services Bureau had opened up a branch there. We used it as an educational centre to teach local Afghans Arabic and delivered humanitarian aid from there. It was morning and we were sitting down on the floor talking when I heard the sound of a Russian Jeep pull up with its distinctive sound of Soviet engineering. Dr Khalil Hanani knocked on the door and I got up to invite him in.[15] I loved and respected this man, and he remains to this day a man of upright character and true to the spirit of the great commander he served as communication and logistics officer. He had gained his PhD after Sheikh Musa al-Qarni visited us in 1991 in north Takhar.[16] Sheikh al-Qarni said that post-invasion Afghanistan would need educated men to rebuild the country and offered scholarships to help facilitate that. Massoud put forward a list of people and Officer Khalil was one of them. Usually there was a lot of friendly banter between us but that day he was stony faced and troubled, it was as if winter had arrived early. 'Emir Sahib', he said, 'wants to see you.'

I was puzzled—it must have been something important. I threw something on quickly and jumped in to the car. Dr Hanani drove me to Massoud's house in silence without any of the usual chit chat or jokes. I came to the house and was let in with the same sombreness. When Massoud saw me, he bade me sit, as if to prepare me psychologically, he poured me tea, stirred in the sugar and started an introductory talk, the sort of talk one gives to introduce bad news. 'You know Abdallah,' he said, 'Jihad is a difficult road, we have all buried people we loved.'

He did not need to tell me, I surmised what he would say next and burst into tears. I knew there and then that the sheikh, my future father-in-law, had gone over to the other side. We sat on the floor of that room and cried together like little children. I don't know for how long I cried but that is all I, a grown man, a warrior, could do. Every soul tastes death, it is the only certainty in life after all. But that still didn't make the departure any easier. When I looked at it, I could still say that God was generous in taking his soul at that time. Had it been three weeks before during a previous attempt it would have been an even bigger disaster. I was told that on that occasion an Afghan caretaker had found an improvised explosive device hidden in the pulpit where the sheikh was due to give his Friday sermon. Thank God he had found it: had it exploded during the sermon hundreds would have been killed, injured and maimed.

I only found out later what happened. Sheikh Abdullah had, as was his want, asked his son Hutheifa to accompany him to the local mosque named after a Yemeni martyr, Sabu' al-Layl: that was where the Arab Afghans prayed. But Hutheifa had woken up late, so the sheikh said that he should go and shower and prepare himself for the Friday prayer. He asked his youngest son, the sixteen year old Ibrahim, a young man of remarkable intelligence, to go with him alongside his oldest, Mohammed. The three jumped in the car and started towards the mosque. A little while later, my mother-in-law who was in the kitchen plucking a chicken heard an explosion; this was common in Peshawar. Nevertheless a premonition told her that something was wrong. She called the Arab Services Bureau office and asked Abu Adel where the sheikh was.[17] Abu Adel reassured her that everything was fine. But she insisted that they go and see what happened. So he went out in the direction of the explosion, followed by Abu'l Harith, Sheikh Abdullah's nephew. As they came closer they beheld the macabre spectacle. A roadside bomb had blown the car to bits, the legs and the body parts of the sheikh's two sons were hanging off the branches of trees but he appeared asleep, his body was intact, just his nose was bleeding. We take that as a good sign that God accepted him as a martyr. God willing.

All the Arabs went mad at the news, they started to scream, cry, sit down on the roadside completely lost. I can only imagine that we tasted that momentary madness that Umar bin al-Khattab, the second Caliph of Islam, must have felt on the passing of the Prophet. A sense of complete and utter loss, helplessness and despair filled the Arabs. They were mad men or headless chickens not sure as to what they should do.

We decided there and then that I should head to Peshawar, even though there was a risk that we might get caught by the winter snow, but the roads were no longer dangerous since we didn't have to worry about the Russians or the Communists anymore. So I set out with a trusty guide and trekked across seven mountains to get to Peshawar. I could not attend the funeral that had been held in Pabbi very quickly after his death.[18] Everyone attended the funeral except Hekmatyar and Osama. Osama was in Saudi Arabia at the time. I don't know why Hekmatyar didn't attend, but I am sure Osama would have been devastated by the news and would have attended if he could.

When I say that everyone attended, I do mean everyone. Even the likes of al-Zawahiri was there crying his eyes out even though only a few days before he and his friends had been spreading calumnies against him. He was a vociferous opponent of Sheikh Abdullah due to his Muslim Brotherhood links and wouldn't even pray in the same mosque where the sheikh prayed. I am convinced that his loud tears were affectation because he wanted to show the sheikh's followers how attached he was to him. But God knows how much he schemed, how much he hated him and how he turned Osama into the man who can order the death of Ahmed Shah Massoud and those innocent souls that died on 9/11 and today. The Brotherhood that had been fostered by the sheikh was now in tatters and the Arab Afghans became factionalised.

As to who killed him, every guest-house was buzzing with theories, some accused the Iranians and others the Saudis, everyone one had their theory. Many fighters in the guest-houses accused the *takfiris* of killing him, after all they were responsible for poisoning the atmosphere in Peshawar and turning Osama into one of them. Others pointed to the handiwork of the intelligence services. Here some accused the Russians and others the Israelis; Sheikh Abdullah after all was Palestinian and dreamed of liberating Jerusalem, the Israelis were just nipping the problem in the bud. But Islamists were probably not a great worry for Mossad at the time for them to assassinate him—they were far too busy with the PLO.

Others dismissed Russian machinations: 'Why', they would ask, 'would they focus on killing him and not the other *mujahideen* leaders? The war had already been won by the *mujahideen* by that point. The Russians are rational actors, why would they go after an obscure sheikh with little impact on the ground after they had pulled out of the country? Why not go after Rabbani, Hekmatyar, or Massoud for that matter? But they did not go after the others. Why not? Why didn't we see other assassination attempts?'

Some, smarting from the Jalalabad defeat, pointed an accusing finger at the Pakistani ISI. Afghanistan after all was and remains intrinsically tied to the destiny of Pakistan. There was always a fear that if Afghanistan was not under their sphere of influence, then India would manipulate the circumstances in Afghanistan in order to encircle Pakistan. This fear, the fighters argued, led the ISI always to bank on Pashtuns and men who were more amenable to their national interests. There was a recognition that whilst Pakistan is a Muslim country, in order to preserve its integrity the state needed to have their man in Kabul. This is why despite the War on Terror, Pakistan kept the channels to the Afghan Taliban open nor have they renounced the Haqqanis like the US wanted them to do. It was simply a case of realpolitik.

Some believed that the ISI had discovered very early on that Ahmed Shah Massoud was not their man.[19] He was not malleable and too independent for their liking. The Jalalabad offensive showed many participants in the Jihad that Pakistan had its own agenda and it did not necessarily coincide with their own. Both sides of course respected each other, but Massoud did not do their bidding. So when Hamid Gul, the intelligence chief, promised Prime Minister Benazir Bhutto that they would take Jalalabad and Kabul easily as long as Massoud held the Salang pass and the latter rejected the plan as unworkable, it gave the ISI a very clear message that this Tajiki *mujahid* was not their man. But ISI also recognised that neither was he Iran or India's man: what Massoud wanted was an independent sovereign Afghanistan, and that was impossible for the Pakistani national interest. And so the Pakistani state began to lean towards supporting Hekmatyar more aggressively. I don't know how much truth there was to that theory, but you could sense inklings of it in Peshawar. Hekmatyar received more funding and equipment than the rest. It could also explain why he took the unilateral decision to take Kabul on his own, for it would mean that he would have hegemony of the country which would of course be in the interest of Islamabad.

But how did this link to Azzam's assassination? Some of the fighters argued that when the Jalalabad offensive began Sheikh Abdullah was not in the sights of the ISI at all. But the battle was a disaster and we lost many good men on those days in 1989. The Afghans had not told the Arabs that they had broken up to celebrate Eid and they were pounced upon and had to retreat.

It was at that moment that Sheikh Abdullah visited Massoud. He returned energised and praised Massoud to the sky, to the extent that he described Massoud as a modern-day Napoleon in a press conference in Kuwait. That message would worry the ISI. The sheikh's superstar status in the Muslim world effectively meant that he could direct funds and give legitimacy to the Massoud faction and so their man, Hekmatyar, would lose out and that would harm Pakistan's national interest. And so the ISI made a calculated decision to eliminate him—this then is the conspiracy theory and God knows best about the matter. I did hear however, that after a twenty-eight year hiatus, Sayyaf made a visit to the Kingdom of Saudi Arabia and there in an interview he claimed that he knew which hand was behind the assassination of Sheikh Abdullah Azzam and that he would reveal it in due course.[20]

After Sheikh Abdullah's death that anchor that kept many of the Arab Afghans to take sides in the conflict was gone and there began a steady slide towards partisanship and extremism. However, that is not to say that it was inevitable. In 1990, after the National Commanders Shura meeting where commanders including Massoud, Haqqani, Abdul Haq and others attended to resolve the political deadlock that the politicians in Peshawar were facing, Massoud was invited to Islamabad for a meeting with the military top brass including the likes of Lieutenant General Asad Durrani, the new head of the ISI and General Aslam Baig, head of the Pakistani army. Massoud accepted the meeting and made a good impression on them; however, whether he changed their attitude towards him was debatable. On his return to Afghanistan he stopped over in Peshawar for two weeks where he stayed as a guest of Professor Burhanuddin Rabbani.

Massoud's arrival in Peshawar was immense, he was mobbed by the Afghans in Peshawar and the whole atmosphere of the city changed. But moreover, for us at the MAK it had a tremendous impact. The guest-houses were buzzing with news of the arrival of this legendary commander. Massoud visited Abdullah Azzam's house where I, Wael Julaidan and others were treated to the hospitality of my mother-in-law whose cooking skills were almost as legendary as the fighting abilities of the Lion of Panshir. I should add that bin Laden didn't attend due to him being away in the country but I am in no doubt that he would have attended had he been in Peshawar at the time. For several hours she serenaded Massoud with the finest Palestinian cooking from Maqlouba to pastries. We also tried to do an interview with him, but it had to be cut short when one of the questioners asked him, what he would do if he met Abdullah Azzam in Peshawar? He just broke down in tears and couldn't continue the interview. He was immensely moved by the experience of sitting in the house of a great ally and friend of the Afghan Jihad. Of course, the fact that this man was hosted at Abdullah Azzam's house made a profound impression on the Afghan Arabs, despite the rumours concerning him.

ASSASSINATION

The MAK set up a meeting where we invited all the Peshawar humanitarian organisations, Red Crescent, the Arab Afghans from the guest-houses and many others to attend a Q&A session with Massoud. After making a speech, we opened up the floor to questions from the audience. The Arab Afghans asked Massoud about strategy, what would happen after the fall of Kabul and much, much more. These questions dispelled so many myths and rumours that the likes of Qari Saeed who had made those preposterous accusations earlier asked me if I could help him to reconcile with him. So when Qari Saeed went to Massoud, trying to apologise, Massoud didn't even pay his apology any attention, it was a bagatelle, he just hugged him and asked him how he was and that was the end of the matter. Massoud left the Arab Afghans glowing for days. I suspect that had Massoud made regular visits to Peshawar, that impression would have remained and it would have gone a long way in preventing many of the Afghan Arabs turning towards extremism and taking sides. But Massoud had bigger priorities than what a handful of Arabs thought of him. So once the impact of his visit had worn off in Peshawar, the rumours that had been years in the making resurfaced. So much so that it was from the hearts of some of those men in Peshawar that his assassination came about.

PART IV

INTO THE WILDERNESS
AND RETURN TO THE MOUNTAINS

17

INTO THE WILDERNESS

I don't wish to give another history lesson with regards to Algeria here, but I believe that a brief overview must be given in order to explain the trajectory of my life. Especially since the Algerian civil war in the early 90s had a massive impact on my life and indeed on the politics of the Middle East even if few can make that direct link. In many ways what Europe is faced with currently, with the fear of grizzled hardy returnees, Algeria has already experienced. I myself am a returnee grizzled only by time. At the time of writing, with Syria embroiled in a civil war rather than revolution, we have men from Europe who fought in Syria and are, in many ways, experiencing similar dilemmas to those I faced during my wilderness years after the Russians had left.

I have never made it a secret that I am part of the Islamic movement in Algeria and remain unashamedly so today. My links with the Islamic movement leaders during my time in Afghanistan was good. Even in Afghanistan, whenever I could, I tried to follow events in my home country on news services. I snatched phone conversations or asked Algerians for news on Algeria's political situation. I was hopeful about events in Algeria because in many ways it was going in the opposite direction to that which Afghanistan was going in. Whilst Afghanistan was increasingly heading towards civil war, Algeria was heading towards democracy.

Algeria's independence, though bloody and brutal in many ways, had always been characterised by a unity of purpose. The FLN had been an umbrella organisation and managed to unite the various currents whether socialist, nationalist, Islamist or liberal and direct them towards removing French authority in the country during the 50s and 60s. Afghanistan had been the opposite, it had a purpose but it had failed to achieve unity. Despite the oaths of unity and loyalty taken inside the Kaaba the Afghan leaders returned to their old ways at the cost of so many more lives. The idea that the West had destroyed the unity of Afghanistan in my experience doesn't ring true. It was the Afghan leadership who destroyed the future of their country. Nevertheless, the victory of the Afghans over the Soviet Union buoyed the Islamic world with confidence. It had inspired the Intifada, given birth to Hamas, General Bashir and the late Hassan al-Turabi[1] had gained Sudan with mixed results, and of course the FIS was making headway in Algeria.

Now, the Afghan leaders all believed, as do the Taliban today, that only their group represented the 'state', they could not accept multi-party politics. Algeria post-independence became a one-party state. Algerians though, still hoped for a multi-party state with a fully functioning democracy where civil society was strong. And it had figures within Algeria that worked for it throughout, and so the tradition was still very much alive within Algerian society. But in October 1988 under the Chadli Bendjedid government, riots broke out and spread across Algeria, as a consequence of austerity measures. The social despair, the fall in oil prices, and the slowness of political reform led to the youth protesting in Algiers which subsequently spread to other cities. Realising that the government was losing control they announced changes in the constitution and opened up the country to a multi-party political system. It is here that one Abbas Madani, a nationalist and Islamist who had spent seven years in the French gaols, emerged triumphant. This academic from Sidi Uqba in Biskra province in East Algeria, with a PhD from SOAS University of London, mobilised his party. Over time the academic had increasingly blended his nationalism with the Islamic movement which was geared towards the Algerian context. Whilst the other Islamist parties hesitated for fear of arrest, Abbas Madani in alliance with Salafists led by Ali Belhadj, went out on to the streets and registered as a political party. It was a bold move since it was perfectly natural to believe this new-found liberalism was a trap. In their experience they had been cut down to size: Nasser had done so in Egypt and it was not implausible that the same thing might happen here. However, Abbas Madani seized the moment and emerged as the main leader of the opposition.

Madani and Belhadj's FIS was set up in September 1989 and won local council elections in June 1990 securing 93 per cent of town councils. They seemed to be far more effective too, they were praised for their efficiency and probity, and their social work was outstanding. They dealt with the earthquake in Oran, Tipaza province far more effectively than the government. But the real earthquake for the Algerian state and indeed for the European partners was the question, where exactly was this young party taking Algeria? Rather naively, not dissimilar to the Muslim Brotherhood in Egypt, they began to worry the Deep State. Some members were making incendiary comments geared towards their support base, but the comments worried the international community. Abbas Madani was likened to Ayatollah Khomeini, some were making noises that after Algeria they would march on France. Others said they would have democracy once and then the Shariah of God will be implemented. This form of populism may have been attractive at the time to the FIS but it also showed that they lacked political maturity and did not know how to behave within state structures. And I should add here that I was not immune to those sorts of slogans; it was only the fall of Kabul, the conflict in Algeria, 9/11 and indeed the tumult I have witnessed with the Arab Spring that has led me to re-evaluate and reassess my own assumptions about those times.

But it couldn't last. When the Algerian state tried to curb this parallel government where the FIS controlled the local councils Madani called for national strikes in May 1991.[2] The strikes succeeded and crippled the country. The government were forced to climb down but they also realised that this was the time when they had to shut down the FIS. By January 1992, the military had cancelled the second round of elections and staged a coup.[3] They arrested senior party members and eventually declared a state of emergency. Soon the security apparatus of the state rounded up local councillors and FIS supporters and dumped their bodies in black body bags on the street.

During the period before the crack-down, as I said, I watched events keenly in Algeria. And there was a period after the death of Abdullah Azzam that my newlywed wife and I decided to honeymoon there. Although it wasn't really a honeymoon. Firstly, on arrival the Algerian authorities welcomed us by detaining us for three days. They interrogated us as to the purpose of our trip and to gather intelligence. But thereafter, my wife saw very little of me, because my return to Algeria was like the return of a celebrity due to my relationship with Abdullah Azzam and the Jihad in Afghanistan. I must have seen thousands of people and visited every inch of the country during that period. And yet as the repression continued, the country was slowly but surely being led down the path of civil war. Young Algerians started to head to the mountains of Algeria in numbers. This then was the cause of their radicalisation: the actions of the government first drove men to the mountain and pushed the moderates away.

But that is not to deny that there weren't any *takfiri* elements in the mountains overlooking Algiers. Even during the heyday of the FIS there was always an element amongst the Algerian Islamic movement that accused the FIS of apostasy and heresy by taking part in a democratic system. I have already mentioned the likes of Dr Ahmed who vehemently denounced the FIS for participating in democracy. Whilst Islam as a monolithic tradition of course doesn't have a view on democracy and throughout its history has existed alongside kings, emperors, caliphs and even non-Muslim rulers, in the modern context, democracy was problematic. To some thinkers democracy was intrinsic to a secular world system founded on godless materialistic principles of the West, and it was simply impossible to separate the two. The FIS and other Islamist parties disputed that assertion. Some viewed democracy as a tool for holding a ruler to account and removing an oppressive ruler without bloodshed. Despotism and succession disputes meant that Muslim empires had been afflicted with these maladies in the past.

In my view of course, those sorts of analogies that suggest that participating in democracy is tantamount to apostasy are false. For don't Jihadists have bank accounts in banks that deal with interest? And yet does the fact that they house their money in banks that deal in usurious transactions mean that they condone usury? So why does this logic not also apply to democracy? In our case the FIS vehemently believed that democracy was the best political culture to resolve our issues peacefully. During the years of peace, those voices who expressed militant ideas had no space in the political discourse. Their rhetoric of gaining power through the sword had no weight with the FIS. In sum, the liberal political climate where people could take part in political life meant that those who advocated the bullet instead of the ballot box just didn't have any support and they remained a fringe group similar to the extreme far right in the UK. However, when the Years of Lead entered with many young Algerians fleeing to the mountain and the real prospect of armed insurrection began, their radical call reappeared and gained credence. Extreme times often lead to the middle being marginalised and the radical becoming the norm. For they could say: 'See we told you so. This is what happens when you take on democracy'. This is not dissimilar to Muslim activists telling American Muslims that their political activism and participation in the US has not stopped Trump's Muslim ban. All political effort has been in vain and Muslims have no place in America. And many will no doubt buy that narrative.

And this anger and feeling was given an ideological basis through the pronouncements of Ayman al-Zawahiri, Dr Fadl, Abu Qatada,[4] and Abu Musab al-Suri.[5] It was their propagation and preposterous statements that gave their ideas validity. Their message swallowed up moderate voices and saw the birth of the GIA, Armed Islamic Group, the Algerian equivalent of Islamic Jihad in Egypt. Whilst initially the goals of the GIA was unclear and saw many young men flocking to it soon their agenda became pretty clear. They were essentially a group who believed that their actions were sanctioned by God, and so the killing of civilians, journalists and others were permissible because these people subscribed to an infidel system and by virtue of that were apostates or *murtadd*. Becoming an apostate in traditional Islamic law could lead to the judiciary sentencing you to death.[6] Of course the GIA was not the judiciary, they were bandits at worst and vigilantes at best. It was this sort of thinking that lead a Tunisian to assassinate Massoud because he believed Massoud was an apostate.

Similarly, the GIA, led by Djamal Zitouni, the son of an Algerian poultry farmer with little religious training, passed a death sentence on the FIS leaders which included me, Rabeh

Kabeer, Anwar Haddam, Qamar-Eddine Kharban and Salman and Ousama, the sons of Sheikh Abbas Madani. The statement was published by *al-Ansar* in London whose editor in chief was Abu Qatada. At the time he even supported the GIA's criminal actions that included the murder of women, children and preachers. How he justified such actions was exemplified by his justification of the GIA's killing of the revered preacher Muhammad al-Saeed. Abu Qatada wrote the following:

> Muhammad Al-Sa'id is unique...but his name must not be over-looked without looking into the reasons behind his killing...those who want to open a dialogue with the tyrants or open contacts with foreign tyrants like Gaddafi and others, or work for the return of democracy, must be killed without dignity.[7]

Words such as these have serious consequences. Abdelbaki Sahraoui, a FIS leader, was murdered in Paris on 11 July 1995. It was no wonder that the Algerian Intelligence, the DRS, could manipulate the GIA and weaponise them against the FIS.[8] Through their atrocities they tried to tarnish all Islamists in the same way many governments are using ISIS to tarnish all Islamists. There were many accounts which suggest that the dark hand of the Algerian state was involved in massacres and atrocities. The Bentalha massacre in 1997 for instance was an obvious example. Some claimed that it was the GIA who killed 400 men, women and children in cold blood in full view of the Algerian army; others claim that it was the Algerian security forces that killed them masquerading as the GIA.[9]

Whilst there is no doubt that some Afghan Arab Algerians were involved in setting up the GIA, most of these came after 1993 when the Soviets had left and the Afghan factions were fighting amongst themselves. In my view it would be wrong to label them *mujahideen* since they were fighting other Muslims in a civil war. These tiny unruly Algerians were turned into convenient bogeymen by the Algerian government to conceal their own crimes just like Assad has done in Syria, killing thousands in the name of fighting terrorism trying to destabilise the country. The Algerian military junta put thousands in concentrations camps in the desert, assassinated, tortured and sent to death many good men in the name of fighting extremism. Moreover, the Algerian security services realised that the GIA could be infiltrated. After all, most of these men were ignorant and lacked political and religious finesse epitomised in Djamal Zitouni. It was no wonder that these ignorant devils, for that is what they are, were able to wipe out entire villages and towns because 'God willed it'.

For me though the prospect of returning to my beloved country was scuppered. General Khalid Nizar, the Algerian defence minister designated me as the *capo* of the Arab Afghan agitators. I was the Algerian state's arch enemy and super terrorist. I was shocked by the accusation. I didn't even know who some of these people were. As for the ideologues that supported this group, I did not know who they were. I had met Abu Qatada briefly in Peshawar before he sought refuge in the UK. The meeting had been uneventful in someone's house, tea and small talk that's all it was. He was a secondary school teacher in Peshawar and was not there to fight Jihad and I contend that he still does not know the difference between a Makarov and a Barretta let alone how to take them apart. I never considered him a *mujahid* then and I became increasingly puzzled by the likes of Al-Jazeera and other broadcasters touting him, Omar Bakri, Hani Siba'i,[10] and Abu Muhammad al-Maqdisi[11] as belonging to some great line of Jihadi scholars when their combined hours on the field of combat amounted to nothing. In what way were they Jihadi scholars, and how did they speak for the likes of me? It really infuriated me. Similarly I watched incredulously as Al-Jazeera put on the likes of Abdel Bari Atwan commenting on bin Laden as an expert when Atwan had very little experience of the Afghan

Jihad. I would have understood if it was the likes of Olivier Roy, Sandy Gall or Lyce Doucet—these people had spent considerable time in Afghanistan, and Roy had written an academic text book—but putting Atwan on really confounded me. It was either editorially dishonest or simply incompetent.

After the guest-houses had become factionalised, I would come across Algerians who would confront me about my support for the FIS. I wouldn't apologise for my beliefs. They would be upset at my political position and we would part ways. In Peshawar however these ideological positions had not crystallised until much, much later. And you could walk around in Peshawar holding different views but as the 90s went on and *takfir*-ism began to take root, attitudes hardened. That is when you had to be careful.

I still remember the surreal experience of meeting Abu Musab al-Suri in Khartoum quite by chance in 1994. I was invited by Hassan al-Turabi to the Popular Arab and Islamic Conference in April 1994. The late Turabi was a brilliant intellect and had previously invited me and my mother-in-law to Sudan in 1991 out of respect for Sheikh Abdullah. After the fall of Kabul I had helped the Sudanese secure an embassy there and that had endeared me to them. So in 1991 we had flown in from Pakistan where he hosted us in true Arab fashion full of kindness and generosity. I could see how Turabi could be the intellectual powerhouse behind President Omar Bashir who had come to power through a military coup in 1989.

When I flew from Pakistan in 1994 to the conference as a representative of the FIS the circumstances had changed. Algeria was embroiled in a civil war, I was also looking for a place to call home until things in Algeria were resolved. Turabi's conference was held in the plush Hilton in Khartoum. His diplomacy had managed to get a wide spectrum of people of various political inclinations and sympathies to attend. There were some groups of course that Westerners found abhorrent and likened the conference to a *Terrorist Internationale* but they were not viewed thus by many in the Arab world or the Muslim world. Some attendees such as the PLO were viewed as resistance groups fighting the Israeli occupation, whilst others such as Ennahda were likened to the Christian democrats in Germany. So in attendance were members of the PLO, Hezbollah and representatives of the Rabbani government, *mujahideen* factions and many others. My plans were to network with various groups, see old friends from Afghanistan and pay Osama bin Laden a courtesy call and see whether Sudan could be my temporary home before returning to Algeria. Bin Laden was also in attendance at the conference and used that opportunity to petition the Afghan government whether he could return to Afghanistan. He told the Rabbani government that Saudi Arabia was putting pressure on the Sudanese government for hosting him and asked the Rabbani government for political refuge. When the representatives returned to Kabul they discussed Osama's request to return to Afghanistan and decided that if Osama could tolerate living under civil war conditions there were no issues on their part. He had after all helped the *mujahideen* with his money and resources. Once bin Laden was given the green light he chartered a private jet that flew into Jalalabad and stayed there until Jalalabad fell three months later to the Taliban and that is how Osama was introduced to the Taliban. It was strange how Osama paid back such good will with so much destruction.

It was on one of those sunny mornings in Khartoum, when I was asked to lead the morning prayer, Fajr. Normally, you are expected to give a talk or reminder afterwards since you have been honoured to lead the prayer. After having finished the prayer I sat down to give a small reminder to the attendees at the mosque. From the corner of my eye I spotted some Algerian GIA members at the mosque, I had seen them in Peshawar. Curiously, they came up to me and let me know that they would not take part in this circle of knowledge. That was not a problem at all, no one is obliged to sit in a circle of knowledge in any case, one is free to do what one wishes. I just found it odd that these men made it a point of telling me, as if they wanted me to know that they were boycotting me. They went off and I continued unfazed by such an encounter.

Later that day Abu Rida, a friend, relayed a message that Abu Musab al-Suri wanted to meet me. I agreed, there were no issues in meeting him. I had met him in 1986 quite by chance in Madrid when I had travelled to Spain to see my parents there. At the time, I feared that the Algerian military junta which was cracking down on the Islamists and would not allow me to re-enter Algeria, might trouble my parents on account of me. So I arranged to meet them in Madrid in Autumn 1986. It was there that having offered my prayers in a mosque I met a group of Syrians who had fled the crack-down of the Syrian regime following the failed Hama uprising in 1982. The uprising had led to the utter defeat of the Brotherhood and the flattening of the ancient city.[12] One of those men was Suri, a tall red haired man with green eyes—he was from Aleppo and part of the Muslim Brotherhood offshoot, Fighting Vanguard, a militant group renounced by the Syrian Brotherhood. This Combatant Vanguard had taken up arms against Hafez al-Assad's repressive regime. The group had called for an uprising in a conservative Sunni town in the heart of the fertile plains of Syria. Hafez's response was swift and brutal: thousands of people died as his brother mercilessly flattened the city into submission. Suri who had fled to Spain married a Spanish convert and became a Spanish national. I met Suri in a suburb of Madrid. My impression of him and his group was not positive, he was full of criticism for the Syrian Brotherhood that verged on contempt. They believed that the Syrian Brotherhood was responsible for the failure of the Syrian uprising. Later on they published a book on the Syrian Brotherhood entitled 'The Syrian Experience'; it was a commentary on the communiques of the Syrian Brotherhood.[13] I would have welcomed such a book if it was constructive criticism but it was also filled with invective and bitterness. It was no wonder Suri's anger could diffuse into the men that he led.

Many have depicted him as a brilliant strategist but I found Abu Musab al-Suri to be unremarkable in my first encounter. He was polite enough and asked me general questions about the situation in Afghanistan and how one could get there and what the living conditions were like. I informed him of what he wanted to know over tea and the meeting went amicably. Years later I bumped into Abu Musab al-Suri, he had made several journeys to Afghanistan and even moved his family over there. By then he had written that vitriolic tract against the Syrian Muslim Brotherhood. I noticed then, that he had this rising dark anger in his heart, the sort of anger that could border on outright hostility towards his opponent. When he hated you, he really hated you. I could not find a reason for it except his experiences with the Syrian regime and the twenty-five or so Syrian intelligence services that still exist to this day, that have the ability to produce men such as these. It is worth remembering that brutal regimes produce brutal men and it is difficult to transcend that pain inflicted on you and retain a degree of humanity in your heart.

When I met him in a flat in Khartoum I remembered him again. He informed me that those Algerians, his followers, didn't sit in the morning gathering for a reason and that today I had a choice to make. Either I was on the side of the 'Democrats' or on the side of '*Minhaj al-Sahih*'—the correct path. He was behaving like a Spanish inquisitor, examining my faith even though that was something abhorrent to the Islamic tradition. The Prophet had forbidden it. Moreover who had given him the authority to do so? Was he a legal jurist?[14] Nevertheless he explained that these young Algerians didn't want to sit in the lecture until I 'clarified my creed.'

Why did I need to clarify my position with the FIS? And what if it was not to his liking? What would happen then? It was such a surreal experience. And so this inquisitor asked me about the FIS and their adherence to democracy, to fighting, and delved into all sorts of theological questions. But I wasn't going to be bullied by this man, it just goes against the Algerian national character, so I argued with him for two or three hours that day and in the end he had made up his mind about me. I was on the wrong side and, by implication, I was his enemy. I was no longer part of their caravan and he released a tape denouncing my political views. Even though Suri had never met them he expressed such a level of hate towards the FIS leadership it surprised me. Having fallen on the wrong side of Suri and his group meant that I had to be careful in Khartoum because I felt that these men were willing to kill me for what I held in my heart. They didn't say it but you could see it in their eyes. Suri and his friends were later implicated in the Madrid bombings in 2004. The disease of the inside will manifests itself on the outside.

I saw these attitudes in the men that Osama bin Laden was surrounding himself with too. On the same visit I decided that I would out of courtesy pay a visit to my old comrade in arms. Osama had left for Sudan, due to the dispute he had with the Saudi government over the invasion of Iraq in August 1990. He was now a businessman in Khartoum and settled there alongside some old veterans from the MAK: Abu Hajer, Abu Ibrahim, Abu Ubaidah al-Banshiri, Abu Hafs al-Masri and of course al-Zawahiri and his men. Osama at the time was not a committed militant. He flitted from being a legitimate businessman to a political or militant leader. He was at the crossroads and many of the MAK veterans were involved in running his business ventures that centred around agriculture and construction. But he was also surrounded by Zawahiri's *takfiri*s. When I turned up at Osama's, unannounced admittedly, there was a hostile guard with a Kalashnikov eying me suspiciously.

'What do you want?' said the guard gruffly.

'I want to see Abu Abdullah', I replied.

'Who are you?'

'Abdullah Anas.'

Instead of going to see if Osama was in, the guard launched into a diatribe about my credentials as a *mujahid* and implied that I was some sort of heretic. 'Go!' he said turning me away from the villa and insulting my dignity and honour. I was so incensed by the treatment that I told Osama what had happened through one of my contacts and demanded redress. He was upset at the way I had been treated by his man. The guard however, denied he had meant it the way I had taken it. When I was invited to lunch, Osama purposefully made it a point to have the same man who had offended me serving us. That is when I confronted Osama about the men he was surrounding himself with. Why was it necessary for armed men to take over the whole street and cause his neighbours inconvenience in this suburban street? Was it necessary to place a truck there? Who would want to attack him and why? 'Turabi', I said, 'is a statesman, he doesn't need armed guards and honours his guests, why do you?'

Osama didn't say anything, he couldn't respond. Yet at the same time I believe that some of the men he brought with him from Afghanistan were of the same ilk that they had always been when I had met him. Abu Hajar might have said things to prove his credentials to the *takfiri*s but he didn't hold those beliefs. I am certain of that because he expressed his disappointment at them when I met him last in Khartoum. Abu Ibrahim, his brother-in-law, when he returned to Iraq during the war in 2003, was an inveterate opponent of Abu Musab al-Zarqawi's tactics and beliefs, so much so that he returned to Sudan. Abu

Ubaidah al-Banshiri and Abu Hafs, both men, strange as it seems, remained great admirers of Ahmed Shah Massoud and I just couldn't understand how things went so wrong. And I contend that this was because of the poisonous ideology of these *takfiris* that became a cancer in the *Ummah* and needs to be rooted out by us Muslims.

18

PESHAWAR

As I said previously, the death of Abdullah Azzam had created a vacuum in Peshawar amongst the Afghan Arabs. People were coming up with crazy ideas not dissimilar to those we have seen in Syria and Iraq but on a far greater scale. After the Soviets left, there were instances that were so curious that the mind boggles. There were slogans that were bandied around Peshawar that were far removed from the realities of the conflict. Imagine hearing a point of creed and theology being the very crux to all of Afghanistan's solutions. 'If', said the slogan, 'you don't have loyalty and disavowal, all your effort is in vain and your are wasting your time.' This concept known as *'al-wala wal bara'* in Arabic crudely put required Muslims to refrain from befriending or loving non-Muslims and imitating their beliefs and customs. This ludicrous slogan argued that an obscure point of religious creed from a thirteenth-century medieval scholar, Ibn Taymiyyah, would solve all of Afghanistan's problems. And it was believed that the only man who was able to teach this creed in Peshawar was Abu Qatada who had gathered round him a small coterie of followers from North Africa.

In Peshawar we had Abu Humam Muhammed al-Rifa'i, a veritable 'Abu Bakr al-Baghdadi-lite'.[1] This Jordanian doctor ended up running a caliphate from a London council estate. He claimed leadership of a billion Muslims and set his little emirate up not too far from Peshawar. It resulted in some families in London selling their homes in order to join this makeshift caliphate. I didn't understand his pull however, I myself had found him unremarkable. I had met him in 1983 through a colleague Dr Abu Hutheifa, Mashour Khalafat, in Peshawar. Al-Rifa'i worked for the Red Crescent as a physiotherapist for amputee victims. He had been a student in Pakistan studying radiotherapy but changed course. I would bump into him every few days in one of the guest-houses where he was meeting some friend or another. He was polite, friendly and devout—that was all that could be said of him. Many years later after the fall of Kabul I met him again. We had prayed the sunset prayer, Maghreb, at the mosque and an audience of thirty to forty had gathered to ask me what was going on in Kabul. The Pakistani imam acted as my translator as I informed the audience of the events that I had seen. It was amidst this talk that a man with a beard that reached all the way to his chest asked me whether the Afghan factions were applying Shariah. I looked at who the questioner was and discovered that it was Abu Humam himself, I didn't quite get the thrust of the question so I asked him for clarification. 'I mean', he said as the crowd gathered around us, 'do they apply all of it? Are they applying it in its fullest sense?'

It put me in a dilemma. If I replied yes, that would be a lie and if I said no, then I knew what he would say: we needed a caliphate that applies Shariah in its totality. See, you can never satisfy an extremist. Yet, I didn't want to humiliate him or enter into a long-winded argument with him. So I replied that the question needed a full explanation and this place wasn't the appropriate place for it. I later asked what had happened to Abu Humam and

I was told that he had left for Britain, declared himself a caliph and was shipping families to his caliphate 20 km from Peshawar. He caused immense problems to his followers, some of whom were, simply put, rogues, criminals and murders. Just as ISIS followers came together and declared Abu Bakr al-Baghdadi caliph, so too did the followers of Abu Humam, and if you rejected their leader they kidnapped, killed and extorted. They even took part in drug dealing to fund their misguided project. Even Abu Qatada, someone who supported the GIA, denounced Abu Humam's mad project when he arrived in London.

In fact I saw what these criminals did first hand for once I had to protect a family from his goons. One of his followers, a mother, refused to marry her daughter off to some of his men. And in so doing she had disobeyed the caliph. Knowing what the repercussions would be the mother came to us for help and we protected her with armed guards around our home making sure that those bandits didn't come in to seize her daughter. Another time my mother-in-law received a phone call from a Pakistani nurse from a local hospital informing me that there was a nameless English convert woman dumped in the hospital. The hospital didn't know what to do with this foreigner and out of desperation they got in touch with someone who was known to be in touch with foreigners. We had to pick her up from hospital before the armed men returned in their armed pickups to take her away. My mother-in-law had to go to the hospital to try to find out who she was. Having these sorts of men marauding the countryside it was no wonder that the security apparatus was getting jittery, this *takfir*-ism was spreading. These men now identified me as a marked man, and I noticed that there were people who would no longer pray behind me whether in Peshawar, Khartoum or London due to my membership of the FIS. *Al-Ansar* magazine published diatribes against me in London advocating my death. And yet here I was in the most difficult of circumstances labelled as the source of Jihadi agitation by the Algerian state whilst at the same time I was also an avowed enemy of the GIA. Those days were indeed years of lead for me and my family.

But it couldn't be helped; the civil unrest in Algeria and my own enlarged political role in the FIS meant that some of these things were expected. I was forced to take a more active role in the politics of the FIS following the crack-down by the Algerian military junta. The party was in disarray, and it had different competing visions about what do to in Algeria and the message it should convey to the world. Due to the ban, and many members acting autonomously, the party was sending out mixed messages to the various Western countries, so of course I had to help give it some direction. Remember that I was not psychologically shocked by the crack-down in Algeria. I had been insulated from the shock of being at the cusp of power one moment and the next running for one's life. The crackdown had a massive psychological impact on the FIS leadership in the same way the crackdown of Gamal Abdel Nasser on the Muslim Brotherhood no doubt had on their development.

On a personal level I too had different considerations. War changes you. As the old proverb goes one's entry into the toilet is not the same as one's exit; in other words I was a different person after nearly a decade of fighting in Afghanistan. In many ways, I was disappointed and disheartened. Yes, we had removed and expelled the Russians but the infighting between the Afghan leadership had meant that our dream of Islamic government, if you will, had not been realised. I used to blame my father's generation regarding the FLN nationalists: 'you got the French out of the country,' I would lament, 'you achieved martyrdom, you performed feats of heroism and self-sacrifice, but you failed to build a state that secured our freedoms.' I did not imagine that one day I would be in that same position. What had we achieved? We fought, we killed, we sacrificed and for what? I realised that sometimes the people are able to achieve the first stage of removing an oppressive ruler but the same people who have sacrificed themselves due to the lack of political maturity and political culture do not have the ability or cultural capital to start forming a state from scratch. This has been shown by the example of Egypt with the fall of Hosni Mubarak. Egypt was united by his fall but post-Mubarak they could not maintain this unity. I have noticed this experience in my father's generation of 1962 and with us in 1992 and it is continuing to happen now. The Muslim world can provide you with hundreds of martyrs but very few world-class statesmen who can resolve the issues that afflict us so.

I was also a married man, that too changes you. Although I got engaged before my father-in-law's death, I married soon after his passing. And now I had another responsibility that God would ask me about on the Day of Judgement. Have I looked after my wife and children? Have I done my duty by them? God placed an obligation on me to them as a father and husband. So naturally my calculations were different than when I was carefree. With my family I decided to leave Afghanistan and seeing that I couldn't return to Algeria, I settled in Pakistan with my wife who was at the time carrying my second child. My firstborn was about to start school. Moreover, I also knew that my position in Pakistan was becoming untenable due to my association with the FIS amongst this new influx of Afghan Arabs of the *takfiri* variety. I also knew that I was viewed with suspicion by the Pakistani ISI too. There was even an occasion when the ISI raided my house looking for me. Sometimes the authorities did it for bribes, other times they did it with political intent to send a message. In this case, the Algerian intelligence services were involved, as I was told later by one of the Algerian officers charged with trying to arrest me. And so it was time to start winding down affairs in Peshawar.

However, a new crisis was brewing in the heart of Europe. Following the break-up of Tito's Yugoslavia ethnic tensions had started to flare up in Bosnia Herzegovina. For a long time ethnic tensions had been building up in the country. Long before the genocide began Serbian radio presenters and press began talking about ethnically cleansing Muslim Bosniaks. They were already using language that we are very familiar with today. On April 1992 the Bosniaks were attacked, and I felt it was a duty for me to start looking into the matter. I made several trips to Croatia in 1992 to see if setting up a MAK office would be useful. I also crossed over to Albania, staying with friends, gathering intelligence and making my assessments. But I was getting so much grief in Pakistan that I couldn't follow through with the project.

We were also in the process of repatriating the Afghan Arabs to their home countries so I couldn't stay long in the Balkans. Most of the Afghan Arabs had been persuaded not to take part in the civil war in Afghanistan which was now in full swing. We published a fatwa in order to persuade them not to take any sides. To most of the returnees we gave two to three hundred dollars and bought them a one-way ticket to a country of their choice. All in all we repatriated 2,000 fighters. The Yemenis had it the easiest: Sheikh Abdel Majid Zindani had struck a deal with the late President Ali Abdullah Saleh, who was mobilising the Yemenis to fight the socialists. The Afghan Arabs from Saudi Arabia and the Gulf returned unhindered with few problems with the exception of Osama bin Laden who went to Sudan. As for the Egyptians they would be killed or imprisoned with a heavy dose of torture, Iraqis would be killed on arrival as would the Tunisians, Syrians and Libyans. With Algerians and the Moroccans it was on a case-by-case basis. Many Algerians and Moroccans returned without any problems and lived out their lives without any issues even during the civil war. The Libyan fighters numbered at the most fifty after 1991, Moroccans thirty,

Tunisians twenty to thirty and Algerians numbered a few hundred; the majority of whom did not join the GIA.

As for me, I didn't quite know where to go and from 1992 onwards until my coming to the UK, my wife and I lived out of suitcases and it worried me no end. Financially I was in dire straits, I was not in charge of the accounts of the Arab Services Bureau, every transaction had to be accounted for by a financial council and signed for by two signatories as Sheikh Abdullah had stipulated. I could not simply increase my salary even if I wanted to. I can remember at one point I was walking around the streets of Istanbul praying, almost willing my heavily pregnant wife not to give birth because it would cause us so many complications with regards to the nationality of the new-born. She was a Palestinian with Jordanian nationality who could not put her new-born child on to her passport if the father is a foreign national, which I was. I could not put the child on my passport because my visit to the Algerian embassy would result in my arrest. My child would effectively be stateless and we may have been stuck in Turkey as a result. In the end Providence decreed that my child was born in Pakistan because my wife managed to return to her mother in Pakistan. It was during this period that I also travelled to Sudan at the invitation of Turabi to see if I could make a life for myself there, and from there I visited Yemen to explore that possibility too. But all these places were unsuitable for me. And in any case perhaps I was in denial at the time, I had not fully accepted the fact that the Algerian civil war would last that long. And I hoped we could return to Algeria as soon as the problem was resolved. I had not yet surrendered myself to the thought that this would be a long civil war. You see, as a fighter you have a sense of dignity and you cannot just surrender that way. It appears almost ignominious.

But when 200,000 lives were lost, and peace talks, endless negotiations, the atrocities and deaths of people I loved continued, it dawned on me that perhaps I needed to find a more permanent solution. And so for the first time I started to look beyond the Muslim world. America was never a consideration for me. I was *persona non grata* in France already. I had obtained a visa from the French embassy in Kabul to visit Paris on a dry run to see if the place was suitable for a political exile. I remained in Paris for a while seeing whether this could be the place where I could settle with my young family. But when it came to renewing my visa I was arrested by the police, detained and told that I was a security threat. I suspect that my arrest had much to do with France's unethical relationship with the Algerian state.[2] However, I was fortunate enough to be deported to Pakistan and not to Algeria.

It was in such circumstances, that the UK was becoming a prospect for refuge. The country seemed and remains very much like the country of the Abyssinian king, the Negus. It had a just ruler, adhered to its laws, it was multicultural and friends told me that it was like Londonistan.[3] There were men from all political persuasions, from Rachid Ghannouchi, to Brotherhood types like Kemal Helbawi, to the stranger types like those of Hezb ut-Tahrir who I found to be naive in their political outlook. There were of course the sort I didn't agree with living there too such as Abu Qatada, Abu Musab al-Suri living in Neasden and other *takfiris* too.[4] But in the end I set my heart on going to the UK.

I managed to obtain false passports and fly from Istanbul into Heathrow airport as a political refugee in November 1995. I was followed by another friend who due to a lack of funds managed to put his six children on one passport, one of those 'children' turned out to be older than him and had given birth to him! The immigration officer was very kind and respectful and dealt with us without any of the security measures that we experience today. In those days the prejudice and hostility towards migrants just wasn't there.

In fact, so impressed was my friend that he prayed for their guidance to Islam and as he did so, his mother told him not to pray for their guidance. Sadly, his mother associated Muslims with oppression and worried that if these immigration officers became Muslims they too would become like those Muslim rulers who oppress many of its people today. It is a testimony to how low we as Muslims had fallen in terms of our ethics.

And the poison and prejudice we face today on a daily basis, in my view, has been created by some Muslim loudmouths and extremists who should have understood that the things they were spewing off in public would have landed them in the gallows in Muslim police states. They could have contributed to building this society and contributed to it positively.

It was difficult to enter the UK as a political refugee. I had always had my dignity, especially as a warrior one feels this more intensely, because it is so tied up with honour, courage and other traits of manhood. To turn up in a country, cap in hand asking for political asylum is always difficult. My ego, my *nafs*, was bruised. In the Muslim world I would be recognised and treated as a distinguished person, now I was just like any other person. Now the dream, the vision I had chased were in tatters, and here I was signing my name claiming political asylum. It was immensely hard at the time but eating humble pie was immensely beneficial for me spiritually. God teaches you in every period of your life.

Whilst I missed the mountains of Afghanistan, I busied myself with two things. One was my personal development; I needed to learn the language and acclimatise myself to my new found home fast. I needed to get my children enrolled into school, help my wife set up home and so forth. I also needed to pay attention to what was going on in Algeria and so I busied myself with writing articles for *Sabil*, a journal representing FIS views. I spoke out against the atrocities committed by the military junta and the

GIA in Algeria. I did not realise at the time though, that *al-Ansar* magazine, the mouthpiece for the GIA was published in London. Not only was the editor Abu Qatada in London but the GIA had its fair share of supporters in the city too.

For me *al-Ansar* was probably the progenitor to *Dabiq* magazine in its extremism. It capitalised on the alienation of the Algerian diaspora in Europe which suffered from marginalisation in France and watched from afar the horrendous bloody war occurring in their mother country, and at the same time they began to awaken religiously. Islam was now becoming important for their identity and spirituality. With these feelings of alienation and pain Abu Qatada's magazine poured more fuel to the fire encouraging disaffection. Of course here, I am in no way absolving the French state for not apologising for the historical wrongs done to Algeria nor its marginalisation of the north African diaspora, nor its links to the Algerian generals. I believe the French state could go a long way to resolve its issues with extremism if it resolved that matter and dealt with its North African French citizens fairly.

In the nineties *al-Ansar*, though it was registered to an address in Sweden, was actually edited by Abu Qatada in London. Abu Qatada had his own column entitled *Bayna Minhajayn*, 'between the two ways'. There were distributors in all the major cities in Europe from Paris and Brussels to Naples. It had a large readership in France due to the North African diaspora settled in France. It was interesting to note that some of the killers of Massoud were distributors of this magazine and had an indirect link to the terrible Paris attacks in November 2015.[5]

The contents of this magazine dissected the creed of scholars, denounced them and highlighted their 'deviancy'. They denounced the likes of Rachid Ghannouchi[6] and others as Mutazzilites whilst sending Eid greetings from Zahawiri;[7] they also published communiqués from the GIA and of course published articles that denounced me and took my words out of context. They said that I refused unity, when the truth is that I wanted unity without the extremism of such groups as them. At the time some voices within the leadership felt that I had gone too far because they saw it as politically advantageous against the military junta, but for me it was clear that no benefit could come from a deal with the devil. I include an extract below from one of their communiqués:[8]

ABDULLAH ANAS LEADS THE GREAT SEDITION

'Rank hatred has already appeared from their mouths: What their hearts conceal is far worse'[9]

In an explosive interview with *al-Hayat* newspaper in London on Tuesday 28 March 1995. Abdullah Anas announced his rejection of unifying the Mujahideen in Algeria within the framework of the Armed Combatant Group [GIA]...he demands that the West arrest the supporters of the Armed Combatant Group in Europe. He incites the West making false accusations saying that they [GIA] call the general Muslim population apostates, that they kill women, children and the innocent and by so doing imploring the pleasure of the West towards the client Islamic parties that signed the Rome document.[10]

Some of al-Ansar's people were implicated in the 1995 Paris Metro bombings by the GIA and followed a similar pattern to what we see today. For example, look how similar the background of an ignorant Algerian terrorist Khaled Kelkal[11] is to that of Salah Abdesalam, the surviving Paris Attacker of 2015. Both became devout recently, both were petty criminals of limited intellect. Kelkal had already been involved in the assassination of the FIS leader Abdulbaki Sahraoui in July 1995 in Paris. Sahraoui was opposed to extending the civil war to France. Kelkal then went on to carry out a string of bombings in France eventually being killed by the French police. The trail of this bombing campaign however went all the way back to London because the communiqué of the attack was made through *al-Ansar* magazine.[12] As the *New York Times* wrote at the time:

> In a statement published last weekend in a clandestine bulletin called *El-Ansar*, circulated in London, the Armed Islamic Group said, 'France's engagement in Algeria's moving sands verges on suicide.' The bulletin also printed a map of Paris showing the Eiffel Tower being blown up, threatened 'military strikes at the very heart of France and its big cities,' and reprinted an earlier claim signed by Abu Abderrahman Amine, a pseudonym for one of the Armed Islamic Group's leaders, taking responsibility for the earlier attacks this summer.[13]

As the article suggests all the tropes found in *Dabiq* magazine and tactics used by ISIS were already present as early as the 1990s. So we have to ask ourselves are the communiqués of GIA so dissimilar to ISIS? Doesn't ISIS use the same tropes in its imagery, from using the image of the Eiffel Tower to the same murderous language that the GIA used? And doesn't the editor of *al-Ansar* not bear some responsibility for those ideas becoming prevalent currently?

Of course there were others too. Abu Humam,[14] the self-appointed caliph, was living on a council estate in London's Edgware Road. You had Abu Musab al-Suri living in Neasden also editing *al-Ansar*, he had also opened an office in London doing research on conflict in 'Muslim countries' and arranged press meetings for Osama bin Laden. But for me, I needed to be wary of the GIA, especially after the death of Sahraoui in Paris. There were even reports of the GIA having a hit list that wanted to take out FIS members.[15] I recall going to pick up some meat from my local Algerian butcher in Lewisham. As I ordered the meat I saw the butcher raising money for 'our brothers in Algeria'. Having purchased the meat I was about to throw the change in the box when I asked the butcher who these brothers were. I discovered subsequently that these brothers the butcher was talking about was the GIA. I left quickly surprised at how deeply the GIA's ideas had penetrated the Algerian community in London. I also saw GIA supporters distributing magazines speaking against me and denouncing my views. They did not at the time know that I was in the UK. The secret only emerged when I did an interview with *al-Hayat* newspaper based in London, then they launched full frontal ad-hominem attacks on my character and credentials.

But though they attacked me none of these so called 'Jihadi' scholars wanted to debate me openly. I found that odd, did they have something to hide? They were willing to debate the likes of ex-Muslim Brotherhood member Kamal Helbawi and others, but they deliberately requested that they not debate me. It upset me, because I believed that they were twisting Azzam's views and taking them out of context, that they had hijacked him.

But even so, I did not busy myself with lunatics and their preaching during the nineties. My concern was focused on the Algerian civil war and of course trying my best to settle in my new milieu. Though I missed Afghanistan, the mountains were becoming part of the distant past, a period of my life that I had left behind. But the friendships I made lasted, especially the bond between me and Ahmed Shah Massoud. That could never be abandoned. We talked often but I could sense in his voice that the civil war was taking its toll on him. The rise of the Taliban too and the country being divided into north and south was difficult to bear. Sometimes the two parties would open up negotiations and the Taliban would demand his total unconditional surrender, that was impossible and the war would start again. Unconditional surrender was something Massoud could not do. He told them that many times, he had fought the Communists and now he was fighting the same sort of totalitarian ideas on behalf of his people. It broke me to hear his weary voice, he was becoming increasingly cornered. His warnings against the rise of al-Qaeda as an organisation were interpreted as just that: the cries of a cornered fox.

But he had seen it before, many of us had: this organisation if it was not quelled would burst out into the world and wreak havoc. And in many ways looking at what is going on all over the world Ahmed Shah Massoud was right. He is not given enough credit for that by the world and especially the Muslim world. Had we listened this organisation wouldn't have spread like a cancer. Nothing good has come from it. Nothing. I challenge any one to show me one place where that organisation has entered and it has done something good to the people it ruled.

By 1995 Osama's increasing closeness to Zawahiri and his return to Afghanistan in May 1996 meant that his mind had been more or less made up. Osama was now a militant leader. He had landed in Jalalabad under the auspices of the Rabbani government, and a few months later the Taliban entered the city victorious. He reached out to the Taliban and formed an uneasy partnership with them. Osama, though never fully committed to the Taliban, realised that he could cooperate with them under the auspices of an old comrade Jalaladin Haqqani in Paktia province. The relationship was mutually beneficial. The Taliban used Osama's zealots as foot soldiers against Massoud's men and in return they were allowed to run autonomous camps in and around Jalalabad and Kandahar. Mullah Omar though asked him to move to Kandahar where he could keep an eye on him and his activities. With Osama's return, the growth of his camps with its pool of fanatical al-Qaeda fighters meant that things took a turn for the worse for Massoud. But what the Taliban failed to realise was that these men had no allegiance to anyone but bin Laden, and respected no emir but bin Laden. Mullah Omar should have realised it when bin Laden declared war on the Western crusaders and Jews in 1998 without his knowledge, but he didn't. And why should he? He was a simple *mullah* from a small village in southern Afghanistan with little education outside of the *madrasa*. And so in those camps Osama and his men plotted and planned until their fruits were felt on 11 September 2001.

19

TO THE MOUNTAINS

I remember the day as if it was yesterday. It was 9 September 2001, I was chairing a meeting with some FIS members when I received the news. Two men had detonated a bomb hidden in a camera, they were European Arabs, and both had died. Initially, I heard reports that Massoud was badly hurt but still alive.[1] I later called his brother, the Chargé d'affaires, Ahmed Wali, who told me that it was far worse.

'How bad?'

'A martyr, God willing.'

My world was shattered. I returned home went straight to my room, closed the door and stayed there alone with my grief. I experienced the same grief that I had when Sheikh Abdullah passed away. I didn't want anyone to comfort me, for no one could comfort me apart from Him. I hope that God will fulfil that promise He makes His servant when he loses his best friend and he remains patient; that He will reunite them in Paradise. This is how it was in those days.

I only found out from the Afghan Ambassador that my dear friend had died at the hands of two Arabs from Brussels, both members of the Tunisian Fighting Group, the equivalent of the Algerian GIA. They had posed as journalists with a letter from an Egyptian activist and exile in London called Yassir Sirri.[2] I did not know much about the latter except that he was an opponent of the Egyptian government and belonged to the same party that Omar Abdul Rahman belonged to. I got his number through my contacts and met him in Edgware Road, west London. From his account I realised that he had himself been duped by the men. Whilst he had been working in a bookshop in Baker Street some men had come asking for a letter of introduction for Ahmed Shah Massoud. Yassir Sirri,[3] realising that this was an opportunity for a scoop and potential for making some money by selling the film to Western media, had given them the letter of introduction. He didn't check the credibility of these men and busied himself getting in touch with his media contacts. So the men travelled to Afghanistan as journalists concealing their bomb in the camera. They had waited for days in order to interview Massoud and when they finally met for a sit-down interview they detonated their bomb. The cameraman was killed instantly, the interviewer was killed later when he tried to escape from his prison cell. It was said that Osama had ordered his killing. Massoud and Osama had never met; the latter knew of his military prowess and contribution, why he decided to side against him when neutrality would have been better was beyond my comprehension.

Two days later whilst still grieving over the loss of my friend, I turned on the TV and saw the most extraordinary images that my eyes had ever beheld. A plane flew into the Twin Towers in New York followed by a second plane. It was something out of a disaster movie. The world quickly forgot that Massoud had been killed and focused all its attention on the loss of those two towers. President George W. Bush came out and made statements that told you exactly where you were meant to stand on the Twin

Towers: either you were with America or you were against her. Similarly Osama echoed words which also said that either you were with al-Qaeda in solidarity or you were with the US. The worst thing about it was that both of these world visions were false narratives. Absolutely false. It eliminated nuance and looked at the complex world in absolutist terms.

From the US perspective, I knew that US policy towards Afghanistan was complicated and its interests were not wholly unified. Yet to send troops to invade a people who had nothing to do with al-Qaeda was wrong. Moreover, the Taliban had asked for proof or evidence of the crime. That too was a reasonable thing to ask of another country. This is how extradition orders are produced, one produces the evidence and then the respective state considers its position and acts accordingly. Yet for them to expect that the whole of the Muslim world should stand in solidarity with them after al-Qaeda, an organisation they were sheltering had angered the international community, seemed unreasonable. How could al-Qaeda justify the deaths of thousands of Afghans in order to attack innocent civilians in the twin towers? They knew that the reaction would be swift, the consequences for the population would be immense and yet they still continued. Why? Is that an organisation that thinks about the *Ummah*, the pan-Islamic Muslim community, or only of its own interests? Is that how al-Qaeda thinks about its mission, is it so blind that it is willing to accept the dumping of more bombs in Afghanistan just to fulfil its mad vision? I was not willing to accept this bipolar world because I knew this to be to false vision. Just because the US committed atrocities in Iraq did not mean that al-Qaeda should be my teacher. The act of showing enmity towards non-Muslims just because their compatriots were oppressing Muslims was contradicted by a simple Panshiri who, whilst climbing with some journalists, was being extraordinary helpful to them. I was annoyed, and asked him why he was being so helpful to them?

And he simply replied: 'Why not? What is wrong with helping them? Isn't there a Godly reward in being kind and generous to strangers, wayfarers and guests?' The Panshiri was not living in a them-and-us kind of world. Most Muslims were like that. It made a profound impression on me. I have made friends from the UK, Japan, America, France, and even former Soviet soldiers, and I was not about to be dragged into this bipolar world of good and evil, of light and darkness. The world was nuanced and complex, the Algerian and Afghan civil wars had taught me that.

Now when the rhetoric was being bandied about, my Arab friends stood and listened fixated to the firebrands on Al-Jazeera and then they saw that I was unmoved by this 'Jihad' of al-Qaeda against the Americans. But what had happened to me? Why could I not take such an absolute position? Had I died or something? Had I sold out? Even my wife started to look at me as if there was something wrong with me. Her friends were all taking sides on this imagined 'clash of civilisations' and I wasn't even moving, I was listless. The truth was I was sitting and watching a football match or a film where I knew the ending so I couldn't get into it.

That is not to say that I was some lover of American foreign policy, far from it. The US invasion of Iraq had given birth to terrorism and blind sectarianism and much, much more. As has become increasingly clear the US-led invasion of Iraq was criminal and constituted terrorism just as much as the actions of Assad or al-Qaeda and her sisters. I do believe that the likes of Bush and Blair should be held accountable just as we hold African dictators to account for war crimes in The Hague.

But what was I to do? I was already a marked man by the likes of the Algerian government. During the nineties and the early noughties Arab activists were getting brazenly assassinated in the streets of London with impunity. There were enough GIA supporters in London already that could stick the knife in. Then when Bush made that infamous statement and launched his War on Terror, they labelled Abdullah Azzam as one of those men who had founded al-Qaeda, and here I was in London, his son-in-law enjoying the fruits of British democracy. People were being rounded up left, right and centre, and here I was a friend of bin Laden going about my daily business. I was expecting to be renditioned to Guantanamo at any moment. Many of my friends due to their associations with Osama were getting put on terror lists. Wael Julaidan for instance was deemed a terror financier, and put on a list from which he has only recently managed to have himself removed.[4] Others like Abu Rida, Mohammed Loay Beyazid, was implicated for things that he had no part in. There were wild theories flying around that he was linked to trying to obtain uranium and dirty bombs from the post-Soviet nations as they floundered due to the collapse of the USSR. But it was, as he told me when I met him in 2015, complete nonsense. The US had tried to extradite him but the Sudanese government stepped in and told them quite adamantly that Abu Rida had little to do with 9/11. In fact, the US investigators found little evidence for any of their suspicions and he even invited them to Sudan and took the investigators on the felucca ride on the Nile explaining what his role was in the Afghan-Soviet conflict. Abu Rida, my Syrian companion who had accompanied me to Mazar Sharif, was from an established family in Damascus. His mother, a graduate of the University of Beirut was also employed by the UN and he had all the refinements and connections of Damascene society. He was far from being an Islamist and had no connection to the Islamic movements whatsoever. After graduating in the United States he was immensely moved by the plight in Afghanistan and he joined the war effort. However, the MAK soon discovered that Abu Rida had a knack for logistics, the buying and selling of goods which I believe as a successful businessman, he still uses skilfully. The MAK employed him for that purpose and he built up good connections with suppliers during the war. When the war came to an end he opted to settle in Sudan since he could not return to Syria due to the brutal Assad regime and the possible danger it might cause his family. In Sudan he started up a business and resides there still. Unfortunately for him, he got tarnished due to his association with Osama.

These were just two examples of people falling into the dragnet of the war on terror. What about the son-in-law of Abdullah Azzam? I knew all the same people and was more senior than Abu Rida, so would it not be unreasonable to expect that I was implicated? Moreover, though I did not know the master-mind Khalid Sheikh Mahmoud, I knew the family of this Baluchi *bidoon*.[5] I was good friends with his brothers, one of them was my friend, Abu Hafs who was involved solely with charity work and the other brother, Abed, died during the war in the battle of Jalalabad in 1989. Mahmoud used to teach the Afghan refugees in Sayyaf's camp, he never fought the Soviets nor took part in the civil war that ensued. I believe he probably became a militant once the ISI kicked out all the Arabs from Peshawar and they had to go to Afghanistan, that's probably when he got close to Osama bin Laden and turned into the man who committed those atrocities. With such contacts a CIA analyst sitting in Langley could easily join the dots together and assume that I was someone who needed to be arrested, snatched, extradited or renditioned. Men who knew far less than me had ended up in Bagram and Guantanamo. One of my close friends Mohammed Amin, a friend of Osama bin Laden who fought alongside Massoud, was renditioned to Bagram for his association to Osama.[6] In fact, he had fallen out with Osama bin Laden and left for Massoud. Mohammed Amin came from the Hadramawt valley in Yemen but was born in Medina, the Prophet's city, and was resident in Saudi Arabia just like Osama bin Laden. The only difference was that the latter had Saudi nationality. Mohammed Amin had to renew his residency periodically. Both were longstanding friends who travelled to Afghanistan together. After the end of the war Amin could no longer return to Saudi Arabia and returned to Sanaa, Yemen's capital, to carry on with business. On one such business trip to Bangkok he was arrested by the Thai authorities and then detained until he was interrogated by the Americans. He told me himself that the Americans blindfolded him, and kept him tied up for hours on a plane. It was only when he tasted the water that he knew that he was in Afghanistan. He ended up in Bagram air base where the Americans committed unspeakable crimes. He was interrogated and for ten years he was held without charge: he wasn't even an enemy combatant, he hadn't been captured in Afghanistan. He protested his innocence but Amin told me that he fulfilled all the conditions: he had fought in Afghanistan and he knew bin Laden; that was enough. When they asked him if that was true, he could not deny it, and so they held him thus for years. Not until his family raised the case with the late President Ali Abdullah Saleh was some attention put on his case. But Ali Abdullah Saleh wanted two million dollars to just 'de-radicalise' the likes of him because of course that sort of thing was big business there and here in the UK currently, so the Americans refused. Amin's father appealed to the Saudis seeing that he was born in Medina, but the Saudis said he wasn't one of their nationals so could not be repatriated to the kingdom and so he was forgotten again. It was only when Amin became extremely sick and the Americans didn't want to take on such a liability that they let him go. So in such dangerous circumstances, I decided to remain silent despite the fact that the press was continuously haranguing me and asking me to comment on a situation. I restrained myself, as I knew that my words could easily be twisted and taken out of context. But I guess there was one thing that did save me from the clutches of the Americans: my past pronouncements against al-Qaeda had vindicated me.

And I would have been silent still, had these self-appointed spokesmen not appeared on Al-Jazeera Arabic claiming to articulate the ideas of Sheikh Abdullah. Who were these people? These Salafi-Jihadis who claimed to have been Afghan Arabs, didn't know anything about Jihad and yet here they were pontificating. Why? Who gave them the authority to speak? Irrespective of the legal arguments, why were the likes of Abu Qatada expending millions in legal aid in order to remain in the country and not get deported to a Muslim country?[7] Where is the dignity and honour in that? Where is the manliness from those who claim to be 'Jihadi'? Whoever is not grateful to people is not grateful to God. It was the comments of these rabble-rousers and advice from friends that made me rethink my position with the media.

I asked myself, whether I could appear in front of God and justify myself to him if I just remained silent. And the answer was a resounding no. I couldn't remain silent and so I made tentative steps to explain my position. People didn't like the fact that I didn't endorse bin Laden or al-Qaeda or the Taliban for that matter. I later met men who had spent time in Seydanayya prison, Syria,[8] who became leaders of Ahrar al-Sham who told me that they watched my broadcasts then and harboured dislike for me. But afterwards, when they had experienced war they realised that I was right and they apologised. I also put out my account of the Afghan Arabs to *al-Hayat* newspaper, revealing those things that needed to be revealed, hoping to affect the Arab media landscape which in some ways had fallen into the trap of the War on Terror too. And whilst I faced criticism for my positions and nuance, it seems that by now, it had become quite clear that the false narrative that al-Qaeda and the US were pushing was truly a failed project. God made it such that though my enemies slandered me for my position, God protected my reputation.

TO THE MOUNTAINS

The US invasion of Afghanistan had taken its toll on its people. On one hand you had the Taliban demanding that the Islamic Movement of Afghanistan, known as the Northern Alliance in the West, side with it against the invaders. On the other hand the Rabbani government asked why they should join a movement that had brought the fault on itself? Similarly, the Americans were in Afghanistan to fight al-Qaeda—a handful of Arabs—and yet why had all Afghans become al-Qaeda in their eyes? Incredible crimes were committed against a long-suffering people. This war was going nowhere.

In 2006, I felt that this conflict could not be solved militarily. In Jihad the enemy had to be clear, in reality the conflict in Afghanistan was not clear. People were dying for no reason. I felt that as a former *mujahid*, maybe I should do something about it. Moreover, I had also become a naturalised British citizen and it afforded me more scope to move and travel. I hoped that I could renew the legacy of my father-in-law in Afghanistan. I remember the night before his assassination how he had been knocking on the doors of all the leaders begging them to remain united, to negotiate and not fall into infighting. I hoped to renew that legacy once again. I remember the letters he sent to Massoud pleading with him to remain steadfast and patient and always take the road towards peace.

So it was with this idea in mind that I went to the Afghan embassy at Princes Gate in London to visit an old friend of mine, a *mujahid* and a military attaché to the embassy, Colonel Muslim Hayat. He was an immensely good man. In that visit, I told him that the conflict in Afghanistan didn't have a military solution and that it would only lead to more bloodshed. Colonel Muslim agreed with me and I proposed to visit Afghanistan to see if there was any possibility for opening up dialogue with the various parties.

Colonel Muslim agreed and offered his support, and as we sat in his office watching Al-Jazeera, the governor of Kandahar came out for a press briefing on a military operation. Colonel Muslim reminded me that I knew that governor appearing on the screen, it was Assadullah Khalid from my days in Afghanistan. Khalid might just be the perfect contact to get the ball rolling. He was an old friend of Sayyaf, so I called him and proposed the same idea and he too seemed enthusiastic. Khalid had come to the same conclusion too; Afghanistan knew very little about al-Qaeda and at the same time why should NATO troops stay in Afghanistan? Both parties were dying. People should know why they are fighting and dying. It didn't make sense to the mother receiving her dead son in Oslo or a mother receiving her dead son in Kandahar. So sensing that the time was right, and encouraged by former *mujahideen* friends in London, I decided to return to the mountains not in anger but in peace after a decade-long absence.

I flew to Kandahar to meet Hajji Assadullah Khalid who received me well and I stayed with him for two days. Khalid got me in touch with the brother of President Hamid Karzai, Abdul Qayyoum Karzai. Nowadays President Hamid Karzai is often mistaken for his brother, Abdul Qayyoum. But few realise that President Karzai had always been involved with the *mujahideen* and their messy politics. Whilst the former president is often depicted as an embattled leader or a stooge of the West, few realise that Karzai was a follower of Sibghatullah Mojaddedi's party, the National Liberation Front, and served in the interim government and lost his father to the Taliban. Karzai's brother, Abdul Qayyoum on the other hand, was American-educated and a successful businessman in Afghanistan and the US. Khalid believed that a conversation with the president's brother would help to smooth the proposal through with the president himself.

So I paid a visit to Abdul Qayyoum Karzai in Kandahar and we had a productive meeting. He too liked the idea and spoke to his younger brother about the proposal. Of course we should not forget that no one will ever say that they don't want peace, but often the stumbling blocks are such that peace might not serve their own interests. All parties might gather for peace talks but put such stringent conditions that peace becomes near impossible. Then, all sides will blame the other for the breakdown all the while claiming that they love peace. That has been the way since time immemorial. But nevertheless, the visit was on the whole successful and I found myself on a plane to Kabul where I sat with the Afghan president.

President Hamid Karzai was happy to receive me and honoured me because of my links with Sheikh Abdullah Azzam. He was also happy that we conversed in Persian. He was immensely fond of the language and its poetry. We talked about the proposal at the palace for two hours. Karzai was positive about the idea of peace talks with the Taliban. I think everyone had become war weary, Karzai too was increasingly beleaguered by pressure from the international community. Once I got the agreement from Karzai, I approached the Taliban side in the hope that they too might be positive to these overtures.

I remained in Kabul for another twelve days, and I renewed my contacts with Marshal Faheem, Rabbani, Sayyaf and many others in the capital. It seemed that all my old friends were keen on achieving some sort of peace. Everyone was in agreement that the Americans had to leave, but the question was always how? Should the Americans leave immediately or should there be a gradual withdrawal? Or until the Afghan national army was effective? There were also other issues to contend with. One group, namely the Taliban, wanted the original *mujahideen* leaders to join them in repelling the Americans, but the original *mujahideen* parties believed that fighting the Americans wasn't their fight since it was the Taliban who had brought them to the country in the first place by allowing militant factions like al-Qaeda in their midst. Why should they bear that heavy burden?

I used my stay in Kabul to get in touch with the Taliban. I was initially worried as to how I might be viewed by them. Time has a way of forgetting, might the Taliban view me as an informant paid by the British security services now that I was naturalised? Or would the British security services view my overtures in a suspicious light due to my connection with Abdullah Azzam? Fortunately the British ambassador in Afghanistan was aware of my actions and I was left to get on with my project. My intentions were not misunderstood, thank God.

In the end I discovered a group of Taliban supporters who stayed in Kabul. There was the former Taliban ambassador Abdul Salaam Zayeef[9] who had returned to Kabul after being detained in Guantanamo having been seized by the Pakistanis, the foreign minister Mullah Ahmed Mutawakkil, Abdul Hakim Mujahid the Taliban's representative to the United Nations,[10] and Mullah Arsala Rahmani the Taliban Minister for Education.[11] Some of these men would later join the Afghan Peace Council at considerable risk to their personal safety. These Taliban dignitaries lived in Kabul having been assigned security guards. They received me cordially when I paid them a visit. Especially the late Mullah Arsala Rahmani knew me due to my friendship with Jalaluddin Haqqani. All of them respected and honoured me from the Afghan-Soviet war. Then, after the pleasantries and small talk which went on for several hours, I made my proposal for peace.

Although these Taliban members were no longer involved directly with the Taliban, they still had significant influence and channels within the organisation to pass the proposal on. And they were eventually convinced that this war was a blind alley without any clear goals and benefitted no one. In fact, some of them told me that the Taliban wasn't even aware of al-Qaeda's plans when they found out about it on the news. As I left they promised to pass on the idea to those in the Taliban that had the ability to initiate peace.

My wife told me my return to the mountains in 2006 had rejuvenated me. I felt immense joy at seeing the mountains of Afghanistan and I felt that perhaps I could walk in the same footsteps as my late father-in-law. But of course the first visit was just that: the first step; there now had to be a second and third step. I also realised that it was no good getting one's hopes up, for peace negotiations are long and painful and don't always end in peace. One thing I learnt from my days in Afghanistan was that as mediator I had to be independent and tread very softly. So for instance, if I accepted money from any state actor, I would have to accept their agenda and it would compromise me as an honest broker. So in order to maintain my independence I had to organise my affairs every time I went out. It was a costly initiative from a financial perspective. Eventually in March 2007, I travelled to Saudi Arabia to see Wael Julaidan and another companion, Abu Sahl. Julaidan by now had a travel ban imposed on him due to the UN designating him a financier of terrorism which, frankly speaking, wasn't true. Julaidan always believed that al-Qaeda had destroyed Afghanistan and it was the people of Afghanistan who were paying the price for their actions. Nevertheless, I could see how an outside investigator could interpret the evidence in a different light due to his influence being felt everywhere whether in the aid or the war effort against the Soviets. When I went to see him Julaidan was very supportive of my initiative and got me in contact with Abu Sahl and his lawyer, Dr Mansour Salih. It was this lawyer who proved to be instrumental in the negotiations.

At first, Dr. Salih was not optimistic about the plan when I met him in a hotel lobby in Riyadh. 'The truth', said Dr Salih, 'is that the royal family is tired of Afghanistan because they had supported it and now it has come back to bite them. Bin Laden has given them too many problems and they don't want to reopen that file. Afghanistan was too much of a headache. Just look at the hotel we are in, we have so many security measures because of this issue.' Blow back was an issue then as it is now, and I understood that sentiment completely.

'Do your best,' I replied leaving it in the hands of God, 'I will do what I can.'

'I will try my best to push the peace initiative', Dr Salih promised without raising my expectations too much.

'If', I told him, 'the way is closed, it is closed, I am not an ambassador. God knows that I have tried my best.'

Three months later, Dr Salih called me out of the blue, 'I am in London for a few days, let us meet.' When we met, he informed me that there had been progress. 'The peace initiative', he said, 'was not wholly unacceptable and has gained some traction and it would be a good idea to visit Afghanistan together.' And so we flew to Kabul. There I introduced him to the people he needed to know from all sides in order to report back to those in charge. By now Dr Salih was also convinced by the idea, and the fact that he believed in it, meant that he put his energy and drive behind it and gave the peace initiative more oomph. He left Kabul with the idea that Afghanistan was ready for tentative peace talks. Later on, it was the Afghans who made the request to Saudi Arabia to facilitate peace talks.

I however, had to take a step back, after all these years just like I learnt in Mazar Sharif that day when I thought I could solve the disputes between parties just by visiting Massoud, this thing was bigger than me. It is important to realise that, even though this might have been my child, for the sake of peace, if that really was the goal, one had to step back. After all I was not a state nor was I a representative of the state. But nevertheless even though I was no longer needed I was still invited to Riyadh, Saudi Arabia where I was promptly informed that the green light for peace talks in Mecca had been given. I was joyful. The talks began in 2008, and I went to Saudi Arabia to see how the various parties negotiated.

Now, how successful those talks were remain to be seen but at least the idea that a peaceful settlement is the only way forward had been introduced into the conflict. There were of course other small steps towards peace, from Mullah Omar opening an office of the Taliban in Doha, Qatar to more recently, Hekmatyar being brought in from the cold in the spring of 2017.[12]

And in fact, though I took a back seat at state level, in terms of relations between Saudi Arabia and Afghanistan, I did use my influence as a veteran advising various committees on coming to an agreement. The Europeans and Arab states also wanted to resolve the situation in Afghanistan as many of their sons were serving in a conflict that didn't seem to have a point. And so I travelled from Paris to Doha advising European and Arab stake-holders in trying to come to a peaceful solution. I was also taken on as an adviser to Rabbani's High Peace Council. But peace too has its martyrs: Rabbani was assassinated by the Taliban, as were others. But even that assassination showed that the Taliban were in disarray, for they released two communiqués; one claiming responsibility for his killing and the other denying responsibility for his killing. And despite the passing of Rabbani the peace talks remained on track and returning to the mountains has in some small way led to Hekmatyar finally coming in from the cold and engaging with the peace process. That then is a testimony to the strength of that idea.

A decade on and peace talks are still in progress, they stop, start and stall. Some of the leaders of the *mujahideen* are no more. Since the initial peace talks more developments and more talks have happened. I myself have attended several sessions of the Foundation for Strategic Research where all factions came together for forty-eight hours to discuss candidly how to recon-cile. And yet, here we are still trying to reconcile in 2018. Whilst internal dialogue between the factions is good, what the Afghan factions need—whether Hazara, Sufi, Panshiri, Pashtu or

Taliban—is neutral outside support. I have been assured by Pakistani, Gulf, and European government officials that all they want is to see peace in the region but you get the feeling that perhaps they are still pursuing their own national agendas and interests. What they do not understand is that now looms a new threat on the horizon, which will affect all of them. ISIS, that *takfiri* group that seem to revel in blowing up innocent civilians are here and they are gaining serious ground in Afghanistan. It seems that even al-Zawahiri cannot control what he has unleashed and we will see an increase in death and violence if the parties do not come together to resolve the issue. Stabilising Afghanistan is the only option.

Nevertheless I ask myself, will all this blood, treasure, and peace initiatives have been worth it? Is this an issue of being afflicted with attitudes and mentalities that we have as we shed the shackles of colonialism? Maybe, it is the role of outside actors, neighbours or nation-state actors with agendas that do not want to see peace in Afghanistan. Or perhaps in the light of the Arab Spring, the Syrian conflicts and others in the Muslim world, it is simply the case that we are our own worst enemies, we shed blood with ease and we squabble, unwilling to tolerate each other's positions. I see that this seems to be the issue of our times. I pray that God removes this affliction from our souls. Sometimes one's Jihad is not against one's external enemies but against one's own inner enemy.

EPILOGUE

It is ironic that I, Abdullah Anas, having left for the mountains hoping to achieve martyrdom, to kick out the Soviets, have become so vehemently opposed to bloodshed. I believe now more than ever, that being a peacemaker is the greatest Jihad.

Why? Because we live in such confusing times. It is as the Prophet predicted, there will come a time when the killed will not know why he was killed and neither will the killer know as to why he killed. As such we cannot look at the world in black and white terms. Neither can we afford to have mentalities that remain ossified, we cannot let various titles cloud and hide the issues that are really at stake. Adding the word 'Islamic' '*dawah*' or 'sheikh' to something does not change the nature of the thing. Adding the word sheikh to Osama or Zawahiri does not change the fact that they are men with no formal religious training. Their pronouncements do not suddenly become fatwas.

The Muslim world can easily find martyrs but what it urgently and desperately needs are statesman, negotiators, advisors, scholars, and intellectuals who understand their times and peoples. We must re-examine how we as Muslims interact with the outside non-Muslim world and indeed within the Muslim world and hope therein to find peace.

We need to reassess this idea of offensive Jihad. Times have changed, there isn't a justification for it any more in the world that we live in. We don't live in an age of empires. Much blood has been shed and these men who caused it then 'repent' and regret what they did because of an idea. But think about it, how easy was it to take a life? Do these men not realise what sacrilege it is to take one soul, Muslim or otherwise? It is almost tantamount to infidelity. This is something that isn't stressed enough amongst our youth. Killing has become too easy for all sides. It is not for no reason that God warns Muslims not to shed blood, it is as if he was warning Muslims, that whilst we may no longer fall into brazen polytheism we will shed our coreligionists' blood without conscience and compunction.

Whilst I agree that foreign policy has indeed impacted the thinking of our youth in the Muslim world, this 'exiting' factor does not mean that we should harbour unacceptable ideas. This idea that al-Qaeda has propagated is found in ISIS. For what are ISIS' tactics but the same tactics that al-Qaeda used to taunt the US with? And who in the end suffered? Afghans, Iraqis, Somalis, Yemenis and many others who became victim to this so called 'War on Terror'.

I will never denounce Jihad; Jihad will continue to the end of days. As a Muslim I know this to be a noble deed, the peak of perfection—where man can be the most beastly, he chooses to be humane. Jihad has rules, it decides, who, where, and when to fight. It does not choose the path of revenge and hatred but rather the path of mercy. Fighting is not something to look forward to but sometimes you have to fight to defend home and hearth and that is something I believe in. And if such things should occur again, I would not hesitate to return to the mountains again.

And yet whilst defensive Jihad will always be valid as long as there is oppression and occupation, offensive Jihad what is known as *Jihad al-Talab*, on the other hand, is no longer valid. Islamic jurisprudence has always divided Jihad into its defensive and offensive components. Offensive Jihad as understood by many jurists and lawyers of the past, allowed the fighting of non-Muslims in order to remove the impediments that prevented Islam from spreading in those countries. Namely, if the the political powers that be in a country did not allow for the peaceful preaching of Islam, Muslims could fight them.

I don't believe those conditions based on evidence then, are valid and will be valid in the future. I find them unconvincing. I believe that the door must be closed, and that the excuses, reasons and conditions that many of the jurists gave for Jihad's offensive use do not apply in our modern age. Why should we fight a people irrespective of their religion just to bring them into the sphere of Islam even if they don't convert? I don't believe this to be acceptable then or now. Remember these jurists were discussing their times when territory was fluid, nation states did not exist and did not possess weapons of mass destruction that could wipe out an entire nation with the press of just one button!

Moreover, I think as Muslims we have to re-examine our past. For sure Islamic history has produced great men and women but Islamic history is part of human history and has been driven by impulses that drive us all. Some of these conquests were used to satisfy Umayyad or Abbasid imperial ambitions. When we 'opened up Spain' we called it 'Fath' or liberation but when imperial powers did it to us in the nineteenth century we called it imperialism and aggression. We need to move away from salvation history and be fair with ourselves. Admittedly, that is not easy. We should be able to be honest with our past and moreover come to terms with it. Something traumatic has happened to us called colonisation and that has changed us forever. We cannot go back to a glorious golden age of Andalusia. We have to accept Divine decree.

Now we are in urgent need for our thinkers to re-examine our past and question it and help us come to terms with it. How does the idea of offensive Jihad sit with the idea of there not being any compulsion in our faith? If God wanted he could have made everyone believe in Islam and yet he gives us the freedom to choose our faith. In the UK right now, I can set up a TV channel and providing I fulfil my OFCOM license I can say Islam is true and Mohammed is the Messenger of God and more. So long as I don't incite hatred against another and I give a fair and balanced view, I am free to proselytise, pray and so on. So what need do I have to remove the impediments in this country? The conditions and circumstances of the medieval era or imperial times are different from the times that we live in. It is no good to cite Ibn Taymiyyah, a thirteenth-century scholar's opinion towards non-Muslims when he had the Tatars knocking on his door, the response is going to be drastically different from our own. Perhaps instead of relying on a thirteenth-century scholar and thinker we should try to come up with our own thinkers.

Our thinkers need to look at what should be done about offensive Jihad against countries that oppress Muslims or put immense restrictions on Muslims such as China or indeed Myanmar. This is an interesting debate which scholars and jurists of the Muslim world need to discuss and answer. Moreover in the light of the Arab Spring, so much has been said about Quranic injunctions to obey the ruler even when they oppress you. We rely on books again from the medieval scholars who lived in the times of sultans and kings when the state itself was small in comparison to now. We demand obedience when perhaps it is an obligation to speak up against the rulers' transgressions. Why have these concepts ossified within our tradition? In fact, why do Muslims say democracy for instance is forbidden in our Islamic tradition when we find many of those same elements in the political life of the early Muslims? It is not to reform but to look again at our past and come to a solution that allows for dialogue, and accountability in the decision-making process. The privilege of citizenship and political power should not be monopolised by one group or another, whether they be a liberal, Muslim Brotherhood or of any other political persuasion. It is the abuse of these privileges, and the presence of despotic rulers and the inability of some of the opposition to offer an inclusive vision for all its members, that has created some of the tragic situations that I have mentioned in this book.

NOTES

1. FROM WHENCE I CAME

1. I have relied on Alistair Horne's *A Savage War of Peace: Algeria 1954–1962*, New York: New York Review of Books, 2006 for the narrative events of Algerian independence.
2. For a discussion on those tactics and comparison to ISIS Jihadists, see Tam Hussein, 'Paradise lost: The Rise and Fall of Abu Bakr al-Baghdadi', MENA ETC, 24 March 2017, http://www.tamhussein.co.uk/2017/04/paradise-lost-rise-fall-abu-bakr-al-baghdadi/.
3. The cruelty of the siege of Algiers is best reflected in the fictional novel based on real events of Jean Lartéguy, *The Centurions*, London: Penguin, 2015 with foreword by Robert D. Kaplan. One of the main protagonists is based on Paul Aussaresses, a notorious French commander who used torture to break the siege. See Douglas Martin, 'Paul Aussaresses, the man who tortured Algerians dies', *New York Times*, 4 December 2013.
4. *Ulama* (plural) for *Alim* (sing.) means learned scholars.
5. See Al-Jazeera profile of Mahfoudh Nahnah: http://www.aljazeera.net/amp/encyclopedia/icons/2014/11/20/محفوظ-نحناح.
6. I am aware that Syed Qutb is a controversial figure in the West and is seen as a radical figure. But Qutb's works can be interpreted in various ways and as such both the Brotherhood and Salafi-Jihadists claim him as their own, and he is interpreted differently according to the ideas subscribed to. Certainly the case can be made for both: he is an ambiguous figure, and his views certainly hardened following his imprisonment

by Nasser, but he cannot be ignored in understanding the Islamic movement. See for instance an interpretation of Muqtedar Khan, 'Syed
Qutb—John Locke of the Islamic World', Brookings, 28 July 2003,
https://www.brookings.edu/articles/syed-qutb-john-locke-of-the-
islamic-world/. Similarly, I am aware that Abdullah Azzam can be
interpreted in many ways. See for instance Thomas Hegghammer, *The
Caravan: Abdullah Azzam and the Rise of Global Jihad*, Cambridge:
Cambridge University Press, forthcoming, who looks at him in a different light from Abdullah Anas.

7. See John W. Kiser, *Commander of the Faithful: The Life and Times of
   Emir Abd el-Kader*, Archetype, 2008 and also Ira M. Lapidus, *A History
   of Islamic Societies*, Cambridge: Cambridge University Press, 1988, also
   Albert A. Hourani, *History of the Arab Peoples*, New York: Faber and
   Faber, 1992.

8. See also 'Asharq Al-Awsat interviews Umm Mohammed: The Wife
   of Bin Laden's Spiritual Mentor', 30 April 2006, https://eng-archive.
   aawsat.com/theaawsat/features/asharq-al-awsat-interviews-umm-
   mohammed-the-wife-of-bin-ladens-spiritual-mentor. The wife of
   Abdullah Azzam describes how they met and his background.

9. Founded by the Iraqi Jurist Abu Hanifa in Baghdad in the eighth century. See Jonathan A.C. Brown, *Misquoting Muhammad: The Challenge
   and Choices of Interpreting the Prophet's Legacy*, Oneworld Publications,
   2014, also George Makdisi, *The Rise of Colleges: Institutions of Learning
   in Islam and the West*, Edinburgh University Press, 1981, also Wael
   Hallaq, *An Introduction to Islamic Law*, Cambridge University Press,
   2009, and *The Origins and Evolution of Islamic Law*, Cambridge
   University Press, 2005.

2. ON THE ROAD TO AFGHANISTAN

1. Members of the Islamic movement or *Harakat al-Islamiya* in Arabic are
   also known as *Harakatis*. In Afghanistan this refers to the modernist or
   Brotherhood-inspired Islamic revivalist political movement that differed
   from the Tablighi movement which draws its inspiration from the
   Deobandi movement in the Indian subcontinent and Afghanistan.
   Sometimes the former's members are also referred to in the West as

Islamic modernists. For simplicity I will refer to them as Islamists in line with the Arabic term, *Islamiyūn*, in this book.

2. See David B. Edwards, *Before Taliban: Genealogies of the Afghan Jihad*, University of California Press, 2002.

3. Sayyaf, Abdur Rasul, later Abd al-Rab Rasul Sayyaf became the leader of Ettehad-i Islami bara-yi Azadi-yi Afghanistan (Islamic Union for the Liberation of Afghanistan). According to Edwards, Sayyaf with his eloquent Arabic and connection to the Gulf managed to internationalise the Jihad in the Muslim world. See David B. Edwards, *Before Taliban*, pp. 289–90.

4. See Edwards, *Before Taliban*, p. xi.

5. See the obituary of Burhanuddin Rabbani, BBC, http://www.bbc. co.uk/news/world-south-asia-14992226. There are differences as to who emerged as the main leader of this cluster of activists. Hezb and Jamiat-i Islami narratives differ so I have relied on outside sources to verify and give as accurate semblance of events as possible. For instance some accounts suggest that Jamiat-i Islami began after 1976 not 1972 after the split between Rabbani and Hekmatyar.

6. Alex Strick van Linschoten, Felix Kuehn, *An Enemy We Created: The Myth of the Taliban-Al Qaeda Merger in Afghanistan*, London: Hurst, 2012, p. 455.

7. In Afghanistan the word 'Engineer' is an honorific title to any one affiliated to the faculty. The student may never have graduated or may have studied only for several months nevertheless he takes on the title Engineer. These sorts of honorific titles were also given to medical students who may still be referred to as a 'Doctor' even if they never finished their medical degree.

8. See the obituary of Burhanuddin Rabbani in *The Guardian*, https://www.theguardian.com/world/2011/sep/21/burhanuddin-rabbani-obituary.

9. Rodric Braithwaite, *Afgantsy: the Russians in Afghanistan 1979–89*, Profile, 2012, p. 139.

10. See Ludwig W. Adamec, *Historical Dictionary of Afghanistan*, Scarecrow Press, 4th edn, 2012, p. xlvii.

11. The plan similar to Guevara's idea of revolutionary cells that would

lead the people didn't work. Olivier Roy, *Islam and Resistance in Afghanistan*, Cambridge University Press, 1990, pp. 75–6.

12. Ludwig W. Adamec, *Historical Dictionary of Afghanistan*, p. 195; see also Steve Coll, *Ghost Wars: The Secret History of the CIA, Afghanistan, and bin Laden from the Soviet Invasion to September 10, 2001*, Penguin, 2005, p. 113.

13. Mawlawi Younes Khalis was the leader of Hezb-i Islami Afghanistan, and he too had links with Muslim Youth organisation and fled to Peshawar after his son was arrested by the Daoud regime. According to Edwards he ran a small shop in Peshawar but later took on the mantle of Hezb-i Islami when it had been disbanded after the Hekmatyar-Rabbani split. See Edwards, *Before Taliban*, pp. 270–71.

14. Gailani, Sayyid Ahmad was a descendant from one of the Muslim world's greatest saints, Abdel Qadir al-Jilani, (d. 1119) the founder of the Sufi brotherhood or the Qadiri *Tariqa* diffused in the Caucasus, Central Asia and the Middle East. Gailani was the leader of Mahaz-i Milli Islami Afghanistan, National Islamic Front of Afghanistan, which he founded in 1978. Although the Sufi *pirs* did not have such a large impact on the Afghan-Soviet conflict in comparison to the others. Traditionally *pirs* or sufis hailing from a holy lineage were respected for the influence they exerted in Afghan and indeed Muslim society.

15. Mujaddidi, Sibghatullah, leader of Jabha-yi Nejat-i Milli Afghanistan, the National Salvation of Afghanistan, was the grandnephew of a famous sufi, Hazrat of Shor Bazaar. The Mujaddidis descend from the great religious reviver or as he was known Mujaddid (hence the name), Ahmed Sirhindi, the seventeenth-century scholar, sufi and jurist whose family settled in Afghanistan. Traditionally they were an influential family. Sibghatullah Mujaddidi had a secular education but later chose to study in Cairo's al-Azhar University and followed Ghulam Muhammad Niyazi a year later. The former graduated in Islamic jurisprudence in 1953. He later went into exile in Copenhagen following Daoud Khan's coup only returning to Peshawar in 1978.

16. Mohammed Nabi Muhammadi, leader of Harakat-i Inqilabi-yi Islami Afghanistan, Islamic Revolution Movement of Afghanistan. Nabi was a respected scholar and member of parliament for Barak-i Barak in

Logar province in 1969. He was a vociferous opponent of the Communists in Parliament. He also had a good relationship with Muslim Youth and so was seen as a compromise candidate for the leadership when the Hekmatyar and Rabbani split occurred. Nabi's party was seen as one that could act as the umbrella organisation for both.

17. This *Tazkiya* also occurred with foreign fighters in Syria joining battalions, they would be asked for a recommendation.

3. THE ROAD TO SHOLGARA NEAR MAZAR SHARIF

1. Abu Mus'ab al-Zarqawi or Ahmad Fadil al-Nazal al-Khalayleh was a Jordanian national from the village of Zarqa who became the founder. of al-Qaeda in Iraq. Zarqawi went to fight in Afghanistan in 1989 but only caught the tail end of the war when the Soviets had already left. It was said that he met Abu Muhammed al-Maqdisi, his mentor, in Peshawar. He returned to Jordan where he was arrested for plotting attacks in Jordan and imprisoned. Inside prison it is believed that he met Abu Humam al-Rifa'i and became further hardened in his views. Zarqawi was released in 1999 as a result of a general amnesty. He fled to Pakistan and subsequently to Afghanistan following a series of terror plots in Jordan. Zarqawi met al-Qaeda but had an uneasy relationship with them, and he set up his own camps in Herat, Afghanistan. He was involved in militant activity till his death in June 2006. After 9/11 Zarqawi participated in fighting the US invasion. In 2003, Zarqawi moved to northern Iraq following the invasion of Iraq and was involved with some of the worst sectarian violence in the country.

2. Ayman Mohammed Rabie al-Zawahiri is the current leader of Al-Qaeda. He is from an established Cairene family, and trained as a surgeon at Cairo University. He joined Islamic Jihad whilst working in a Egyptian military hospital. From Saudi Arabia he moved to Pakistan in the mid 80s where he worked as a medic in one of the hospitals. Though separate, Zawahiri announced the merger of his organisation, Islamic Jihad and al-Qaeda in 1998. He remains at large and involved with the Syrian conflict where he has sided with the Nusra Front as opposed to ISIS.

3. Abu Hamza al-Masri, Mustafa Kamel Mustafa, was former preacher of Finsbury Park mosque. He was a known radical Imam in London dur-

ing the nineties. He was convicted on incitement and other charges and, despite appeals, was extradited to the US relating to hostages in Yemen in 1998, where he remains incarcerated. His son Sufiyan Kemal is currently fighting in Syria. Jamie Grierson, 'Abu Hamza's son stripped of UK passport', *The Guardian*, 2 April 2017 https://www.theguardian.com/world/2017/apr/02/abu-hamzas-son-stripped-of-uk-passport.

4. Abu Qatada al-Filistini, or Omar Mahmoud Othman, is a Jordanian national of Palestinian descent from Bethlehem. Critics accuse him of being an al-Qaeda member but this does not seem to be accurate. After a brief stint in Peshawar in the 90s, Abu Qatada sought political asylum in the UK and received it in 1993. There, he busied himself with Islamist activity, teaching and delivering his sermons on Fridays in Lisson Green Fourth Feather's Youth Club. He was known to be a supporter of and provided advice to militant groups such as the Algerian GIA. He was the editor of *al-Ansar* magazine in London. In London he was involved with several disputes including Abu Humam al-Rifa'i the 'caliph of Lisson Green' and more famously with Sheikh Abdullah el-Faysal who was associated with Takfiri and Jihadi thought in the 90s. Both the Algerian and Jordanian governments asked for Abu Qatada to be extradited due to his alleged links to militancy in the respective countries. Abu Qatada was repeatedly imprisoned and released under various charges from anti-terrorism laws to immigration to bail violations. Eventually he was deported to Jordan in 2013 to stand trial for a terror plot in 1999. He was cleared of the charges on the grounds of insufficient evidence.

5. According to Abdullah Anas this family had originally fled Saddam Hussein, then could not return to Samarra after the sectarianisation of Iraq under Maliki and later because ISIS controlled his town. Abu'l Jud remains in limbo to this day.

6. Mawlawi is an honorific term in South Asian culture which denotes extensive religious learning. It usually describes someone who has completed higher studies in a religious seminary. It is similar to the word 'sheikh' used in the Arab world. Mawlawi is Arabic in origin stemming from the word Mawla which means protector.

7. Abu Usayd lost his life in the mid-2000s in Waziristan, Pakistan. Due to him fighting in Afghanistan he could not return to Syria and remained

in limbo in Waziristan until I received news that he had been killed, the cause of which remains a mystery.

8. Wael Julaidan, also known as Abu'l Hassan, was one of the founders of the Arab Services Bureau in Afghanistan alongside Abdullah Anas. He was also president of the World Muslim League, Arab Red Crescent and so forth. Later on he became associated with bin Laden's al-Qaeda and placed under a worldwide embargo by the United Nations which was lifted in 2014. Abdullah Anas maintains that Wael Julaidan was not a supporter of al-Qaeda. See the 'Treasury Department Statement on the Designation of Wa'el Hamza Julaidan', 6 Sep. 2002: https://www.treasury.gov/press-center/press-releases/Pages/po3397.aspx. Julaidan has succeeded in winning his case to remove his name from the sanctions list. He is now free to travel after his name was delisted in 2014. See United Nations, Security Council, 'Al-Qaida Sanctions Committee Deletes Wa'el Hamza Abd al-Fatah Julaidan from Its Sanctions List', 26 Aug. 2014, https://www.un.org/press/en/2014/sc11534.doc.htm.

9. Qadi is also an Arabic word for a judge or jurisprudent.

4. IN SEARCH OF MASSOUD

1. See for instance the extraordinary account by Marcela Grad, *Massoud: an Intimate Portrait of the Legendary Afghan Leader*, Webster University Press, 2009. Grad collects the accounts of the people who met Massoud and paints an extraordinary picture of him.

2. For CIA and ISI support of Hekmatyar see Steve Coll, *Ghost Wars: The Secret History of the CIA, Afghanistan, and bin Laden from the Soviet Invasion to September 10, 2001*, Penguin, 2005, pp. 119–20. The CIA 'embraced Hekmatyar as their most effective and dependable ally.'

3. Massoud claims to have received only eight stinger missiles out of the two thousand missiles supplied by the CIA according to Gary Schroen, in Steve Coll, *Ghost Wars*, p. 12.

4. No direct reference but see Hashmat Moslih, 'Afghanistan in the Shadow of Ahmed Shah Massoud' Al-Jazeera, Sep. 2014, https://www.aljazeera.com/indepth/opinion/2014/09/afghanistan-shadow-ahmad-shah-mas-2014997826874331.html.

5. Sahib is an honorific respectful title of Arab origin. Amir Sahib was the honorific title that Afghans used for Massoud. Afghans never called him

by his surname, the same way many Muslims never called the Prophet Muhammed by his name, rather they call him Rasool Allah, 'The Messenger of God' or Nabi, 'the Prophet'; similarly Massoud would be called Amir Sahib out of reverence. In fact, anyone of distinction would be referred to this way in common with the subcontinent in general.

6. Qari is also a religious title which refers to someone who can recite Quran in one or more Quranic recitation styles applying also the correct rules of Quranic pronunciation, *Tajweed*.

7. A Quranic *surah* or chapter.

8. The art of Quranic recitation.

9. Mohammmed Abu Asim was an Iraqi Kurd from Erbil and was killed attacking a Communist base in the battle of Andarab in late 1986. Abdullah Anas buried him with his own hands.

6. MY FIRST BATTLE WITH MASSOUD

1. See also Sandy Gall's account of KHAD and KGB cooperation in *Afghanistan: the Agony of a Nation*, Bodley Head, 1988.

7. HEKMATYAR

1. According to a report by International Crisis Group, Qari Saeed presented himself to the GIA leadership, Mansour Miliani, as a Qutbist and represented Ayman Al-Zawahiri's Islamic Jihad group in Peshawar. Qari convinced Miliani that he was under the leadership of Ayman Al-Zawahiri, and Miliani accepted their support. See International Crisis Group, 'Islamism, Violence and Reform in Algeria: Turning the Page', ICG Middle East Report Nr. 29, Cairo/Brussels, 30 July 2004. Available at: https://d2071andvip0wj.cloudfront.net/29-islamism-violence-and-reform-in-algeria-turning-the-page.pdf. The former Col. Mohammed Samraoui of the DRS from the Algerian Intelligence and Security Directorate in his *Chronique des années de sang*, the *Chronicles of the Years of Blood*, recounts how the security services had infiltrated the GIA and carried out extra-judicial killings and more. He claimed that Qari Saeed was an DRS asset. Abdullah Anas finds this claim extremely implausible, even though he was surprised at him falling under Zawahiri's influence and joining the GIA in 1992, because Anas knows his family and knows him so well that the assertion seems unlikely.

2. Ali Amin al-Rashidi also known as Abu Ubaidah al-Banshiri, was an Egyptian policeman who joined the Afghan Jihad fighting alongside Ahmed Shah Massoud despite being associated with the *takfiri* organisation Islamic Jihad. His brother was involved in the assassination of the Egyptian president Sadat and left Egypt following the security crackdown on Islamists. He gained his name al-Banshiri due to participating in the battle of Annahrayn and took part in the Battle of Jaji in 1987. He was part of Osama bin Laden's inner circle. He drowned in lake Victoria following the capsizing of a ferry in May 1996.

3. Mohammed Atef al-Masri, Sobhi Abu Sitta, also known by his *nom de guerre* Abu Hafs al-Masri became one of Osama bin Laden's senior deputies in al-Qaeda and was perhaps the most experienced militarily. Before going to Afghanistan he served in the Egyptian military and as a police officer before joining Islamic Jihad. He went to Afghanistan following the assassination of President Anwar Sadat 1981. He has been linked to the Black Hawk Down incident in Somalia in 1992 when eighteen US marines died, and was purportedly the mastermind behind the US embassy bombings in 1998. He was killed in November 2001 and was one of the founding members of al-Qaeda.

4. Arab names are extremely confusing for Westerners. In Arab traditional society, whether Muslim or non-Muslim, knowing one's forefathers is a source of pride and is one distinctive characteristic of Arab as opposed to 'Ajam (non-Arab) societies. Arab names traditionally consists of a name, *ism*, e.g Osama, followed by a *nasab*, *ibn* or *bin* meaning son, which is followed by the father's name. Osama bin Laden means Osama the son of Laden. In the Quran, Eesa ibn Maryam, Jesus the son of Mary, is a rare expression. Rarely is the child's mother given attribution, and the fact that Jesus is referred to as the son of Mary serves as a device to negate the Christian position that God is the father of Jesus. Sometimes an Arab might just be referred to by his father's name for example, the famous historian Ibn Khaldun, the son of Khaldun. He might also have a *laqab*, a nickname, which can be a descriptive epithet or title. Abu Hamid Muhammad al-Ghazali, an eleventh century scholar and mystic for instance had a *laqab*, *Hujjatul Islam*—the proof of Islam. It is an indication of his status. The great Seljuk vizier Nizam al-Mulk

is another example, whose real name was Ali, but was known by his title and status: 'The Order of the Realm'. Arab names might also have a *nisbah*, the place you are from. For instance, al-Farisi or al-Britani, from Persia or Britain. In modern Jihadi terminology the *nisbah* is used sometimes to denote a battle one has taken part in. For instance, Abu Ubaidah al-Banshiri, a senior member of al-Qaeda, took part in Massoud's battles and became known as Panshiri even though he was an Arab. The Companions who took part in the Prophet's battle of Badr in 624 CE added al-Badri to their name; in other words they were the veterans of Badr and thereby had a special status in the early Muslim community. It is worth Nothing that in traditional Arab culture staying with a people for more than forty days meant that one became of them as the Prophet relates in one of his sayings. In the case of many British Jihadists with identity issues currently fighting in Syria, they might add a *nisbah* according to where they are from, al-Britani (Britain), or where their fathers are from, al-Somali (Somalia) or what they follow, e.g. al-Salafi (they follow Wahabism), and will use them interchangeably. 'Kunya' or paedonymic is also used by many Arabs interchangeably. Being a father is an honour in Muslim cultures. A man can be referred to in relation to his first born son, so Osama bin Laden was also known as Abu Abdullah, meaning Father of Abdullah (his first born). If the man has no son, then he will be known by the daughter's name, as in Abu Maryam: the Father of Mary. The Kunya is a sign of respect and honour. In Syrian culture, a man might be known as the possessor of his father. So Abu Walid literally means 'Possessor of Walid' that is my father's name is Walid. The problem occurs when every single son of Walid calls himself Abu Walid. Here it is being used as a patronymic. Confusingly, Kunya is also used as a *nom de guerre* amongst modern Jihadists to hide their real identity or what they aspire to, hence a lot of Jihadists adopt the name Abu Dujanah after the famous warrior companion to emulate him. Kunyas have also been used by many secular Pan-Arabist or Marxist Palestinian militant organisations; Abu Nidal is one example. It can also be used affectionately to denote closeness and as a nickname. The famous companion who was known as Abu Hurayrah, the father of kittens, was called thus because of his love for cats. Kunyas can also be used to denote mastery of a profession. 'Umm'—meaning 'Mother'—is the female version. So Osama bin Laden means Osama the son of Laden, his 'Kunya' is Abu Abdullah, because his first born son is Abdullah, and the mother of Abdullah would be known as Umm Abdullah.

5. God is Most Great.

6. There is no power or might but God's.

8. POLITICKING IN PESHAWAR AND THE ENTRY OF EXTREMISTS

1. There are of course other accounts that suggest that the Taliban emerged as early as 1983 according to some of their members. This account according to Abdullah Anas seems to be implausible. See Alex Strick Van Linschoten and Felix Kuehn, *The Taliban Reader: War, Islam and Politics*, London: Hurst & Co., 2018, pp. 13–15; see Abdul Salam Zaeef's account.

2. See James Rupert, 'Afghanistan Rebels Lose Key Battle', *Washington Post*, 8 July 1989, https://www.washingtonpost.com/archive/politics/1989/07/08/afghanistan-rebels-lose-key-battle/074ff765327d-4a60-b8ab-ed118a87ba50/, see also Richard M. Weintraub, 'Bhutto Asserts Role in Afghan Policy', *Washington Post*, 22 May 1989, https://www.washingtonpost.com/archive/politics/1989/05/22/bhutto-asserts-role-in-afghan-policy/72feb814-a569-4325-807c-a95d891d3fc8/. The Jalalabad offensive according to Bill Collum for the *Washington Post*, 'The CIA Bungled it', notes that Hekmatyar's men were also involved in having kidnapped and tortured Massoud's men. In fact, the reporter says that three quarters of *mujahideen* internecine warfare is linked to Hezb-i Islami.

3. Ludwig W. Adamec and Frank A. Clements, *Conflict in Afghanistan: A Historical Encyclopaedia*, ABC Clio, 2003, pp. 106–8. The authors say Hekmatyar received the 'bulk of the support from the United States channeled through Pakistan... His *mujahideen* group was the most destructive antisocial unit, carrying out a number of terrorist attacks in Afghanistan'.

4. It is important to define terms here—for whilst we will use the word

extremist we will use it according to how it has been defined by the Prophet Muhammed not how it has been defined by many Western analysts. This is for the following reasons: the word extremism has become loaded and agenda-led and overused in the West, so much so that it has become a badge of honour to extremists. However, the Prophet uses the word '*mutanatti*' and this is the word Anas means when he uses the word extremist. Abdullah b. Massoud, one of the Companions of the Prophet and a great narrator of *hadith* in Islam [2670] has said that the Prophet said: 'the *Mutanatt'een* will perish!' He said it three times. What does this mean? Extremism as defined by the Prophet is the lack of mercy, and ease, and an excess of harshness and zealotry in behaviour, faith and religious matters. So when Anas uses the word extremist this is what he means.

9. THE BROKEN TRUCE

1. For instance, Commanders Faheem Khan, Ghada, Mohamed Pana, Salih Registani, Muslim, Mohammed Aryanpour, Sarmuallim Tariq, Syed Ekramuddin, Bismillah, Abdullah, Amir Mujahid, Syed Najmuddin and others.

2. Hamid Gul had advised that a slow drawn out war of attrition against Jalalabad would lead to success but it was General Baber's advice of a full frontal assault that prevailed according to Henry Kamm, 'Pakistan Officials Tell Of Ordering Afghan Rebel Push', *New York Times*, 23 Apr. 1989, https://www.nytimes.com/1989/04/23/world/pakistan-officials-tell-of-ordering-afghan-rebel-push.html. Kamm also notes that 14,000 Afghan rebels pushed for a conventional all-out war against the regime. They were woefully inadequate and indisciplined. There were issues of indiscipline where government forces were massacred as they were surrounded as well as the creation of 30,000 to 40,000 refugees according to Western diplomatic estimates. See Henry Kamm, 'The Lessons Of Jalalabad; Afghan Guerrillas See Weaknesses Exposed', *New York Times*, 13 Apr. 1989, https://www.nytimes.com/1989/04/13/world/the-lessons-of-jalalabad-afghan-guerrillas-see-weaknesses-exposed.html.

3. Abdul Haq was a charismatic *mujahideen* leader and part of the Hezb-i Islami Yunus Khalis faction. He was an able Pashtun commander who did not take part in the ensuing civil war following the fall of Kabul.

He returned after 9/11 and was executed by the Taliban on 26 Oct. 2001. See Anatol Lieven's interview with him here: https://carnegieendowment.org/2001/10/14/on-road-interview-with-commander-abdul-haq-pub-818. On the Jalalabad offensive he said 'It is dumb to attack Jalalabad ... because it is dumb to lose ten thousand lives ... There's no way the mujahidin can take the city now', in Robert Kaplan, *Soldiers of God*, New York: Vintage Books, 1990, p. 166.

4. There were repeated accusations by human rights groups that Hekmatyar's group was involved with eliminating his enemies. See for instance the death of Sayed Bahauddin Majrooh, Anthony Hyman, 'In Memoriam: Professor Sayed Bahauddin Majrooh', *Central Asian Survey*, 7:2–3 (2007): 209–12, DOI: 10.1080/02634938808400639. See Barnett Rubin, 'Hard Choices for Peace', *The New Yorker*, 18 Oct. 2016, https://www.newyorker.com/news/news-desk/hard-choices-for-peace-in-afghanistan, who links the academic's death to Hekmatyar and his followers. See also The Afghanistan Justice Project, 'Casting Shadows: War Crimes and Crimes against Humanity: 1978–2001', documentation and analysis of major patterns of abuse in the war in Afghanistan, https://www.opensocietyfoundations.org/sites/default/files/ajpreport_20050718.pdf.

5. Mamdouh Mahmud Salim was an Iraqi Arab who will be discussed later in the book. The media has depicted him as a very senior member of al-Qaeda and close to Osama bin Laden and associated with the American embassy bombings in East Africa. He is currently serving life without parole. See for instance Benjamin Weiser, 'Reputed bin Laden Adviser Gets Life Term in Stabbing', *New York Times*, 31 Aug. 2010 https://www.nytimes.com/2010/09/01/nyregion/01salim.html.

6. Professor Abdul Sabur was assassinated by unknown gunmen on 3 May 2007, see http://news.bbc.co.uk/1/hi/world/south_asia/6618127.stm.

7. See Human Rights Watch Report in 1991, V: 'Human Rights Violations by Elements of the Afghan Resistance', https://www.hrw.org/reports/1991/afghanistan/5AFGHAN.htm.

10. WHEN KABUL FELL, MY WORLD FELL

1. Mustafa Shalabi was the director of al-Kifah. See Peter Lance, 'The Prince of Jihad is Dead', *Huffington Post*, 18 Feb. 2017 https://www.huff-

ingtonpost.com/entry/the-prince-of-jihad-is-dead-will-the-blind-sheikhs_us_58a8a6fde4b0b0e1e0e20ba7.

2. A place to pray rather than a mosque per se, that is it didn't hold the obligatory five daily prayers in congregation as mosques do, and didn't necessarily have an imam or provide other pastoral services.

3. Mary B. W. Tabor, 'Slaying in Brooklyn Linked to Militants', *New York Times*, 11 Apr. 1993, https://www.nytimes.com/1993/04/11/nyregion/slaying-in-brooklyn-linked-to-militants.html.

4. This Quranic chapter is considered to be important for it has references to Jihad and fighting and moreover, although the chapter is called *Taubah*, repentance, it does not start as do other chapters with the *Bismillah*—that is with the words 'in the Name of God the Most Merciful the Most Beneficent'. Sheikh Omar's PhD thesis was on this chapter.

5. There are differing accounts regarding Mawlawi Jamil ur-Rahman Husain (1933–92). Adamec et al say that he broke with Hekmatyar in 1982, grabbed power in Kunar and imposed an Islamic regime. See Ludwig W. Adamec and Frank A. Clements, *Conflict in Afghanistan: A Historical Encyclopaedia*, ABC Clio, 2003, p. 134. However, Kevin Bell, 'The First Islamic State: A Look Back at the Islamic Emirate of Kunar', *CTCsentinel*, Vol 9, Issue 2, Feb. 2016, https://ctc.usma.edu/the-first-islamic-state-a-look-back-at-the-islamic-emirate-of-kunar/ makes some interesting observations about Jamil ur-Rahman's emirate including the adoption of elections which was not tolerated by Hekmatyar. He describes this emirate as a precursor to the Islamic state but also shows that Salafis have the ability to take part in elections. He also suggests that Abdullah Rumi may have worked for *al-Jihad* magazine and posed as a journalist and worked with Bunyan Marsous. Interestingly Bell says that Jamil ur-Rahman was lionized by Osama bin Laden, the Syrian cleric and Londoner Abu Basir al-Tartusi now in Turkey, Muqbil bin Hadi al-Wadi'i, and Rabi' Hadi al-Madkhali. Bell claims that al-Tartusi spent five months working with al-Rahman's *mujahideen* and later went to Jordan mentoring Abu Musab al-Zarqawi, the eventual leader of the Islamic State's predecessor organisation, al-Qaeda in Iraq (AQI). That according to my research and interviews with those who knew Tartusi seems inaccurate.

6. Known as the Imarat al-Tawhid, 'The emirate of the unity of God'.

7. Wahabi is a pejorative term used for the Salafism of neo-conservative Muslims who believe in the teachings of Abdul Wahab al-Najdi. Abdul Wahab's teachings are similar to protestant Christianity claiming to return to the source and that the centuries of Islamic jurisprudential traditions of the four schools were wrong and distorted the Prophet's original teaching. They follow mostly the teaching of the thirteenth-century scholar Ibn Tayymiyah and others. Outside of the Gulf many Muslim scholars see them as deviants and go as far as labelling their doctrines and teachings a sect similar to the Khawarij. So calling someone a Wahabi was tantamount to implying that they did not belong to Sunnism. The Saudi Kingdom in Arabia is an alliance between the Wahabites and the House of Saud who formed their state in rebellion against the Ottoman caliphate who claimed to be the defenders of orthodoxy. The formation of the KSA resulted in them claiming religious orthodoxy's mantle by being the protector of the two holy sanctuaries, Medina and Mecca. Yet whilst the KSA has developed, the doctrine of the Wahabis has remained narrow and has not managed to keep up with the modern state. It has caused the KSA to be viewed as a strange anomalous entity in the Middle East. Mohammed bin Salman's erstwhile modernisation efforts and the subsequent marginalisation of the Wahabi clerics could in effect erode their legitimacy.

8. Abd el-Sattar Dahmane, a Belgian of Tunisian descent living in Brussels. He purportedly trained with al-Qaeda in 2001 in Jalalabad. His wife Malika el-Aroud or Oumm Ubaydah followed him to Afghanistan. Following Dahmane's assassination of Massoud and his own death, el-Aroud returned to Belgium. She became connected to Fatima Aberkan, as well as Tarek Habib Maaroufi who was a follower of Abu Qatada and distributed his magazine in Brussels. Maaroufi was implicated in Massoud's killing. Whilst Maaroufi abandoned radical Islamism, el-Aroud and Aberkan continued. They became linked to the Zerkani network based in Molenbeek, Brussels. Khalid Zerkani its leader was also someone who apparently had links to Afghanistan training camps. Zerkani built up a network linked to criminality and Jihadism. Some of his followers, the most famous Abdelhamid Abaaoud, became linked to

the Paris attacks. See https://www.nytimes.com/2008/05/28/world/
europe/28terror.html also Pieter Van Ostaeyen in 'Belgian Radical
Networks and the Road to the Brussels Attacks', in *CTCsentinel*, Vol. 9
Issue 6, 2016. See also Alex Strick van Linschoten and Felix Kuehn
*An Enemy We Created: The Myth of the Taliban-Al Qaeda Merger in
Afghanistan*, OUP, 2012.

9. See also Mustafa Hamid and Leah Farrall, *Arabs at War in Afghanistan*,
Hurst & Co, 2018, pp. 154–5. I am aware of course that with regards
to Mustafa Hamid—or as he is known Abu Walid al-Masri—analysts
have questioned his testimony, as have his own people namely Ahmed
Hassan Abu'l Khayr who criticises Hamid in this document held by
the US Directorate of National Intelligence: https://www.dni.gov/files/
documents/ubl2016/english/Letter%20to%20Professor%20
Mustafa%20Hamid.pdf. Nevertheless there seem to be two components to the Jalalabad offensive in March, a full frontal assault that
lasted six weeks. Then there seems to be another push on 5–7 July.
Irrespective of this, accounts agree that Osama bin Laden suffered
heavy losses in the campaign. See also Peter L Bergen, *The Osama Bin
Laden I Know: an Oral History of al-Qaeda's Leader*, Free Press, 2006,
pp. 87–92.

10. He was the leader of the National Front for the Salvation of Afghanistan.
He was the first appointed president after the fall of Kabul in 1992.

11. 'Afghanistan: From Coup to Rebel Victory', *New York Times*, 26
Apr. 1992, https://www.nytimes.com/1992/04/26/world/afghanistan-
from-coup-to-rebel-victory.html.

11.　POWER AND ITS BITTER FRUITS

1. For a detailed analysis of the fall of Kabul see John Sifton, Human Rights
Watch, 'Blood-Stained Hands: Past Atrocities in Kabul and Afghanistan's
Legacy of Impunity', 6 July 2005, https://www.hrw.org/report/2005/07/
06/blood-stained-hands/past-atrocities-kabul-and-afghanistans-legacy-
impunity#7ea268.

2. See for instance allegation of gang rape that Abdul Rashid Dostum
ordered on one of his political rivals in 2017, Rod Nordland and Jawad
Sukhanyar, 'Afghanistan Police Surrounded Vice President's House',

New York Times 21 Feb. 2017, https://www.nytimes.com/2017/02/21/world/asia/abdul-rashid-dostum-afghanistan.html.

3. Jalalaluddin Haqqani also makes a similar assertion in 1992, when he says that Arabs who stay in Afghanistan [a] Do not abandon military training [b] Allow corrupt elements to enter their organisation which leads to factionalism and problems between Afghans and them [c] That they don't form parties that compete with Afghan parties and get involved in the internal struggles of the country. See Anne Stenersen, *Al-Qaida in Afghanistan*, Cambridge University Press, 2017, p. 36.

12. THE ESTABLISHMENT OF THE ARAB SERVICES BUREAU

1. Ibn al-Khattab, Samir Salih Abdullah al-Suwailim, was a Saudi fighter of Arab Circassian descent. According to his brother he went to Afghanistan in 1987 at the age of 17. After fighting in Afghanistan he explored efforts to go to Chechnya and Dagestan to open up camps there and eventually found his way to Chechnya where he fought in two Chechen wars. He is linked to several Chechen commanders including Shamil Basayev, Abu Muslim Shishani (later fighting in Syria: see Bill Roggio, 'Chechen al Qaeda commander, popular Saudi cleric, and an Ahrar al Sham leader spotted on front lines in Latakia', FDD's *Long War Journal*, 27 Mar. 2014, https://www.longwarjournal.org/archives/2014/03/chechen_al_qaeda_com.php) and Abu'l Walid and others. Whilst some have suggested that he was affiliated to al-Qaeda, Abdullah Anas and Mustafa Hamid refute that even though Osama bin Laden encouraged him to join. He died in March 2002 by a poisoned letter. For two very interesting interviews concerning Khattab see Carlotta Gall, 'Muslim Fighter Embraces Warrior Mystique', *New York Times*, 17 Oct. 1999, https://www.nytimes.com/1999/10/17/world/muslim-fighter-embraces-warrior-mystique.html and also Mowaffaq Al-Nowaiser, 'Khattab, the man who died for the cause of Chechnya', *Arab News*, 4 May 2002 http://www.arabnews.com/node/220601.

2. Prince Turki b. al-Faisal al-Saud was the Director General of the KSA's intelligence services from 1977 to just before the 9/11 attacks in 2001. He was intrinsically linked with the Afghan Jihad and negotiations with the Taliban.

3. Mohammed Zia ul-Haqq was Pakistan's president from 1978–88. He is credited with Islamising the country and hence his support for the Afghan Jihad. He died in a plane crash in 1988.

4. This refers to the Creed proposed by Ibn Taymiyyah, the thirteenth-century Syrian scholar, who divided creed thus. This has been taken on by the Wahabi scholars of Saudi Arabia but not by the rest of Sunnidom who remain Ashari and Maturidi. Even Osama bin Laden was Ikhwani in outlook and not wholly Wahabi.

5. Abu Talal al-Qasimi was the first person renditioned by the US in Croatia and then transferred to Egypt where he was executed. Human Rights Watch, 'Black hole: Fate of Islamists rendered to Egypt', 5 Sep. 2005, https://www.hrw.org/report/2005/05/09/black-hole/fate-islamists-ren-dered-egypt. See also Jane Mayer, 'Outsourcing Torture', *The New Yorker*, 14 Feb. 2005, https://www.newyorker.com/magazine/2005/02/14/outsourcing-torture. For Abu Talal al-Qasimis connection to Abu Faraj al-Masri see Kyle Orton, 'The Demise of Ahmad Mabruk: Al-Qaeda in Syria and American Policy, Syrian Intifada', 4 Oct. 2016, https://kyleorton1991.wordpress.com/2016/10/04/al-qaeda-in-syria-and-american-policy/#more-3060.

6. On the latest movements of Mohammed Showqi Islambouli, some analysts believe that Islambouli is part of the 'Khorasan' group in Syria. See Thomas Joscelyn, 'US strikes al Qaeda's "Khorasan Group" in Syria', FDD's *Long War Journal*, 8 Apr. 2016, https://www.longwarjournal.org/archives/2016/04/us-strikes-al-qaedas-khorasan-group-in-syria.php. Islambouli has been closely linked to al-Qaeda according to Joscelyn.

7. Rifa'i Ahmed Taha Musa was a senior member of Gamaa Islamiya, according to the US, he has been linked to numerous terror plots from kidnapping American citizens to assassinating former dictator Hosni Mubarak. Rifa'i became closely linked to al-Qaeda, after the Arab Spring he travelled to Syria and became part of what became known as the 'Khorasan' group. He was working on a reconciliation between various actors including Ahrar and Nusra Front. Musa was killed alongside Abu Firas al-Suri and Abu Sulayman Belgiki.

8. 'Sadat killing mastermind freed', BBC News, 29 Sep. 2003, http://news.bbc.co.uk/1/hi/world/middle_east/3147598.stm.

9. On Mohammed Hasan Khalil al-Hakim or Abu Jihad al-Masri, see Bill Roggio, 'Senior al Qaeda leader thought killed in North Waziristan strike in 2008', FDD's *Long War Journal*, 1 Nov. 2008 https://www. longwarjournal.org/archives/2008/11/senior_al_qaeda_lead_2.php. Hakim has been described as al-Qaeda's external operations manager and propaganda chief and linked to various terror attacks in Egypt.

10. Note that this name, Bunyan Marsous, was also used by a Libyan Misratan coalition formed in the summer of 2016, which launched an offensive against ISIS in Sirte and defeated them that same year. See Mary Fitzgerald, 'Armed groups', in 'A quick guide to Libya's main players', European Council of Foreign Relations, http://www.ecfr.eu/ mena/mapping_libya_conflict#. The significance of the name comes from the Quranic Chapter '*Al-Saff*', 'The Ranks', verse 4: 'Truly Allah loves those who fight in His cause in battle array, as if they were a solid cemented structure.' The 'solid cemented structure' refers to Bunyan Marsous which implies unity and determination.

11. Both '*ribat*' and '*al-murabitoon*' are significant in Muslim tradition. Historically it refers to the Murabitoon, a North African dynasty that established an empire across Spain and North Africa in the eleventh century fighting back the Christian gains in Andalusia at the expense of its Muslim princedoms. In Islamic tradition the word *ribat* has military and spiritual connotations. In its military sense it is a frontier outpost and garrison town where one guards against the enemy. Many cities in North Africa such as Rabat, Morocco came about as a result of that. The one who garrisons the *ribat* is a '*murabit*', '*murabitoon*' being the plural. However, later during the medieval period these *ribats* became places where one could undertake voluntary defence of Islam. Often Muslim volunteers, many of them sufis, would join a *ribat*: it was seen both as a spiritual venture where one undertook spiritual devotion as well as taking part in fighting the enemy. This stems from the numerous prophetic traditions that mention the virtue of guarding the frontier posts of Islam. Later on these *ribats* turned into *khanaqah*s and *zawiyas* for sufi fraternities, with a hospice and guesthouse where *murids*, seekers, met for their spiritual devotions. But the terms *murabit* and *ribat* were seen in a positive light by both sufi and

Jihadi alike. See Jörg Feuchter, 'Ribat', in Emad El-Din Shah, *Oxford Encyclopaedia of Islam and Politics* II, OUP, 2014, pp. 343–5.

12. See on *Jihad* magazine, Peter L. Bergen, *The Osama Bin Laden I Know: an Oral History of al-Qaeda's Leader*, Free Press, 2006, pp. 31–41.

13. THE EARLY ARABS

1. This is a reference to martyrs being married to seventy-two virgins. In the Arabic language, seventy-two signifies many. So seventy-two virgins simply means many.

2. Jalal ul-din Haqqani was a scholar of the Deobandi school and commander and tribal leader who fought against the Russians mostly in south-eastern Afghanistan. He was also the founder of what became known as the Haqqani network and welcomed foreign fighters to fight alongside him. He later joined the Taliban movement.

3. See Vahid Brown and Don Rassler, *Fountainhead of Jihad, The Haqqani Nexus, 1973–2012*, London: Hurst & Co., 2013. Here the authors point out that Haqqani had actually started the *Jihad* in 1973 (*manba' al-Jihad* magazine). He also says there were different Arabs there such as Abu Walid al-Masri, it is also reported that this is how Abu Hafs and Abu Ubaida al-Banshiri came into Afghanistan.

4. The Deoband school is a sub-branch of the Hanafi school of jurisprudence founded in the late nineteenth century and was inspired by Shah Waliullah Dehlawi. The school, named after the place it was founded, was a direct response to the British imperial influence and consequently had a revivalist attitude. It is scholastic in nature, it is strict in adherence to tradition but unlike the Wahabi movement did not reject sufism. Tablighi Jamaat, the Taliban and other groups adhere to the Deobandi school although the Taliban has increasingly fallen under the sway of Wahabi thought.

14. THE INNER CIRCLE

1. Islamic tradition does not dismiss a dream as being merely just that, rather it is seen as a window into the unseen, as a small portion of revelation. There are references to dreams as prophecy in Surah Yusuf (Joseph in the Bible) in the Quran. The Prophet also interpreted dreams

as did early scholars like Ibn Sirin and others. It is a tradition that continues to this day in Muslim societies. Seeing the Prophet for instance, is considered a blessed thing and not everyone is graced with this vision.

2. Sheikh Abdul Majid Zindani, the Yemeni scholar from Ibb who is probably one of the country's most influential scholars. He is a founding member of al-Islah which blends Yemeni tribal politics and Brotherhood ideas with Wahabi thought.

3. The late Mohamed Qutb is the brother of Syed Qutb and a very influential figure in the Islamic movement. He is generally attributed as being Syed Qutb's editor but also an academic in his own right. Lawrence Wright believes that Osama bin Laden attended his lectures, Lawrence Wright, *Looming Tower: Al Qaeda and the Road to 9/11*, New York: Knopf, 2006, p. 79.

4. Abdallah Zayed is the influential and powerful president of the Islamic University of Medina.

5. Mohammed Mahmud al-Sawwaf is an influential Islamic movement figure and al-Azhar graduate from Iraq.

6. Yusuf al-Qardawi is an influential Egyptian scholar linked to the Muslim Brotherhood and host of the programme *Shariah and Life* on Al-Jazeera Arabic. He is the chairman of International Union of Muslim Council and also founded the European Council for Fatwa and Research.

7. According to Sheikh Abdullah Azzam's eulogy of Sheikh Tameem, *The Lofty Mountain*, Tameem was a Jerusalemite whose ancestors had been the rulers of the city. He grew up in a literary family and his father was a considerable poet and Nasserist. Tameem studied under Marwan Hadid, a Syrian Islamist and friend of Syed Qutb. Tameem graduated and became an interpreter in Dhahran, Saudi Arabia where he heard the call of the Afghan Jihad. Marwan Hadid was a militant Islamist from Hama, Syria, and one of the founders of the Fighting Vanguard that precipitated the Hama massacre in February 1982, which crushed the Fighting Vanguard and killed around 20,000 to 40,000 people. See Raphaël Lafèvre, 'The Syrian Brotherhood's Armed Struggle', Carnegie Endowment for International Peace, 14 Dec. 2012, https://carnegieendowment.org/2012/12/14/syrian-brotherhood-s-armed-struggle-pub-50380.

15. INNER OF THE INNER CIRCLE

1. The *tazkiya* tradition is something that transferred over to the battalions in Syria too. Many foreign fighters who joined some of these battalions needed to have a recommendation from friends who would vouch for their credibility.

2. Erbakan was a leading Islamist in Turkish politics and had been PM of the Turkish state.

3. This is in Islamic apocalyptic tradition and is not necessarily part of Muslim creed.

4. Here referring to the late Radwan Nammous or as he is known by his *nom de guerre* Abu Firas al-Suri. Suri was involved in the lead up to the Hama uprising in 1982 being linked to a violent offshoot Fighting Vanguard. Suri escaped to Peshawar where he ran a bookshop and became close to al-Qaeda. His association with Abdullah Azzam was according to Abdullah Anas one of enmity. Suri later emerged in Syria as one of the senior leaders of Nusra Front where he tried to mediate between Nusra Front and ISIS. Talks failed and he was killed by a US airstrike on 3 April 2016 in Idlib.

5. The terms '*Ansar*' and '*Muhajir*' often crop up in Jihadism. It harks back to the golden era of Islam namely when the Prophet was alive. Those companions who made *hijra* or emigrated to Medina were known as the *Muhajir*s or *Muhajiroon*, emigrants. It also implied seniority since they were the earliest Muslims. *Muhajir*s had a different status in the early Muslim community. Similarly, those foreign fighters who went to Syria from Europe call themselves Emigrants or *Muhajir*s too. It's a nod to that tradition. But also because it implies that they have followed the obligation emphasised by many Salafis that one could not live in a non-Muslim country, and so one had to make *hijra*. This explains why many foreign fighters in Syria, for instance, add the epithet *Muhajir*. In contrast, in the early tradition the Medinans who gave the Prophet refuge and helped the *Mujahiroon* escape became known as the *Ansar*, the helpers. This is why some Syrians will call themselves Ansari suggesting that they are natives of the country. Yet again this is a nod to Islamic history.

6. Also known as Sayyed Imam al-Sharif, Dr Fadl was a physician whose

book *al-'Umda fi I'dad al-'Udda* ('The Essentials of Making Ready [for Jihad]') had a major impact on the global Jihadist movement even though he recanted following the 9/11 attacks in 2001 and wrote a text countering his previous arguments in 2004. In 2007 he released *Tarshid al-Jihad fi Misr wa al-Aalam* ('Rationalizations on Jihad in Egypt and the World') from Fayyoum prison. The text though denounced by Ayman al-Zawahiri and other Salafi-Jihadis is considered a definitive rejection of violence by Sharif. See Jarret Brachman, 'Leading Egyptian Jihadist Sayyid Imam Renounces Violence', *CTC Sentinel* Vol. 1 Issue 1, Dec. 2007, https://ctc.usma.edu/leading-egyptian-jihadist-sayyid-imam-renounces-violence/.

16. ASSASSINATION

1. Omar Abdullah Nassif was the president of World Muslim League and King Abdul Aziz University. He is a chemist by profession who is well connected to international universities all over the world.

2. See Zainab al-Ghazali, *Return of the Pharaoh*, translated by Mokrane Guezzou, Islamic Foundation, 2006, p. 97.

3. This is confirmed in an interview by Nabeel Naeem with al-Arabiya on 28 Mar. 2017, https://english.alarabiya.net/en/features/2017/03/28/Former-Egyptian-Islamic-Jihad-leader-Nabil-Naeem-Zawahiri-himself-is-ignorant.html. He was a former member of Egyptian Jihad who had spent time in Afghanistan.

4. The late Muhammed Nasir ul-Din Albani was an Albanian self-taught scholar. Albani lived in Damascus and was the founder of an important strand of Salafism characterised by a rejection of adhering to the four schools of jurisprudence in Sunni thought.

5. Mustafa Hamid says Dr Ahmed arrived in 1988 with some Algerians and Libyans; Abdullah Anas' account contradicts this. Mustafa Hamid and Leah Farrall, *Arabs at War in Afghanistan*, Hurst & Co, 2018, p. 116.

6. A famous companion of the Prophet, a *muhajir*, a scholar and teacher.

7. Emir has many connotations in Islamic traditions. Depending on context it can mean leader, prince, commander or ruler. The question 'who is your emir?' could mean who is your commander or it can mean leader. There are Islamic traditions which advise that one appoint an emir when

there are at least three people embarking on a journey. Emir can also mean Caliph and/or Sultan and may be used interchangeably. Thus one needs to take the word in its context. The level of obedience rendered is also something one has to take into account.

8. For the trial of Massoud and the tension between him and the Afghan Arabs see the account of Musa al-Qarni, Tam Hussein, 'The Afghan Jihad: An Annotated Interview with Musa al-Qarni about Abdullah Azzam and Ahmed Shah Massoud and the tension with the "Afghan Arabs"', MENA ETC, 24 Feb. 2017, http://www.tamhussein.co.uk/2017/02/musa-al-qarni-on-the-afghan-jihad/.

9. He was the younger brother of Qari Saeed, he fought with Jaysh al-Islam lil-Inqadh (IAS) and there was general amnesty after Bouteflika came to power in 1999. He was in no way linked to the GIA.

10. Abdel Wahid stayed on Peshawar after the war and studied for an MA and then returned to Algeria.

11. Anne Stenersen, *Al-Qaida in Afghanistan*, Cambridge University Press, 2017, p. 35, believes that 'after 1989, al-Qaida established a close, cooperative relationship with Hezb-i Islami that appears to be more elaborate than other Mujahideen parties.' My own interview with a high-profile British fighter also confirms that they were linked to Hezb-i Islami's men, on one occasion even meeting Hekmatyar.

12. Abu Rawdah al-Suri according to Anne Stenersen, *Al-Qaida in Afghanistan*, p. 37, formed a battalion, 'Yarmouk battalion' to fight alongside Hekmatyar's factions. On a side note, Yarmouk battalion was named after the famous battle whereby Khalid bin al-Walid, a famous Muslim hero and general, inflicted a decisive defeat on the Byzantines in August 636. This is why many battalions are so named, and the name is evoked even now amongst rebels and Jihadists in Syria.

13. Abu Saeed joined the GIA during the Algerian civil war but later recanted.

14. Ahmed Said Khadr was killed in a raid by the Pakistani security services in 2003. Ahmed Said Khadr's role in al-Qaeda has been ambiguous and he was very likely an associate. This may have come about due to him being a fundraiser during the Afghan Jihad; he also had good relationships with the various factions in Afghanistan. As to the

extent of his contacts with al-Qaeda, that has been debated. Al-Qaeda considers him a martyr whilst his family emphasises his humanitarian work. Ahmed Said Khadr's situation mirrors that of many British and European Muslims working in the Syrian conflict where there are questions whether they have taken part in armed conflict as well as humanitarian work, or made a transition from one to the other. His son Omar Khadr was captured in a raid and sent to Guantanamo bay prison at the tender age of fifteen. See for example Tim Molyneux, 'Guantanamo Child Soldier Omar Khadr was a Victim Twice Over', *Newsweek*, 13 July 2017 http://www.newsweek.com/omar-khadr-al-qaeda-child-soldier-imprisoned-and-mistreated-us-was-victim-635856. See also United States Of America v. Omar Khadr in http://www.internationalcrimes-database.org/Case/968/Khadr/.

15. He is the general consul for Afghanistan in Kuwait.

16. Al-Qarni was born in Bish in Jazan province Saudi Arabia, in 1954. He obtained his doctoral degree in *Usool al-Fiqh*, Principles of Islamic Jurisprudence, from Umm al-Qurra University in Saudi Arabia. He held various professorships and headships related to Islamic jurisprudence at various Islamic academic institutions. He was also a President of the Islamic University in Peshawar. Al-Qarni too travelled to Afghanistan early and became heavily involved in the Afghan Jihad, in particular in relief work and educational activities. He came in contact with Afghan leaders as well as Abdullah Azzam, Abdel Majid al-Zindani, Osama bin Laden and others. See Tam Hussein 'The Afghan Jihad: An Annotated Interview with Musa al-Qarni about Abdullah Azzam and Ahmed Shah Massoud and the tension with the "Afghan Arabs"', http://www.tamhussein.co.uk/2017/02/musa-al-qarni-on-the-afghan-jihad/.

17. Abu Adel is Abdullah Azzam's nephew, from the West Bank. He was imprisoned for thirteen years without trial by the Israelis. He is, as of 2018, serving in the Hamas government in Gaza.

18. Muslim burial rites require that the body is buried within three days. Usually the corpse is covered in simple white cotton sheets. The Janaza prayer or burial prayer is prayed on him before the corpse is committed to the earth. The martyr however is buried in his clothes because he is not considered dead but rather alive in the company of his Lord.

19. See Anatol Lieven, *Pakistan: A Hard Country*, Penguin/Public Affairs, 2011, for discussion on Pakistan's foreign policy dilemmas. See Ahmed Shah Massoud's understanding of Pakistani foreign policy with Piotr Balcerowicz, 'Last known interview with Afghanistan's Ahmad Shah Massoud', Global Geneva, 20 Mar. 2015, http://www.global-geneva. com/last-known-interview-with-afghanistans-ahmad-shah-massoud/.

20. Nasser al-Haqbani, 'Exclusive—Sayyaf to Asharq Al-Awsat: I Know Who Killed Azzam', *Asharq Al-Awsat*, 20 Feb. 2018, https://aawsat. com/english/home/article/1181231/exclusive-sayyaf-asharq-al-awsat- i-know-who-killed-azzam.

17. INTO THE WILDERNESS

1. On Hassan al-Turabi see profile on the Sorbonne-educated Islamist theologian, Ahmed Saeed, 'Hassan al-Turabi: A man with a mission', Al-Jazeera, 6 Mar. 2016, https://www.aljazeera.com/news/2016/03/has-san-al-turabi-man-mission-160306111225056.html also Ahmed Meiloud, 'The legacy of Sudan's Hassan al-Turabi', *Middle East Eye*, 8 Mar. 2016, http://www.middleeasteye.net/columns/legacy-sudans-hassan-al-turabi-1933889656.

2. 'Algeria frees key member of banned Islamic party', CNN, 15 July 1997, http://edition.cnn.com/WORLD/9707/15/algeria/index.html.

3. 'Timeline: Algeria's "dirty war"', Al-Jazeera, 13 Nov. 2010, https://www. aljazeera.com/news/africa/2010/11/20101110142037288752.html.

4. Omar Mahhmoud Othman or Abu Qatada is a Jordanian national who is considered to be one of the most important Salafi-Jihadi scholars currently. He came to Peshawar after the fall of Kabul due to his purported opposition to the invasion of Iraq. He spent a few months in Peshawar teaching in a secondary school before travelling to the UK where he sought asylum. Fawaz Gerges believes that he built up contacts with global Jihadists offering computer services. There doesn't seem to be direct evidence that Abu Qatada ever met bin Laden. See Fawaz Gerges, *Far Enemy: Why Jihad Went Global*, Cambridge University Press, 2005, pp. 223–4. According to my interview with one of his students, Abu Qatada was certainly someone who could get you to Afghanistan as could Abu Hamza al-Masri. Abu Qatada was based in West London teaching

in Four Feathers Club off Edgware Road. During the Algerian civil war
he was editor in chief of *al-Ansar* magazine, widely regarded as a GIA
propaganda outlet. He was held in the UK on immigration violations.
The Jordanians wanted to prosecute him for terrorism charges. The UK
succeeded in deporting him to Jordan despite concerns that the
Jordanians might subject him to torture. He was found not guilty due
to a lack of evidence and currently resides in Jordan. During the Syrian
conflict he has been in contact with many Salafi-Jihadi groups fighting
in Syria.

5. Mustafa bin Abd al-Qadir Setmariam Nasar from Aleppo, Syria is
   descended from an illustrious sufi family. He however, joined the Muslim
   Brotherhood's offshoot the Fighting Vanguard and took part in the
   Hama uprising in 1982 alongside Abu Khalid al-Suri, Mohamed al-
   Bahaiya one of the founders of Ahrar al-Sham in Syria. He then escaped
   to Spain where he received citizenship. Suri lived in Neasden, London
   in 1994 and worked on Abu Qatada's *al-Ansar* magazine and bin Laden's
   media bureau. Although Khalid Fawwaz officially represented Osama
   bin Laden's bureau, the Advice and Reform Committee, Suri was involved
   with the bureau as were other members of Egyptian Islamic Jihad such
   as Adel Abdel Bari (father of ISIS Jihadist Abdel-Majed Abdel Bary)
   and Ibrahim Eidarous. According to Anas, Fawwaz represented bin
   Laden when the latter had not yet transitioned into an out and out militant. The media bureau's aim was to convey bin Laden's ideas and was
   a consequence of Saudi clerics like Salman al-Oudah, Iyadh al-Qarni,
   Awadh al-Qarni and other demanding a consultative council in the Saudi
   Kingdom. Al-Oudah and others set out their demands in a petition entitled 'Memorandum of Advice', *Mudhakkirat al-Nasiha* in 1992. By 1998
   however the bureau had probably become a political mouthpiece for al-
   Qaeda. By then Suri had left for Afghanistan and ran his own camps in
   Kabul and became very close to the Taliban. He became linked to the
   Madrid bombings in 2004 and 7/7 bombings in London. He was captured in Quetta 2005 and rendered to Syria. It is not known whether
   he is still in prison.

6. Many Muslim scholars, writing when a Muslim polity existed whether
   Ottoman or Mamluk or Abbasid, maintain that apostasy warrants the

death penalty. However, in modern times some Muslim thinkers such as Tariq Ramadan have diverged from this idea and believe that a person is free to change his religion due to their being no compulsion in religion. Ramadan believes that apostasy laws came about because many Qureishis became Muslims in order to spy on the nascent Muslim community in Medina. They would be given access to the community and then renounce their Islam and then re-join their enemies, thus subverting and giving succour to the enemies of the Muslims. In this context of the early Medinan city state, apostasy constituted treason and anyone entering Islam would have to think long and hard as to what that meant. For as Ramadan points out Hisham and Ayyash left Islam and then returned to Islam and there were no legal consequences for their actions, there were others such as Ubayallah ibn Jahsh who become Christian and was left completely untouched. See Tariq Ramadan, *In the Footsteps of the Prophet, Lessons from the Life of Muhammad*, OUP, 2007, pp. 76–7.

7. *Al-Ansar*, 132nd issue, 18 Jan. 1995

8. See Naima Bouteldja, 'Who really bombed Paris?', *The Guardian*, 8 Sep. 2005, https://www.theguardian.com/world/2005/sep/08/france. comment.

9. For a more detailed look into the Bentalha massacre see John R. Schindler, 'Two Decades Later, Algeria Protects Mystery of Bentalha Massacre', *The Observer*, 22 Sep. 2017, http://observer.com/2017/09/two-decades-later-algeria-protects-mystery-of-bentalha-massacre/.

10. Hani Siba'i is an Egyptian exile and Islamist ideologue who lives in the UK. He appears regularly as a commentator on Arab TV channels. Siba'i has been linked to Islamic Jihad which led to his arrest according to Mohammed el-Shafey, 'Inside Britain's Gitmo', 12 Oct. 2005. There has also been some suggestion that he fought in Afghanistan but I have not been able to verify that claim.

11. Essam Muhammed Tahir al-Barqawi, a Salafi-Jihadi cleric of Palestinian descent who is said to be the teacher of Abu Mus'ab al-Zarqawi and has played an important role in the Syrian conflict advising the Jihadist factions.

12. For the impact of the Hama massacre see Raphael Lefevre, *Ashes of*

Hama: The Muslim Brotherhood in Syria, London: Hurst & Co., 2013, also Thomas Pierret, *Religion and State in Syria: The Sunni Ulama from Coup to Revolution*, Cambridge University Press, 2013.

13. Abu Musab al-Suri, *al-tajrubah al-suriyyah*—see also Paul Cruickshank & Mohannad Hage Ali, 'Abu Musab Al Suri: Architect of the New Al Qaeda', *Studies in Conflict & Terrorism*, 30:1 (2007): 1–14, DOI: 10.1080/10576100601049928. See also 'Lessons Learned from the Jihad Ordeal in Syria', Combatting Terrorism Center, no date, ref. AFGP-2002–600080, https://ctc.usma.edu/harmony-program/lessons-learned-from-the-jihad-ordeal-in-syria-original-language-2/.

14. There is a Prophetic tradition where one of the Companions killed a man during the battle. Before he killed him, the man uttered the testimony of faith, but the Companion still killed him. When the news came to the Prophet he rebuked the Companion for his action. The Companion replied that the man had only uttered the testimony of faith because he wanted to save his skin and he didn't really mean what he was saying. The Prophet asked if he had opened up his chest to see whether faith had entered his heart? In other words, the issue of creed and faith rests with the individual and God not with any outside agents whether that be an individual or the state.

18. PESHAWAR

1. There is some suggestion by some sources I interviewed that Abu Humam was closely linked to Abu Muhammad al-Maqdisi and was an influential Salafist. He was thrown into prison for several months by the Jordanian authorities in the 90s and met and influenced Abu Mus'ab Zarqawi when he returned from Afghanistan trying to set up Jund al-Sham, weapons were found in his home and he was arrested. Both men were from the village of Zarqa. See Laura Smith, 'Timeline: Abu Musab al-Zarqawi', *The Guardian*, 8 June 2006, https://www.theguardian.com/world/2006/jun/08/iraq.alqaida1. Abu Humam should not be confused with Turki al-Binali the notorious ISIS scholar of recent years. For more see Kévin Jackson, 'The Forgotten Caliphate', *Jihadica*, 31 Dec. 2014, http://www.jihadica.com/the-forgotten-caliphate/.

2. See Naima Bouteldja, 'Who really bombed Paris?'

3. For comprehensive take on Londonistan see Sadek Hamid, *Sufis, Salafi and Islamists: The Contested Ground of British Islamic Activism*, I. B. Tauris, 2016; also Rafaello Pantucci, *We Love Death as You Love Life: Britain's Suburban Terrorists*, Hurst & Co., 2015, pp. 19–49

4. There were others such as the late Abu Iyadh, Seifallah Ben Hassine, the founder of Ansar al-Shariah, he studied with Abu Qatada in London and had contacts in Afghanistan. According to one student of Abu Qatada I interviewed, he was known as Abu Sufyan in London. Abu Iyadh also had extensive links to Tunisian Combat Group. See Thomas Joscelyn, 'Al Qaeda ally orchestrated assault on US Embassy in Tunisia', *CTC Sentinel*, 2 Oct. 2012, https://ctc.usma.edu/belgian-radical-networks-and-the-road-to-the-brussels-attacks/.

5. See Thomas Joscelyn, 'From al-Qaeda in Italy to Ansar al-Sharia in Tunisia', Foundation for Defence of Democracy, 21 Nov. 2012, http://www.defenddemocracy.org/media-hit/from-al-qaeda-in-italy-to-ansar-al-sharia-tunisia/. See also Pieter Van Ostaeyen, 'Belgian Radical Networks and the Road to the Brussels Attacks', *CTC Sentinel*, June 2016, Vol. 9. Issue 6, https://ctc.usma.edu/belgian-radical-networks-and-the-road-to-the-brussels-attacks/. An example could be the Zerkani network which I investigated. Zerkani and his supporters walk in the same footsteps as the adherents of Abu Qatada in west London. They took part in criminal activities because they saw it as war booty and permissible. It suggests that Zerkani's spiritual father was most likely Abu Qatada. One should stress for accuracy's sake, that Abu Qatada had no link whatsoever to Zerkani's activities. Indeed the criminal behaviour of his adherents in Ladbroke Grove or Brussels was not necessarily condoned by him. For Abu Qatada, as his students have explained, believed that it was contrary to the interests of Muslims living in the West. But, to attack or weaken an infidel in his world-view was not necessarily an impermissible position to hold nor was it sinful; thus robbing, defrauding and other such criminal behaviour were not sinful in and of themselves they were just contrary to the Muslim community's interests. It was a pragmatic response. Zerkani wasn't cut from the same cloth as say Fuad Belkacem's Shariah4Belgium and his comparatively amateurish group of agitators. The nineties and early 2000s both in the UK as

well as European countries was a time of intense Islamist activity of different political persuasions. As such Abu Qatada's ideas did hold sway amongst a segment of the North African community in Europe due to the bloody Algerian conflict. In some ways Zerkani was a manifestation of that. As far as we know Zerkani was linked to Seifullah ben Hassine also known as Abu Iyadh al-Tunsi, the founder of Tunisia's Ansar al-Shariah. The latter was supposedly killed in an air strike in 2015 in Libya. Abu Iyadh or Abu Sufyan as he was known in London, was a student of Abu Qatada during the nineties, this has been confirmed to me by one of Abu Qatada's former students. Moreover, Tarek Maaroufi, a Belgian national and Abu Iyadh founded the Tunisian Combatant Group, the Tunisian equivalent of the Algerian GIA, which aimed to establish an Islamic caliphate in Tunisia. According to some accounts Maaroufi was involved in distributing Abu Qatada's magazine *al-Ansar* concerning itself with the Algerian conflict. Maaroufi has now abandoned extremism. Zerkani is also linked to Ms Fatemah Aberkane, Ms Malika el-Aroud, the wife of Dahmane Abd as-Sattar, the killer of Ahmed Shah Massoud. All these figures are directly or indirectly linked to Zerkani and this implies that his spiritual father was Abu Qatada. See also the similarity between Zerkani and Muhammed Haydar Zammar who was also the agent provocateur linked to the perpetrator of 9/11, the Hamburg cell led by Mohammed Atta. Zammar was investigated by the German security services and later renditioned to Syria where he was tortured and then released on a prison exchange with Ahrar al-Sham, the Syrian rebel group. Zammar ended up with ISIS and was captured in Syria by SDF forces. 'Mohammed Zammar: German jihadist "detained by Syrian Kurds"', BBC News, http://www.bbc.co.uk/news/world-middle-east-43821844.

6. *al-Ansar* magazine, Issue 82, 2 Feb. 1995 pp. 12–14.

7. *al-Ansar* magazine, Issue 91, 6 Apr. 1995, pp. 17–19.

8. *al-Ansar* magazine, Issue 90, 30 Mar. 1996, p. 16. This is my translation.

9. This is a Quranic verse from Chapter 3, 'al-Imran', verse 118: 'O ye who believe! Take not into your intimacy those outside your ranks: they will not fail to corrupt you. They only desire your ruin: Rank hatred has already

appeared from their mouths: what their hearts conceal is far worse. We have made plain to you the signs. If ye have wisdom.' I have used Abdullah Yusuf Ali's *The Meaning of the Holy Quran* translation.

10. This refers to the Sant'Egidio Platform of 13 January 1995, where Algerian opposition parties sought to create a peace plan to end the Algerian conflict. See Sofiane Khatib, 'Spoiler Management During Algeria's Civil War: explaining the peace', *Stanford Journal of International Relations*, 24 May 2006, https://web.stanford.edu/group/sjir/6.1.06_khatib.html.

11. Scott Sayare, 'How Europe's "Little Losers" Became Terrorists', *The Atlantic*, 9 May 2016, https://www.theatlantic.com/international/archive/2016/05/europe-counterterrorism-failure-khaled-kelkal/481908/.

12. See Craig R. Whitney, 'Bomb Rips Train Underneath Paris, with 29 Wounded,' *New York Times*, 18 Oct. 1995 https://www.nytimes.com/1995/10/18/world/bomb-rips-train-underneath-paris-with-29-wounded.html. It is important to stress that Abu Qatada's detention was to do with immigration appeals. He has been cleared of terror charges. The Home Office accused him of promoting and giving legitimacy to extremism. It said he had engaged in conduct that 'facilitates and gives encouragement to the commission, preparation and instigation of acts of terrorism'; see Robert Booth, 'Abu Qatada: spiritual leader for deadly Islamist groups?', *The Guardian*, 7 Feb. 2012 https://www.theguardian.com/world/2012/feb/07/abu-qatada-spiritual-leader-islamist?newsfeed=true. Abu Qatada was also cleared of terror charges. On 24 September 2014 he was cleared of terror charges on the basis of insufficient evidence, see BBC News, http://www.bbc.co.uk/news/world-29340656.

13. Craig R, Whitney, 'Bomb rips train underneath Paris, with 29 wounded'.

14. I am aware that some have pronounced his name 'Abu Hamam', but this is how Abdullah Anas pronounces his name, both versions are sound in meaning.

15. Scott Kraft, 'Algerian Opposition Figure Slain in Paris: North Africa: Islamic Salvation Front's co-founder is ambushed in mosque. Killing casts new doubts on peace prospects', *LA Times*, 12 July 1995, http://

articles.latimes.com/1995–07–12/news/mn-23086_1_islamic-salva-tion-front.

19. TO THE MOUNTAINS

1. See also 'Asharq Al-Awsat interviews Umm Mohammed: The Wife of Bin Laden's Spiritual Mentor', *Asharq al-Awsat*, 30 Apr. 2006, https:// eng-archive.aawsat.com/theaawsat/features/asharq-al-awsat-interviews-umm-mohammed-the-wife-of-bin-ladens-spiritual-mentor. In 1997, there was an assassination plot using mysterious powder in his shoes— possibly anthrax: see Steve Coll, *Ghost Wars: The Secret History of the CIA, Afghanistan, and bin Laden from the Soviet Invasion to September 10, 2001*, Penguin, 2005, p. 348.

2. For a detailed account of the assassination see, Craig Pyes and William, C. Rempel, 'Slowly Stalking an Afghan "Lion", the assassins of Northern Alliance chief faced weeks of delays until finally he met with them', *LA Times*, 12 June 2002, http://articles.latimes.com/2002/jun/12/world/fg-masoud12/7.

3. Yasser Sirri is an Egyptian political exile living in London, UK. He has been accused by the Egyptian authorities of being linked to the militant organisation Gamaa al-Islamiyya and sentenced to death in 1998. The UK press linked him to Abu Qatada, and there have been calls for his deportation. Tom Whitehead, 'Qatada associate will stay in UK, court signals', *Daily Telegraph*, 21 Nov. 2012, https://www.telegraph.co.uk/news/uknews/law-and-order/9693489/Qatada-associate-will-stay-in-UK-court-signals.html. See also UK Supreme Court, Al-Sirri v Secretary of State for the Home Department, 2012, UKSC 54, http://www.asylumlawdatabase.eu/en/case-law/uk-supreme-court-al-sirri-v-secretary-state-home-department-2012-uksc-54.

4. *Al-Sharq al-Awsat*, 8 Sep. 2002 المطوع, وائل جليدان منزعج من إضافة اسمه إلى قائمة مولي الإرهاب, http://archive.aawsat.com/details.asp?article=123 390&issueno=8685#.WvQfby-ZNp9.

5. *Bidoon* is someone of Persian, Arab or other descent who was not given nationality following the formation of Kuwait. They have no rights within Kuwait. A famous *Bidoon* family is the ISIS executioner Mohammed Emwazi or Jihadi John.

6. Also known as Mohammed al-Bakri or Amin al-Bakri, see Missy Ryan, 'Pentagon dossier to detail secretive U.S. Afghan detainee policy', Reuters, 24 Apr. 2014, https://www.reuters.com/article/us-usa-afghanistan-detainees-idUSBREA3M26Q20140424; see also interview with al-Bakri's father in Mohammed al-Qiri, 'Interview with Mohammed al-Bakri, father of Bagram Prison detainee Amin al-Bakri', *Yemeni Observer*, 15 July 2015, https://www.webcitation.org/query?url=http%3A%2F%2Fwww.yobserver.com%2Freports%2F10014605.html&date=2010-01-03.

7. James Meikle, 'Abu Qatada extradition battle has cost taxpayers £1.7m, says Theresa May', *The Guardian*, 14 June 2013, https://www.the-guardian.com/world/2013/jun/14/abu-qatada-extradition-theresa-may.

8. The brutal prison is designated for Islamists in Syria. See Amnesty International report, 'Human Slaughterhouse, Mass hangings end extermination at Saydnaya prison, Syria', Feb. 2017 https://www.amnesty.org/download/Documents/MDE2454152017ENGLISH.PDF.

9. See Abdul Salam Zayeef, ed. Felix Kuehn, Alex Strick van Linschoten, *My Life with the Taliban*, London: Hurst & Co., 2010.

10. Abdul Hakim Mujahid condemned the 9/11 attacks and urged Taliban to do so and joined the Afghan Peace Council: see Sanjay Kumar's profile on Abdul Hakim Mujahid, *The Diplomat*, 12 Dec. 2013.

11. See Rod Nordland and Jawad Sukhanyar, 'Member of Afghan Peace Council Assassinated', 13 May 2012. Rahmani was the former Minister for Education for the Taliban: see 'Arsala Rahmani is Assassinated in Kabul', *New York Times*, 14 May 2012, https://www.nytimes.com/2012/05/14/world/asia/arsala-rahmani-is-assassinated-in-kabul.html.

12. Sune Engel Rasmussen, 'Fear and doubt as notorious "butcher of Kabul" returns with talk of peace', *The Guardian*, 4 May 2017, https://www.theguardian.com/world/2017/may/04/afghan-warlord-gulbuddin-hek-matyar-returns-kabul-20-years-call-peace.

BIBLIOGRAPHY

This book is based on the account of one man, Abdullah Anas, conducted between 2016–2018. The notes and bibliography that I add here of course are not extensive. They are attempts at cross-referencing and helping the reader to make connections. It is also to give further background and allow the reader to piece together the account given by Mr Anas by looking at the sterling work done by other writers, researchers, journalists and the like. The aim is not for exhaustiveness but rather for transparency. Moreover, when I feel that some of the figures Mr Anas mentions require further illumination or are controversial to the Western reader, I add a note to signal one's awareness of these issues. The references then serve to give the reader an alternate perspective in the spirit of fairness which is a cornerstone of good journalism. I have deliberately stayed away from Arabic sources since the book is for English speakers who may want to follow them up themselves.

–TH

Books

Adamec, Ludwig W. *Historical Dictionary of Afghanistan*, Scarecrow Press, 4th edn, 2012.

Adamec, Ludwig W. and Frank A. Clements, *Conflict in Afghanistan: A Historical Encyclopaedia*, ABC Clio, 2003.

Braithwaite, Rodric, *Afgantsy, the Russians in Afghanistan 1979–89*, Profile, 2011.

BIBLIOGRAPHY

Brown, Jonathan A.C., *Misquoting Muhammad: The Challenge and Choices of Interpreting the Prophet's Legacy*, Oneworld Publications, 2014.

Brown, Vahid and Don Rassler, *Fountainhead of Jihad: The Haqqani Nexus, 1973–2012*, Hurst, 2013.

Coll, Steve, *Ghost Wars: The Secret History of the CIA, Afghanistan, and bin Laden from the Soviet Invasion to September 10, 2001*, Penguin, 2005.

Edwards, David B., *Before Taliban: Genealogies of the Afghan Jihad*, University of California Press, 2002.

Feuchter, Jörg, 'Ribat', in Emad El-Din Shah, *Oxford Encyclopedia of Islam and Politics* II, OUP, 2014.

Hallaq, Wael, *An Introduction to Islamic Law*, Cambridge University Press, 2009.

Hamid, Mustafa and Leah Farrall, *The Arabs at War in Afghanistan*, Hurst, 2018.

Hamid, Sadek, *Sufis, Salafi and Islamists: The Contested Ground of British Islamic Activism*, I. B. Tauris, 2016.

Hegghammer, Thomas, *The Caravan: Abdullah Azzam and the Rise of Global Jihad*, Cambridge University Press, forthcoming.

Horne, Alistair, *A Savage War of Peace: Algeria 1954–1962*, New York: New York Review of Books, 2006.

Hourani, Albert, *History of the Arab Peoples*, New York: Faber and Faber, 1992.

al-Ghazali, Zainab, *The Return of the Pharaoh*, translated by Mokrane Guezzou, Islamic Foundation, 2006.

Gall, Sandy, *Afghanistan: Agony of a Nation*, Bodley Head, 1988.

Gerges, Fawaz, *Far Enemy: Why Jihad Went Global*, Cambridge University Press, 2005.

Grad, Marcela, *Massoud: An Intimate Portrait of the Legendary Afghan Leader*, Webster University Press, 2009.

Kaplan, Robert, *Soldiers of God*, New York: Vintage Books, 1990.

Kiser, John W., *Commander of the Faithful: The Life and Times of Emir Abd el-Kader*, Archetype, 2008.

Lapidus, Ira M., *A History of Islamic Societies*, Cambridge: Cambridge University Press, 1988.

Lartéguy, Jean, *The Centurions*, with foreword by Robert D. Kaplan Penguin, 2015.

BIBLIOGRAPHY

Lefevre, Raphael *Ashes of Hama: The Muslim Brotherhood in Syria*, London: Hurst, 2013.

Lieven, Anatol, *Pakistan: A Hard Country*, Public Affairs, 2011.

Linschoten, Alex Strick van, and Felix Kuehn, *An Enemy We Created: The Myth of the Taliban-Al Qaeda Merger in Afghanistan*, OUP, 2012.

———, *The Taliban Reader: War, Islam and Politics*, Hurst, 2018.

Makdisi, George, *The Rise of Colleges: Institutions of Learning in Islam and the West*, Edinburgh University Press, 1981.

Pantucci, Rafaello, *We Love Death as You Love Life: Britain's Suburban Terrorists*, London: Hurst, 2015.

Pierret, Thomas, *Religion and State in Syria: The Sunni Ulama from Coup to Revolution*, Cambridge University Press, 2013.

Ramadan, Tariq, *In the Footsteps of the Prophet: Lessons from the Life of Muhammad*, OUP, 2007.

Roy, Olivier, *Islam and Resistance in Afghanistan*, Cambridge University Press, 1990.

Stenersen, Anne, *Al-Qaida in Afghanistan*, Cambridge University Press, 2017.

Wright, Lawrence, *Looming Tower: Al Qaeda and the Road to 9/11*, New York: Knopf, 2006.

Zayeef, Abdul Salam, ed. Felix Kuehn, Alex Strick van Linschoten, *My Life with the Taliban*, Hurst, 2010.

Newspapers and Articles

The Afghanistan Justice Project, 'Casting Shadows: War Crimes and Crimes against Humanity: 1978–2001', Kabul, 2005

Al-Jazeera: 'Timeline: Algeria's "dirty war"', 13 Nov. 2010, https://www.aljazeera.com/news/africa/2010/11/20101110142037288752.html.

———, 'Ahmed Saeed, Hassan al-Turabi: A man with a mission', 6 Mar 2016, https://www.aljazeera.com/news/2016/03/hassan-al-turabi-man-mission-160306111225056.html.

———, 'Profile on Mahfoudh Nahnah', 20 Nov. 2014, http://www.aljazeera.net/amp/encyclopedia/icons/2014/11/20/محفوظ-نحناح

Al-Ahram: 'Jailing of blind sheikh pushes Muslim anger against US, warns son', 19 Jan. 2013, http://english.ahram.org.eg/NewsContent/

BIBLIOGRAPHY

1/64/62828/Egypt/Politics-/Jailing-of-blind-sheikh-pushes-Muslim-anger-agains.aspx.

Al-Ansar Magazine, Issue 132, 18 Jan. 1995.

———, Issue 82, 2 Feb. 1995.

———, Issue 91, 6 Apr. 1995.

———, Issue 90, 30, Mar. 1996.

Al-Sharq al-Awsat, 8 September 2002, وائل جليدان منزعج من إضافة اسمه إل http://archive.aawsat.com/details.asp?articl بدر المطوع ,ى قائمة مولي الإرهاب e=123390&issueno=8685#.WvQfby-ZNp9.

———, 'Asharq Al-Awsat interviews Umm Mohammed: The Wife of Bin Laden's Spiritual Mentor', 30 Apr. 2006, https://eng-archive.aawsat. com/theaawsat/features/asharq-al-awsat-interviews-umm-mohammed-the-wife-of-bin-ladens-spiritual-mentor.

Amnesty International report, 'Human Slaughterhouse, Mass hangings end extermination at Saydnaya prison, Syria', Feb. 2017 https://www. amnesty.org/download/Documents/MDE2454152017ENGLISH.PDF.

Arabiya news: Nabeel Naeem with al-Arabiya on 28 Mar. 2017, https:// english.alarabiya.net/en/features/2017/03/28/Former-Egyptian-Islamic-Jihad-leader-Nabil-Naeem-Zawahiri-himself-is-ignorant.html.

BBC News: 'Professor Abdul Sabur was assassinated by unknown gun-men', 3 May 2007, http://news.bbc.co.uk/1/hi/world/south_asia/6618 127.stm.

———, 'Q&A: Afghan Taliban open Doha office', 20 June 2013, http:// www.bbc.co.uk/news/world-asia-22957827.

———, 'Abu Qatada cleared of Terror Charges', 24 Sep. 2014, http:// www.bbc.co.uk/news/world-29340656.

———, 'Sadat killing mastermind freed', 29 Sep. 2003, http://news.bbc. co.uk/1/hi/world/middle_east/3147598.stm.

———, 'Mohammed Zammar: German jihadist "detained by Syrian Kurds"' http://www.bbc.co.uk/news/world-middle-east-43821844.

Balcerowicz, Piotr, 'Last known interview with Afghanistan's Ahmad Shah Massoud', Global Geneva, http://www.global-geneva.com/last-known-interview-with-afghanistans-ahmad-shah-massoud/

Bell, Kevin, 'The First Islamic State: A Look Back at the Islamic Emirate of Kunar', *CTC Sentinel*, Feb. 2016, Vol 9, Issue 2, https://ctc.usma.edu/ the-first-islamic-state-a-look-back-at-the-islamic-emirate-of-kunar/.

BIBLIOGRAPHY

Booth, Robert, 'Abu Qatada: spiritual leader for deadly Islamist groups?', *The Guardian*, 7 Feb. 2012 https://www.theguardian.com/world/2012/feb/07/abu-qatada-spiritual-leader-islamist?newsfeed=true.

Bouteldja, Naima, 'Who really bombed Paris?', *The Guardian*, 8 Sep. 2005, https://www.theguardian.com/world/2005/sep/08/france.comment.

Brachman, Jarret, 'Leading Egyptian Jihadist Sayyid Imam Renounces Violence', *CTC Sentinel* Vol. 1 Issue 1, Dec. 2007, https://ctc.usma.edu/leading-egyptian-jihadist-sayyid-imam-renounces-violence/.

CNN: 'Algeria frees key member of banned Islamic party', 15 July 1997, http://edition.cnn.com/WORLD/9707/15/algeria/index.html.

———, 'Osama bin Laden: The Most Notorious Terrorist documentary Transcript', 29 Sep. 2001, http://edition.cnn.com/TRANSCRIPTS/0109/29/pitn.00.html.

Crossette, Barbara, 'Failed Coup Attempt Changes Opinions', *New York Times*, 21 Mar. 1990, https://www.nytimes.com/1990/03/21/world/failed-kabul-coup-changes-opinions.html.

Fitzgerald, Mary, 'Armed groups', in 'A quick guide to Libya's main players', European Council of Foreign Relations, http://www.ecfr.eu/mena/mapping_libya_conflict#.

Gall, Carlotta, 'Muslim Fighter Embraces Warrior Mystique', *New York Times*, 17 Oct. 1999, https://www.nytimes.com/1999/10/17/world/muslim-fighter-embraces-warrior-mystique.html.

Goldman, John J., 'Chief Prosecution Witness in Bomb Trial Tells of Lies: Terrorism: Salem testifies Egyptian cleric asked him to kill Mubarak. He admits to relating false stories about his background to FBI', *Los Angeles Times*, 8 Mar. 1995, http://articles.latimes.com/1995-03-08/news/mn-40189_1_egyptian-cleric.

Grierson, Jamie, 'Abu Hamza's son stripped of UK passport', *The Guardian*, 2 Apr. 2017, https://www.theguardian.com/world/2017/apr/02/abu-hamzas-son-stripped-of-uk-passport.

Hassan al-Khayr, Ahmed, 'Letter to Professor Mustafa Hamid', in the archives of the US Directorate of National Intelligence, available at https://www.dni.gov/files/documents/ubl2016/english/Letter%20to%20Professor%20Mustafa%20Hamid.pdf.

Human Rights Watch Report, 1991, V. 'Human Rights Violations by

Elements of the Afghan Resistance', https://www.hrw.org/reports/1991/afghanistan/5AFGHAN.htm.

al-Haqbani, Nasser, 'Exclusive—Sayyaf to Asharq Al-Awsat: I Know Who Killed Azzam', *Asharq Al-Awsat*, 20 Feb. 2018, https://aawsat.com/english/home/article/1181231/exclusive-sayyaf-asharq-al-awsat-i-know-who-killed-azzam.

Hussein, Tam, 'The Afghan Jihad: An Annotated Interview with Musa al-Qarni about Abdullah Azzam and Ahmed Shah Massoud and the tension with the "Afghan Arabs"', MENA ETC, 24 Feb. 2017, http://www.tamhussein.co.uk/2017/02/musa-al-qarni-on-the-afghan-jihad/.

———, 'Paradise Lost: The Rise and Fall of Abu Bakr al-Baghdadi', MENA ETC, 24 Mar. 2017, http://www.tamhussein.co.uk/2017/04/paradise-lost-rise-fall-abu-bakr-al-baghdadi/.

Hyman, Anthony, 'In Memoriam: Professor Sayed Bahauddin Majrooh', *Central Asian Survey*, 7:2–3 (2007): 209–12, DOI: 10.1080/02634938808400639.

International Crisis Group. 'Islamism, Violence and Reform in Algeria: Turning the Page', ICG Middle East Report Nr. 29, Cairo/Brussels, 30 July 2004. Available at: https://d2071andvip0wj.cloudfront.net/29-islamism-violence-and-reform-in-algeria-turning-the-page.pdf.

Jackson, Kévin, 'The Forgotten Caliphate', Jihadica, 31 Dec. 2014, http://www.jihadica.com/the-forgotten-caliphate/.

Joscelyn, Thomas, 'US strikes al Qaeda's "Khorasan Group" in Syria', FDD's *Long War Journal*, 8 Apr. 2016, https://www.longwarjournal.org/archives/2016/04/us-strikes-al-qaedas-khorasan-group-in-syria.php.

———, 'Al Qaeda ally orchestrated assault on US Embassy in Tunisia', 2 Oct. 2012, https://ctc.usma.edu/belgian-radical-networks-and-the-road-to-the-brussels-attacks/.

———, 'From al-Qaeda in Italy to Ansar al-Sharia in Tunisia', Foundation for the Defence of Democracy, 21 Nov. 2012, http://www.defenddemocracy.org/media-hit/from-al-qaeda-in-italy-to-ansar-al-sharia-tunisia/.

Kamm, Henry, 'Pakistan Officials Tell Of Ordering Afghan Rebel Push', *New York Times*, 23 Apr. 1989, https://www.nytimes.com/1989/04/23/world/pakistan-officials-tell-of-ordering-afghan-rebel-push.html.

————, 'The Lessons Of Jalalabad; Afghan Guerrillas See Weaknesses Exposed', *New York Times*, 13 Apr. 1989, https://www.nytimes.com/1989/04/13/world/the-lessons-of-jalalabad-afghan-guerrillas-see-weaknesses-exposed.html.

Khan, Muqtedar, 'Syed Qutb—John Locke of the Islamic World', Brookings, 28 July 2003, https://www.brookings.edu/articles/syed-qutb-john-locke-of-the-islamic-world/.

Khatib, Sofiane, 'Spoiler Management During Algeria's Civil War: explaining the peace', *Stanford Journal of International Relations*, 24 May 2006, https://web.stanford.edu/group/sjir/6.1.06_khatib.html.

Kraft, Scott, 'Algerian Opposition Figure Slain in Paris: North Africa: Islamic Salvation Front's co-founder is ambushed in mosque. Killing casts new doubts on peace prospects', 12 July 1995, *LA Times*, http://articles.latimes.com/1995-07-12/news/mn-23086_1_islamic-salvation-front.

Kumar, Sanjay, 'Profile on Abdul Hakim Mujahid', *The Diplomat*, 12 Dec. 2013.

Lafèvre, Raphaël, 'The Syrian Brotherhood's Armed Struggle', Carnegie Endowment for International Peace, 14 Dec. 2012, https://carnegieendowment.org/2012/12/14/syrian-brotherhood-s-armed-struggle-pub-50380.

Lieven, Anatol, 'Interview with Abdul Haq', Carnegie Endowment, 14 Oct. 2001, https://carnegieendowment.org/2001/10/14/on-road-interview-with-commander-abdul-haq-pub-818.

Martin, Douglas, 'Paul Aussaresses, the man who tortured Algerians dies', *New York Times*, 4 Dec. 2013, https://www.nytimes.com/2013/12/05/world/europe/paul-aussaresses-95-dies-confessed-to-torture.html.

Mayer, Jane, 'Outsourcing Torture', *The New Yorker*, 14 Feb. 2005, https://www.newyorker.com/magazine/2005/02/14/outsourcing-torture.

Meikle, James, 'Abu Qatada extradition battle has cost taxpayers £1.7m, says Theresa May', *The Guardian*, 14 June 2013, https://www.theguardian.com/world/2013/jun/14/abu-qatada-extradition-theresa-may.

Meiloud, Ahmed, 'The legacy of Sudan's Hassan al-Turabi', *Middle East Eye*, 8 Mar. 2016, http://www.middleeasteye.net/columns/legacy-sudans-hassan-al-turabi-1933889656.

BIBLIOGRAPHY

Molyneux, Tim, 'Guantanamo Child Soldier Omar Khadr was a Victim Twice Over', *Newsweek*, 13 July 2017, http://www.newsweek.com/omar-khadr-al-qaeda-child-soldier-imprisoned-and-mistreated-us-was-victim-635856.

Moslih, Hashmat, 'Afghanistan in the Shadow of Ahmed Shah Massoud', Al-Jazeera, Sep 2014, https://www.aljazeera.com/indepth/opinion/2014/09/afghanistan-shadow-ahmad-shah-mas-2014997826874331.html.

Nordland, Rod and Jawad Sukhanyar, 'Member of Afghan Peace Council Assassinated', *New York Times*, 13 May 2012, https://www.nytimes.com/2012/05/14/world/asia/arsala-rahmani-is-assassinated-in-kabul.html.

Al-Nowaiser, Mowaffaq, 'Khattab, the man who died for the cause of Chechnya', Arab News, 4 May 2002 http://www.arabnews.com/node/220601

Open Society Foundation, 'War Crimes and Crimes against Humanity: 1978–2001, Documentation and analysis of major patterns of abuse in the war in Afghanistan,' https://www.opensocietyfoundations.org/sites/default/files/ajpreport_20050718.pdf.

Orton, Kyle, 'The Demise of Ahmad Mabruk: Al-Qaeda in Syria and American Policy, Syrian Intifada', 4 Oct. 2016, https://kyleorton1991.wordpress.com/2016/10/04/al-qaeda-in-syria-and-american-policy/#more-3060.

Ostaeyen, Pieter Van, 'Belgian Radical Networks and the Road to the Brussels Attacks', *CTC Sentinel*, June 2016, Vol. 9. Issue 6, https://ctc.usma.edu/belgian-radical-networks-and-the-road-to-the-brussels-attacks/.

Pyes, Craig and William C. Rempel, 'Slowly Stalking an Afghan "Lion", The assassins of Northern Alliance chief faced weeks of delays until finally he met with them', *Los Angeles Times*, 12 June 2002, http://articles.latimes.com/2002/jun/12/world/fg-masoud12/7.

al-Qiri, Mohammed, 'Interview with Mohammed al-Bakri, father of Bagram Prison detainee Amin al-Bakri', *Yemeni Observer*, 15 July 2015, https://www.webcitation.org/query?url=http%3A%2F%2Fwww.yobserver.com%2Freports%2F10014605.html&date=2010–01–03.

BIBLIOGRAPHY

Rasmussen, Sune Engel, 'Fear and doubt as notorious "butcher of Kabul" returns with talk of peace', *The Guardian*, 4 May 2017, https://www. theguardian.com/world/2017/may/04/afghan-warlord-gulbuddin-hekmatyar-returns-kabul-20-years-call-peace.

Roggio, Bill, 'Senior al Qaeda leader thought killed in North Waziristan strike', FDD's *Long War Journal*, 1 Nov. 2008 https://www.longwar-journal.org/archives/2008/11/senior_al_qaeda_lead_2.

————, 'Chechen al Qaeda commander, popular Saudi cleric, and an Ahrar al Sham leader spotted on front lines in Latakia', FDD's *Long War Journal*, 27 Mar. 2014, https://www.longwarjournal.org/archives/2014/03/chechen_al_qaeda_com.php.

Rubin, Barnett, 'Hard Choices for Peace', *The New Yorker*, 18 Oct. 2016, https://www.newyorker.com/news/news-desk/hard-choices-for-peace-in-afghanistan.

Rupert, James, 'Afghanistan Rebels Lose Key Battle', 8 July 1989, *Washington Post*, https://www.washingtonpost.com/archive/politics/1989/07/08/afghanistan-rebels-lose-key-battle/074ff765-327d-4a60-b8ab-ed118a87ba50/?utm_term=.d5d9ca0dad1d.

Ryan, Missy, 'Pentagon dossier to detail secretive U.S. Afghan detainee policy', Reuters, 24 Apr. 2014, https://www.reuters.com/article/us-usa-afghanistan-detainees-idUSBREA3M26Q20140424.

Sayare, Scott, 'How Europe's "Little Losers" Became Terrorists', *The Atlantic*, 9 May 2016, https://www.theatlantic.com/international/archive/2016/05/europe-counterterrorism-failure-khaled-kelkal/481908/.

Sayare, Scott and Matt Rosenberg, 'New Scenery for Breaking the Ice with the Taliban', *New York Times*, 21 Dec. 2012, https://www.nytimes.com/2012/12/21/world/asia/afghan-factions-hold-informal-talks-near-paris.html.

Schindler, John R., 'Two Decades Later, Algeria Protects Mystery of Bentalha Massacre', *The Observer*, 22 Sep. 2017 http://observer.com/2017/09/two-decades-later-algeria-protects-mystery-of-bentalha-massacre/.

Sciolino, Elaine and Souad Mekhennet, 'Al Qaeda Warrior Uses Internet to Rally Women', *New York Times*, 28 May 2008, https://www.nytimes.com/2008/05/28/world/europe/28terror.html.

el-Shafey, Mohammed, 'Inside Britains Gitmo', ASHARQ Al-Awsat, 12 Oct. 2015, https://www.webcitation.org/query?url=http%3A%2F%2Fwww.aawsat.com%2Fenglish%2Fnews.asp%3Fsection%3D3%26id%3D2124&date=2010-10-06.

Sifton, John, 'Blood-Stained Hands Past Atrocities in Kabul and Afghanistan's Legacy of Impunity', Human Rights Watch, 6 July 2005, https://www.hrw.org/report/2005/07/06/blood-stained-hands/past-atrocities-kabul-and-afghanistans-legacy-impunity#7ea268.

Smith, Laura, 'Timeline: Abu Musab al-Zarqawi', *The Guardian*, 8 Jun. 2006, https://www.theguardian.com/world/2006/jun/08/iraq.alqaida1

Steele, Jonathan, 'Obituary of Burhanuddin Rabbani', *The Guardian*, 21 Sep. 2011, https://www.theguardian.com/world/2011/sep/21/burhanuddin-rabbani-obituary.

al-Suri, Abu Musa, *al-tajrubah al-suriyyah*, see also Paul Cruickshank & Mohannad Hage Ali (2007)

Tabor, Mary B.W., 'Slaying in Brooklyn Linked to Militants', *New York Times*, 11 Apr. 1993, https://www.nytimes.com/1993/04/11/nyregion/slaying-in-brooklyn-linked-to-militants.html.

UK Supreme Court, Al-Sirri v Secretary of State for the Home Department, 2012, UKSC 54, http://www.asylumlawdatabase.eu/en/case-law/uk-supreme-court-al-sirri-v-secretary-state-home-department-2012-uksc-54.

United Nations Security Council, 'Al-Qaida Sanctions Committee Deletes Wa'el Hamza Abd al-Fatah Julaidan from Its Sanctions List', 26 Aug. 2014, https://www.un.org/press/en/2014/sc11534.doc.htm.

United States Treasury Department Statement on the Designation of Wa'el Hamza Julaidan, 9 June 2002: https://www.treasury.gov/press-center/press-releases/Pages/po3397.aspx.

'United States Of America V Omar Khadr'. http://www.international-crimesdatabase.org/Case/968/Khadr/.

Weintraub, Richard M., 'Bhutto Asserts Role in Afghan Policy', *Washington Post*, 22 May 1989, https://www.washingtonpost.com/archive/politics/1989/05/22/bhutto-asserts-role-in-afghan-policy/72feb814-a569-4325-807c-a95d891d3fc8/?utm_term=.c9c28b10bc29.

BIBLIOGRAPHY

Weiser, Benjamin, 'Reputed bin Laden Adviser Gets Life Term in Stabbing', *New York Times*, 31 Aug. 2010 https://mobile.nytimes.com/2010/09/01/nyregion/01salim.html.

Weiser, Benjamin and Lynne F. Stewart, 'Lawyer for "Blind Sheikh" Omar Abdel Rahman, has no regrets', *New York Times*, 24 Feb. 2017, https://www.nytimes.com/2017/02/24/nyregion/lynne-stewart-lawyer-for-omar-abdel-rahman.html.

Whitehead, Tom, 'Qatada associate will stay in UK, court signals', *Daily Telegraph*, 21 Nov. 2012, https://www.telegraph.co.uk/news/uknews/law-and-order/9693489/Qatada-associate-will-stay-in-UK-court-signals.html.

Whitney, Craig R., 'Bomb Rips Train Underneath Paris, with 29 Wounded', *New York Times*, 18 Oct. 1995 https://www.nytimes.com/1995/10/18/world/bomb-rips-train-underneath-paris-with-29-wounded.html

INDEX

INDEX

INDEX

INDEX

INDEX

INDEX

INDEX

INDEX

INDEX

INDEX

INDEX

INDEX

INDEX

INDEX

INDEX

INDEX

INDEX

New York, United States, 116, 153
   September 11 attacks (2001), ix, 4, 38, 137, 142, 170, 171, 195, 207, 218, 244, 246–7
   World Trade Center bombing (1993), xv, 118
New York Times, 242
Niazi, Abdul Rahim, 27
Niazi, Ghulam Muhammad, 27, 28, 33, 270
Nigeria, x, 187
nisbah, 276
Nizam al-Mulk, 275–6
Nizar, Khalid, 222
noms de guerre, 276
non-governmental organisations (NGOs), 149, 150, 203
North Atlantic Treaty Organization (NATO), 254
North West Frontier Province, Pakistan, xii, 31, 45
Northern Alliance, 29, 253
Nosair, El-Seyyid, 118
Nour Eddine, 107
al-Nusra Front, 271, 288

OFCOM, 264
offensive Jihad, 261–5
Omar, Mullah, 97, 121, 137, 244, 259
omens, 12
Oran, Algeria, 217
Oruzgan, Afghanistan, 47
Orwell, George, xvi

al-Otaybi, Juyahman, 173
Ottoman Caliphate (1299–1924), 120–21, 281, 293
el-Ouaer, Rachid Boraoui, 121
al-Oudah, Salman, 293
Oumm Ubaydah, 281
Oxus river, 66

Pabbi, North West Frontier, 42–7, 190, 207
paedonymic, 276
Paghman, Kabul, 131
pakhouls, 66, 76, 132, 200
Pakistan, xii, xvi, 22, 27, 28, 31, 36–9, 104–5, 119
   and Arab Services Bureau, 145, 181, 187
   Azzam, relations with, 108, 145, 181, 187, 189, 208–9
   Bangladesh Liberation War (1971), 28
   Haqqanis, relations with, 208
   Hekmatyar, relations with, 99, 105, 209
   Inter-Services Intelligence (ISI), *see* Inter-Services Intelligence
   and Jalalabad, battle of (1989), 98, 105, 208, 209, 278
   Khadr assassination (2003), 290
   Massoud, relations with, 62, 98–9, 105, 108, 208–9, 210
   and Rahman assassination (1991), 121
   Soviet Union, relations with, 29, 46

335

INDEX

INDEX

INDEX

INDEX

INDEX

INDEX

INDEX

INDEX

INDEX